FREEDOM OF EXPRESSION

FREEDOM OF EXPRESSION IN EIGHTEENTH CENTURY RUSSIA

by

K. A. PAPMEHL

MARTINUS NIJHOFF / THE HAGUE / 1971

Softcover reprint of the hardcover 1st edition 1971

ISBN 978-94-011-8397-0 ISBN 978-94-011-9101-2 (eBook)
DOI 10.1007/978-94-011-9101-2

To the memory of my parents

TABLE OF CONTENTS

PREFACE

This study is an expanded and revised version of a thesis accepted for the Ph. D. Degree by the University of London in 1965. My sincere thanks go to Dr. Bertha Malnick, formerly of the School of Slavonic and East European Studies, for her valuable advice, criticism, and encouragement. Some of the material used in Chapters Three and Four has been published earlier in *The Slavonic & East European Review,* and I am grateful to the Editors of that journal for their kind permission to draw on it for the present purpose. Most of my research was carried out in the libraries of the British Museum and of the School of Slavonic and East European Studies, and I wish to thank the many members of the staff of both these institutions who facilitated my labours. My thanks also go to the ladies of York University Secretarial Services involved in preparing the manuscript for the press. Finally, I must acknowledge the immense debt of gratitude I owe to my wife, without whose co-operation the whole project could never have materialised. The responsibility for all opinions expressed in this book and for all its shortcomings is entirely my own.

Toronto, Canada
December 1970

INTRODUCTION

The eighteenth century for Russia marks the transition from the medieval (i.e. religious) to the modern European (i.e. secular) culture, a process which in relation to most of the nations belonging to the Latin civilisation, was delayed by something like two centuries. In addition, this process in Russia was compressed into a much shorter period of time. The impact of the change was therefore that much greater and its magnitude more apparent, both to the contemporaries and to their descendants: it was, in a true sense, a cultural revolution. The old established concepts, values, and traditions, ranging from the theory of state and political power to manners and the style of attire, were being uprooted and replaced by their Western-European equivalents, generally without mucht thought being given to their suitability or applicability under the local conditions. Simultaneously, the vestiges of the old culture which proved extremely tenacious, in reasserting themselves often modified the imported values or attitudes and altered their character. Whether one sees the effective beginnings of this process in the after-effects of the Time of Troubles or in the reforms of Peter the Great, the fact is that its results did not become fully apparent until the second half of the eighteenth century.

Freedom of expression – by which term I understand the liberty of the individual to utter thoughts, opinions, statements of fact, etc., whether or not they agree with the views of the accepted authorities – was one such modern concept which made its appearance in Russia during this remarkable age. It is closely related to the concurrent development of the practical means of expression, such as literature, theatre, educational institutions, popular assemblies and, last but not least, the printing and publishing facilities. The aim of this study is to examine the circumstances in which the notion of freedom of expression as one of the civil freedoms, or liberties, first became discernible in Russia, the early stages of its development, and its practical application within the political and social system then existing.

This task is fraught with some serious difficulties. Most of them arise from the fact that since the subject is largely a matter of degree and its value is relative, it tends to elude a precise definition. Another problem is its broad character, in the sense of encroaching upon, or overlapping, several academic disciplines. This is why, in setting the terms of reference, I decided to confine the topic to a relatively narrow perspective. Consequently, this study is not, other than marginally, concerned with the philosophical aspect of the problem, it does not investigate the character and intensity of Western influences on Russian thought, and it is not a comparative analysis on an international or intercultural scale. At the same time, I have made no attempt to fit it into some conveniently labelled disciplinary niche, such as intellectual or political history.

The main methodological problem in dealing with double-edged subjects, such as freedom (and, unavoidably, the restrictions upon it) is presented by the tendency to view the issues and events in dialectical terms: as a conflict between the two opposing trends or "camps", personified in "the state" and "the individual". Such dialectical presentation, with its concomitant pitfalls of oversimplification, has been employed in the body of this work for the sake of reasonable lucidity. One of its less desirable results is that, on the pages that follow, the terms "government" and "society" are occasionally employed in what may seem imprecise or ambiguous manner. They in effect mean, respectively, those who have the power to extend or to restrain freedom, and those who desire to use it for the purpose of uttering views or ideas *not* in accord with those of the controlling authority.

One visible characteristic of the reign of Catherine II, the period on which I have concentrated my attention, is the often-noted ambivalence or discrepancy between the policy-making and policy-implementing process. I thought it advisable to employ another dialectical distinction, that between theory and practice, partly in order to show this particular phenomenon in its proper relief.

Traditionally, there have always existed two basic schools of thought with respect to freedom of expression. The first of these can be traced back to Plato and to the early Fathers of the Christian Church. It holds that truth and virtue are absolute values, known to some people whose duty it is to protect them from error or misrepresentation (which, conversely, they are also qualified to identify). The second, a development of the Aristotelian view that each individual should be free in his quest for truth, believes that no one has the right to limit this freedom of choice. Theoretically, both these schools aim at preserving freedom.[1] Both have found their zealous proponents and followers throughout recorded history. In the political context, the first is obviously compatible with an authoritarian, paternalistic structure, the second with a popular democracy.

In transferring this theory onto the more practical plane of the degree, or extent, of freedom of expression obtainable under varying political conditions, we might consider the following three simplified stages, ranging from complete "unfreedom" to the maximum possible freedom:

(1) When there exists an officially proclaimed set of beliefs, applicable to all aspects of life, to which a society is totally committed. In an extreme form of this system not only is all dissent suppressed, but active support of the ruling creed is demanded from writers and other purveyors of articulate thought.
(2) When there is an officially accepted ideology, but it is no longer single and all-embracing. This permits a measure of freedom, within limits set by the guardians or interpreters of the prevailing values. These limits can range from extremely narrow to very broad, in the wide spectrum of systems coming under this category.
(3) When there is no such officially accepted set of values, and ideas are allowed to compete freely. Freedom of expression here is still not absolute: is is circumscribed by the individual rights of the proponents of differing views. This is the total application of the "Aristotelian" principle whereas the "Platonic" one applies, entirely or predominantly, in stages (1) and (2).

It will be evident that the problem of freedom of expression, in the sense of a conflict between the pressures for its extension and the limiting factors, will be most acute, or at least most prominent, in a system falling under category (2). This is precisely why it became discernible in Russia in the second half of the eighteenth century: the transition from (1) to (2) became apparent in that period.

At this point a few words may be said on the important problem of the relationship between civil and political liberties. In modern times, freedom of expression is generally regarded as an aspect of civil, as distinct from political liberties. But this distinction, always somewhat artificial, dates back at the most to the American Bill of Rights. It was not made by such important eighteenth century thinkers as Rousseau or Montesquieu. The belief that these two fields are really inseparable is made clear in the latter's definition of political liberty as "that tranquility of mind which comes from every man's conviction of his own security, as such it is the

[1] For a discussion of this point see W. Gellhorn, *Individual Freedom and Governmental Restraints,* Louisiana State U. P., Baton Rouge, 1956, pp. 50ff.

condition of civil liberty."[2] Being aware of this, I nevertheless found it necessary, for the sake of clarity of the argument, to treat freedom of expression as a civil liberty. Another reason for this is the fact that the same distinction is implicit in the thinking of Catherine II who, as will be seen later, tended to ignore the connection between the two in that she apparently believed that it was possible to make concessions in the civil sphere without affecting the political.

Censorship, in its various forms, must obviously attract a great deal of attention in a work dealing with freedom of expression, I have treated it as one, albeit the most important, part of the negative side of a broader problem. Censorship is understood to mean control over the written matter, exercised by the state or its organs, with the powers to pass, amend, or suppress the material in question. It is, of course, the principal instrument of restraint with regard to freedom of expression in writing, in both aspects of the latter: the freedom to write and the freedom to read. Its early history in Europe is closely connected with the development of printing (the first censor's office was established in 1486 in Germany, at the Archiepiscopal see of Mainz), and the same is true of Russia where the rapid growth of printing facilities raised the issue towards the end of the eighteenth century.

What then, in most general terms, was the status of freedom of expression in eighteenth century Europe? With the exception of Britain and the Low Countries, the official policies towards it, notwithstanding the eroding effects of Renaissance, Reformation, and empirical philosophy, continued to be based entirely on the "Platonic" principle well into the second half of the century. Moreover, it would probably be fair to say that, through the best part of this period, this was agreeable not only to the governments, but to the majority of those of their subjects who where concerned with such problems. What did more than anything else to change this state of affairs was the extension into this field of the theory of Natural Law, the most significant factor in this process probably being the impact of Rousseau's *Contrat Social*. This, in relation to freedom of expression amounted to a clear declaration of the "Aristotelian" principle in the assertion that the individual is the source of all public right. This principle found its embodiment in the American Bill of Rights of 1776 and in the French Declaration of Human Rights of 1789. The long process of secularization of thought, involved in the gradual shift from the theocentric

[2] *Esprit des Lois*, XI, 6, quoted by de Ruggiero, *The History of European Liberalism*, Boston, 1966, p. 55.

to the anthropocentric world-view, begun with the Renaissance and precipitated by the Enlightenment, was thus visibly completed.

In Russia, as we have already noted, this process was compressed into a much shorter time-span. But, by the end of the eighteenth century, it involved directly only a numerically very small fragment of her society; it took more than another hundred years for its effects to be felt at all levels. In the narrower context of our subject, Russia before the eighteenth century and, indeed, until its second half, was still in the stage of total "unfreedom" typical for a medieval (or a modern totalitarian) society. The conditions under which the problem of freedom of expression might arise simply did not yet exist.

In the revolution involved in the rapid transition from the medieval Muscovy to the modern Empire, the old religiously-oriented culture [3] was ostensibly to be replaced by a new one, predominantly secular. What in fact replaced it wat not one but two parallel cultures: one pseudo-European, represented by a segment of the population whose political and social significance was great while its relative numerical strength was small; the other, basically a continuation of the old, inward- and backward-looking, shared by the great majority, but generally ignored, if not despised, by those who had opted out of it. The cultural homogeneity of the Russian people thus ceased to exist for some two hundred years. Attempts to restore it were made, especially during the nineteenth century, but it took another revolution to bring this about.

It is only within the "europeanised" culture of the minority that the concern with and the desire for freedom of expression became apparent in the course of the eighteenth century. For the other, as for its Muscovite antecedent, the problem largely did not exist; if it did, it was usually in its negative aspect. [4] The "Platonic" principle, in its extreme form, was still deeply embedded in the outlook of the majority, including many ostensible adherents of the "westernised" culture.

This last point serves to emphasize the important fact that the two co-existing cultures were never totally divorced from each other or, perhaps more correctly, that they differed more in the superficial than in the essential things. This was true even at the time of their greatest mutual estrangement, at the end of the eighteenth and the beginning of the nineteenth century. They never ceased to interact and influence each other. It might be added that the influence exerted by the "submerged" culture of

[3] By "culture" I understand a set of values and attitudes shared by a people or a group of peoples.

[4] Some examples illustrating this will be found below, especially in Chapter III.

the majority upon the one of the "upper crust" was, quite naturally, considerably greater than vice versa.

The early stages of this encounter and interaction of two different cultural worlds: the one perhaps obsolete but native, the other modern but alien, form the general background to the story told on the following pages. If it serves to throw a measure of light onto a subject which has often been misconceived and more often misrepresented, the author's purpose will be achieved.

The method of transliteration I have used is the one recommended by the Editors of *The Slavonic & East European Review*. The words, names, titles, etc. are rendered in the modern Russian spelling which may not always strictly correspond to the original, i.e., *russkogo* instead of *russkago, oni* instead of *one*. All dates, unless otherwise indicated, are according to the Julian calendar ("Old Style"), i.e., for the eighteenth century eleven, and for the nineteenth twelve days behind the Gregorian Calendar. The bibliography includes most of the works quoted in the text and some (by no means all) others that have been consulted, selected on the basis of presumed potential usefulness to anyone interested in further work in this of related fields. In the classification of sources, the concept of a primary source has been treated with a considerably greater latitude than would be proper in a work of a purely historical character; the broad guiding principle used here was to include in this category all contemporary unpublished material, the published collections of documents, State papers, and such like, and the reliable editions of works and correspondence of prominent literary figures.

CHAPTER I

THE FIRST HALF OF THE CENTURY

Of all the revolutionary changes in Russian life introduced in the reign of Peter the Great, the two most pregnant with consequences were the destruction of the traditional union between the religious and the political principle in the body politic, and the *rapprochement* with Western Europe. Both proved lasting but, as already pointed out, their most important effects were not immediately apparent. It obviously required more than one generation for such cultural innovations as the institutions of learning, the presence of foreign specialists in Russia and the despatch of young Russians to study abroad, to produce visible results in the realm of intellectual concepts and social attitudes. Thus, for most of the first half of the century, the attitude towards freedom in the newly created Russian Empire did not differ much from that in old Muscovy.

The effects of purely political reforms were more immediate and visible. Prominent among those was the strengthening and consolidation of the power of the monarch, primarily at the expense of the Church now relegated to a clearly subordinate position, in theory as well as in practice. The dominant secular power now demanded the same wholesale support and commitment to its aims as the earlier integrated politico-religious structure. There was thus no more room for dissent under Peter and his immediate successors than there had been under the Muscovite tsars; this was made quite explicit in the theoretical exposition of the new system, Feofan Prokopovich's treatise *Justice of the Monarch's Will.*

Yet dissent there had to be in a situation where a revolution was in progress and where its achievements had to be consolidated. This dissent, as is well known, affected all strata of the population, from the tsar's own son to an illiterate peasant in some remote province. Peter suppressed its symptoms with the same single-minded and ruthless determination which he so prominently displayed in all his endeavours. As far as the written word was concerned, his approach was simple: it was useful only where it in some way advanced what he believed to be the interests of his realm, and where it could be kept under strict supervision; otherwise it was dangerous and not to be tolerated. A good illustration of this attitude is his remark made during the visit to a London bookshop in 1698 when, upon being shown a copy of Juvenal's *Satires*, he voiced his strong disapproval, saying that in his country satire was forbidden and anyone guilty of it would be most cruelly punished. He was horrified by the extent of freedom of speech enjoyed by lawyers in England and is said to have observed: "I, too have that ilk at home: I will hang them all as soon as I get back." [1] The same attitude is well reflected in the legislative acts of his reign.

Thus the rather remarkable Edict of 31 January 1701 lays down that "monks have no right whatsoever to write letters of any kind in their cells, nor shall they keep any kind of ink or paper there... if, for some reason, anyone should have to write anything at all, on orders from his superiors, he shall do it openly, in the refectory, and not secretly, since according to the tradition of the ancient Fathers, no monk ought to write anything without [his] superior's approval.[2] This was confirmed in 1722, in the supplement to *Dukhovnyi reglament* (Rules and Regulations pertaining to the Church), [3] with the addition that monks must not keep in their cells "any writings, such as extracts from books or monastic instructions (*sovetnyye gramotki*), without the knowledge of the abbot, on the pain of cruel corporal punishment", and, again, in 1723. [4] In 1718 an edict was issued forbidding anyone except religious teachers, to write anything at all "behind locked doors". The failure to report offenders, regardless of what they might have written about, was punishable as sedition, with the same degree of severity as the offence itself. [5]

A whole series of legislative acts, recurring up to and including the early part of the reign of Catherine II, is aimed at the so-called *podmyotnyye pis'ma,* i.e. usually anonymous letters or pamphlets, left in places where they could easily be found by the intended recipients. This, by the end of the seventeenth century, appears to have become a relatively common method for the subjects of the Muscovite tsar of making their views or requests known to the authorities. It was used in a variety of ways and

[1] Quoted by D. A. Rovinsky, *Russkiye narodnyye kartinki* (Russian Popular Illustrations), V, St. Petersburg, 1893, pp. 263–4.

[2] *Polnoye sobraniye zakonov Rossiyskoy Imperii* – henceforth *P.S.Z.* (Complete Collection of Laws of the Russian Empire), St. P., 1830, IV, item No. 1,834.

[3] *Ibid.*, VI, no. 4,022.

[4] *Ibid.*, VII, No. 4,146.

[5] *Ibid.*, V, No. 3,223.

for varying purposes: sometimes to offer constructive advice which might indeed be accepted and bring honours and promotion to its originator (as in the case of Alexei Kurbatov, a serf of Prince Sheremet'ev, who, in 1699, submitted a project for a new source of revenue in this way), but more frequently – increasingly so as the tempo of Peter's reform accelerated and the resistance to it stiffened – for what we would now call anti-government propaganda. This weapon was used not only by the internal opposition: the Swedes who had the good fortune to intercept, in 1708 at Gdansk (Danzig), the equipment of a printing press with Slavonic type being then transported into Russia by the successors of Jan Tessing, Peter's chartered printer in Amsterdam, apparently lost little time in using it for printing spurious manifestos and propaganda leaflets for distribution in Russia.[6] Peter I reacted promptly by issuing an edict which warned against "letters written in Slavonic... for the purpose of seditious agitation of the people" which must not be believed nor kept by anyone, and prescribed detailed measures for tracing and dealing with those who distributed them.[7] Another edict, dating from the same year (1708) addressed to the people of the Ukraine makes reference to a bogus proclamation obviously from the same source.[8]

Further instances of this type of legislation are: Peter's edict of 25 January 1715 which directs that anyone finding a pamphlet or a letter of any kind is to burn it on the spot, in front of witnesses, without opening or reading it.[9] Catherine I amended this, in 1726, to the effect that any such literature seen or heard of must be reported to the authorities, on the pain of death. At the same time substantial rewards were promised to those complying, as well as amnesty for anyone already having such "letters" in their possession, provided they come forward within one week

[6] Jan Tessing (Thessing), owner of an Amsterdam printing shop, was granted a charter by Peter I, in 1700, for the printing of "drawings and books" in Slavonic, Latin, and Dutch, "for the greater glory of the Great Sovereign amongst the European Monarchs and for the general benefit and profit to the Nation, but nothing that detracts from the Supreme Honour of Our Majesty or the glory of Our Realm must occur in such drawings and books." (*P.S.Z.*, IV, No. 1,751). Tessing died in the following year and, after some time, his master-printer decided to move the enterprise to Russia, with this unfortunate result. (For details see P. P. Pekarsky, *Nauka i literatura v Rossii pri Petre Velikom* (Learning and Literature in Russia at the Time of Peter the Great), St. P., 1862, I, p. 10ff, and II, p. 177. Also V. S. Sopikov, *Opyt rossiyskoy bibliografii* (Tentative Russian bibliography), Part I, St. P., 1904, pp. XLIf; Part V, St. P., 1905, pp. 133ff).

[7] *P.S.Z.*, IV, No. 2,188.

[8] *Ibid.*, IV, No. 2,212.

[9] *Ibid.*, V, No. 2,877. Also cf. VI, No. 3,479.

from an appointed date.[10] Empress Anna reverted to Peter's policy of having the offending material burned by the finder on the spot, and this was repeated and confirmed during the subsequent reigns.[11]

There are many recorded instances of draconian reprisals during the reign of Peter I and his immediate successors against those who wrote without official authorisation.[12] A good example is the fate that befell Ivan Pososhkov, the author of the well known treatise *Book on Scarcity and Wealth* who died in prison, in 1726, whilst under investigation set in motion by the discovery of a copy of his book.[13]

The inference that can be made from these examples is that the power of the written word was by no means underestimated by Peter I and his immediate successors. The prevailing attitude towards it among society, developed in the course of centuries when practically anything that had been written was written under the direct authority of the Church or the supreme political power, was essentially one of trust and respect. The dangers inherent in this credulity being exploited by forces inimical to the regime were only too obvious.[14]

The constriction of independent expression was, of course, not confined to its written form. The measures undertaken to suppress free speech, especially where even the mildest suspicion of a criticism of the policy or the person of the ruler was involved, were even more rigorous. Most cases of this type came under the category of *slovo i delo,* whereby any form of unauthorised discussion of the person or the activities of the tsar could be interpreted as high treason, punishable by death. *Slovo i delo Gosudarevo* (literally, "the Sovereign's Word and Deed"), was the colloquial term, popular in the first half of the eighteenth century, for the crime of high treason, or, as rather vaguely defined in the Code of 1649, "very important matters of State". During the reign of Peter I its terms of reference were extended to cover any form of verbal offence against the person or policies of the Tsar, with no distinction being made between the concepts of high treason and lèsé Majesté. The failure to denounce offenders,

[10] *Ibid.*, VII, No. 4,838.

[11] *Ibid.*, VII, No. 6,150 (Anna); XII, No. 9,105 (Elizabeth); XIX, No. 14,100 Catherine II).

[12] Cf. for example, V. A. Gol'tsev, *Zakonodatel'stvo i nravy v Rossii XVIII veka,* (Legislation and Customs in 18th Century Russia), St. P., 1896, *passim.*

[13] For details see B. B. Kafengauz, *I. T. Pososhkov -zhizn' i deyatel'-nost',* (The Life and Activities of I. T. Pososhkov), Moscow-Leningrad, 1950.

[14] The following passage taken from the "Regulations or Statute of the Committee for Church Affairs" of 1721 (*P.S.Z.*, VI, No. 3,718) may serve to illustrate this point: "... the common people are not capable of telling right from wrong, but cling firmly and stubbornly to what they see written in a book."

whether actual or suspected, carried the same sanctions as the crime itself. The following few examples may serve to exemplify the utmost triviality of some of the accusations.

Thus J.-G. Korb, author of the well-known *Diary* describing his travels in Russia as a secretary to the Imperial embassy, recorded an incident which took place in Moscow in 1698. A wife of a senior official (*d'yak*), passing the bodies of the executed *streltsy* displayed in front of the Kremlin, was overheard remarking with a deep sigh: "Who among the human beings knows whether they were in fact guilty or not?" Upon this being reported to the authorities, both she and her husband were interrogated under torture and, after a prolonged investigation, sentenced to exile, escaping the death penalty only because no proof of "premeditated evil design" was found. In another instance some years later, an official (*fiskal*) denounced for mentioning "the tsar's edict" in a quarrel with an army officer, spent two years under arrest before being sentenced to "merciless beating with rods." Torture and death were meted out to people denounced for discussing the new Imperial title assumed by Peter in 1721, for prophecies, rumours of unusual signs or portents, etc. [15]

Towards the end of Peter's reign the number of prosecutions under this law reached almost unmanageable proportions. People would be denounced out of spite, as a result of petty squabbles and so on, with the result that both the accusers and the accused, as well as the witnesses, would be arrested, tortured, and kept, often indefinitely, in the dungeons of the *Preobrazhensky Prikaz* (and, later, the Secret Chancellery). In 1723 one senior provincial official wrote to Prince Romodanovsky, head of the *Preobrazhensky Prikaz,* drawing his attention to the abuse of *slovo i delo* by "idle rascals" who accost law-abiding people in taverns and in the streets demanding money for drinks under the threat of denounciation. One other common form of abuse was for those condemned to death, corporal punishment, or deportation to invoke *slovo i delo* at the time the sentence was about to be carried out, thus obtaining valuable respite while the case would be investigated anew, almost invariably implicating a further number of usually innocent people. This state of affairs hardly altered after Peter's death, and the excesses of *slovo i delo* continued up to and including Elizabeth's reign, even though the actual punishments became somewhat milder under this last regime. A number of legislative acts by the immediate successors of Peter the Great, while confirming the

[15] Cf. P. E. Mel'gunova et al., *Russkiy byt po vospominaniyam sovremennikov* (Russian Life in the Recollections of Contemporaries), I., M., 1914, p. 74; Gol'tsev, *op. cit.*, pp. 40ff.; M. I. Semevsky, *Slovo i delo!* 1700–1725, St. P., 1884, *passim.*

official view of the gravity of this type of crime, reflect some concern with the abuses and attempt to achieve a more precise definition of its terms of reference.[16] *Slovo i delo* was finally done away with by the Manifesto of 21 February 1762, on the abolition of the Bureau of Secret Investigations (*Taynaya rozysknaya kantselariya*) issued by Peter III.[17]

Thus during practically the whole first half of the century both the letter of the law and the administrative practice were directly inimical to any form of independent expression. New cultural institutions introduced or developed during this period, such as the Academy of Sciences and other educational establishments, the additional printing presses, the first newspaper, etc. owe their appearance and continued existence solely to the supreme political authority whose ends it was their purpose to serve. Any new establishment or enterprise, even if independently conceived, must, in order to justify its existence, be shown to be in some way useful to the government and, in order to ensure that this usefulness is retained, must remain under that government's control. For example, Peter's edict of 17 December 1702[19] ordering the publishing of the *Vedomosti*, the first newspaper available to the general public, conceives its purpose as the dissemination of information considered suitable "for the people of Muscovy and other neighbouring States." The information is to be gathered exclusively from the government sources and published by a government agency.[20] This is the principle generally accepted and shared by the rulers and the ruled alike throughout most of the century. The first instances of its being challenged occur only during the reign of Catherine II, but the attitudes engendered by it extend well beyond the period with which we are here concerned.

The availability of instruments of expression, notably printing facilities, is an important factor which is directly relevant to our subject. At the beginning of the century only one printing press, the Moscow "Printing House" existed in Russia proper. By the end of Peter's reign there were three printing establishments in St. Petersburg: one each at the Senate and at the School of Navigation (both used exclusively for the printing of

[16] *P.S.Z.*, VII, No. 5,004 (Catherine I); VIII, Nos. 5,528; 5,535 (Anna).

[17] *Ibid.*, XV, No. 11,445: "This hateful expression, to wit: *slovo i delo* is henceforth to have no meaning whatsoever and We forbid its use to one and all."

[18] *Ibid.*, XVI, No. 11,687.

[19] *Ibid.*, IV, No. 1,921.

[20] The emphasis in *Vedomosti* (News) was on military matters. The items selected for publication were not tampered with, so that even unfriendly foreign reports of events involving Russia were published *in toto*, without any comment.

decrees and other official publications), and one for religious texts at the monastery of St. Alexander Nevsky; three further presses for printing religious books under the jurisdiction of the Holy Synod were located at Moscow, Chernigov, and Kiev.

In the reign of Peter II the edict of 4 October 1727 [21] authorised the existence of only two printing presses at St. Petersburg, one attached to the Senate, for the printing of government announcements only, and the other newly established at the Academy of Sciences. The "religious" press from St. Alexander's monastery was transferred to Moscow to be incorporated with the one already existing there, to print religious books "as it used to be of old." This edict also established the principle that the Holy Synod was to perform a supervisory function in respect of anything printed both at the Academy of Sciences and at the religious press in Moscow: a clear symptom of a return to the medieval concept.

As long as the only existing printing presses were those attached to the Senate and to religious institutions, the problem of supervision over them could not, strictly speaking, arise. With the establishment of a press at the Academy of Sciences the situation became a little more complicated, and the relevant clause in the edict just quoted obviously attempts to find a simple solution to this problem, on the traditional lines. That this solution was not satisfactory becomes clear from the fact that, in 1743, the government of Elizabeth found it necessary to confirm the exclusive competence in these matters of the Senate and the Synod respectively, but at the same time, to transfer "secular and other books not pertaining to the Church" to the jurisdiction of the former. [22] This, of course, did not solve the problem inasmuch as the thinking behind it was still based on the old principle that anything appearing in print would be either an official government publication (the text-books etc. published in the reign of Peter I certainly fall into this category, as do the *Vedomosti*), or a religious text. This ignored the fact that the Academy of Sciences had begun to publish books which could not properly be fitted into either of these two categories. [23] Moreover, the Academy, as a government institution, could

[21] *P.S.Z.*, VII, No. 5,175.

[22] By a decree of 17 March 1743 (not listed in *P.S.Z.*), cf. M. I. Sukhomlinov, *Materiyaly dlya istorii Imperatorskoy Akademii Nauk* (Source materials for the History of the Imperial Academy of Sciences), VII, p. 341.

[23] Advertisements appearing between 1745 and 1748 in the *St. Petersburg News* show the following titles as published, in Russian, and on sale at the Academy bookshop during these years: *The book of Marcus Aurelius, The True Politics with Poems by Cato, The Honest Mirror of Youth, The History of Troy, Geography: Russian and German, Essential Remarks on the Manifesto by the King of Prussia Against the Court of the Kurfuerst of*

justifiably claim "censorial' jurisdiction over its own output. The Minutes of the Conference of the Academy of Sciences dated 22 March 1745 do, in fact, make this claim and, at the same time, attempt to formulate the principles on which censorship ought to be based. Referring to the translation, prepared by Tredyakovsky, of the *Ancient History of Various Nations* by the French author Charles Rollin, a book "which has already been published in all European languages and could be very useful to the young people who study Ancient History," the Minutes go on to say that

"... the Academy of Sciences, in accordance with the aforementioned Edict [that of 1743], dare not print this History without the permission of the Senate. Therefore [it is resolved] to beg the Senate most humbly for a permission to print the aforementioned book and to sell it to all comers, and to do likewise with other [books] which contain nothing prejudicial to this Empire and to its Laws... Furthermore, the Academy has never published and could not publish, under its own auspices, books which are prejudicial to this Empire or to its Laws." [24]

The principle that the Academy is competent to act as its own "censor" became eventually accepted. In 1748, the then President, Kirill Razumovsky, announced at the Academy conference a verbal edict by the Empress not only permitting, but encouraging the members to translate and publish, in Russian, foreign books on non-religious subjects in which "usefulness and pleasure would be combined with a suitable moral teaching." [25]

In 1747 the Academy press was divided into two separate establishments: one for printing books in foreign languages, and the other in Russian. No further printing presses were established before the seventeen fifties, so that their number by the mid-century remained virtually unchanged since the days of Peter I. It should be noted, however, that the disadvantages of this situation were already becoming apparent, at least to some educated Russians: the historian Tatishchev, in his *Discourse on the Usefulness of Learning* written in the seventeen thirties, recommends establishment of "free" (i.e. privately-owned) printing presses as the best remedy for the deplorable state of the publishing and bookselling trade in Russia. [26] It took another half a century for his wish to become a reality.

Saxony, Travels of Telemachus the Son of Ulysses, Apophegmata. (S. M. Solov'yov, *Istoriya Rossii s drevneyshikh vremyon,* (History of Russia from the Earliest Times), XXII, M., 1963, p. 578.

[24] Sukhomlinov, *Loc.cit.*

[25] P. P. Pekarsky, *Istoriya Imperatorskoy Akademii Nauk v Peterburge,* (The History of the Imperial Academy of Sciences in Petersburg), II, St. P., 1873, p. LII.

One subsidiary point which might be referred to in passing is the question of public demand for printed matter, a not unimportant factor in the development of the printing facilities. This is Russia at the end of the first half of the eighteenth century was very poor indeed, so poor in fact that (Andrey Konstantinovich) Nartov, one of the former pupils and protégés of Peter the Great and the official in charge of the administration of the Academy in 1742 and 1743, conceived the idea, in the best tradition of his mentor, of a compulsory sale of books to the citizens throughout the Empire. According to this, all those in the service of the State, whether civilian or military, were to be ordered to purchase books at the Academy for amounts equivalent to five to six percent of their wages, and the merchants for sums fixed according to their turn-over. This involved only the books in Russian whereas the Academy also held in stock a not inconsiderable number of books in other languages, mostly received from its correspondents abroad. Nartov's proposal provided an equally simple solution to this problem by suggesting that these be disposed of, in the identical manner, in the German-speaking provinces of Livonia and Estonia.[27] Although Nartov's plan was never put into practice, the Empress Elizabeth must have been motivated by somewhat similar precepts when, in 1747, after Tredyakovsky had lost all his property in a fire, she directed him to be issued with 2,000 rubles' worth of books from the Academy, so that he could sell them on his own account.[28] While we do not know how successful he was in restoring his solvency as a result of this grant, we may reasonably surmise that he might have preferred it in some more readily convertible form.

To conclude this sketch of the situation in the field of freedom of expression in Russia up to the middle of the century, it might be worthwhile to quote an incident reflecting the attitude of the Russian citizens of that period to legislation involving printed matter. The legislative acts of Elizabeth's reign show considerable concern in purging such matter of all references to "certain persons known in the previous regime", i.e. to the deposed infant-tsar John VI, Anna Leopoldovna, and members of their family. Thus, in 1742, the Senate ordered all books printed in Russia during the period between the death of the empress Anna and Elizabeth's accession to be returned to the original printing presses for appropriate corrections to be made; in 1748 all non-religious books, whether in Russian

[26] V. N. Tatishchev, *Razgovor o pol'ze nauk i uchilishch,* (A Discourse on the Usefulness of Learning and of Educational Institutions), M., 1887, p. 157.

[27] Pekarsky, *Istoriya . . .*, p. XIII.

[28] *Ibid.*, p. 122.

or in foreign languages, in which such names were mentioned, had to be surrendered to the authorities. Finally, in August 1750, as a result of some foreigners having been caught in St. Petersburg in the process of selling books – in German – which contained references to "certain persons" (or, in the more modern jargon, "non-persons") the Senate issued an edict under this self-explanatory title: "On the bringing forward of Books in Foreign Languages wherein are mentioned the Names of Certain Persons known during the two earlier Regimes: to the Academy of Sciences if such Books had been printed there; on surrendering any other Books of this kind to the Governing Senate, and on the Prohibition to import such Books from Foreign Countries."[29]

The effects of this edict must have exceeded the expectations, as is evident from the fact that it was followed by another one less than two months later (on 10 October 1750), entitled: "On making it known that those who have in their possession Books in Foreign Languages on History, Genealogy, and Geography printed outside Russia, do not have to report them, and that it is not forbidden to bring such Books from abroad, with the exception of those dedicated to Certain Persons by name."

The edict goes on to say that, as a result of the earlier one, all kinds of quite innocuous books, such as those listed in the just quoted heading, had been surrendered to the authorities. It explains that such books are not wanted, that those that had been already handed in can be reclaimed by their owners, and that only books which are dedicated to or written for "certain persons" and prayer books bearing their names are affected.[30]

This incident is probably a good example of the attitude prevalent among society brought up in the traditions of Peter the Great and the stern regime of Anna and Biron.

Another such example is the case of the book by the German pietist Arndt, *On the Principles of True Christianity,* published in Russian translation at Halle in Germany in 1735. Its translator and publisher was one Semyon Todorsky, then a student of theology in Germany. In 1743 Todorsky's (monastic) name appears among the signatories of a memorandum to the Empress Elizabeth requesting the banning of this book as "harmful"; Todorsky also made the report to the Synod on the resulting

[29] *P.S.Z.*, XIII, No. 9,794.

[30] *Ibid.*, XII, No. 9,805. Cf. also A. M. Skabichevsky, *Ocherki istorii russkoy tsenzury (1700–1863 gg.)* – (An Outline of the History of Russian Censorship 1700–1863), St. P., 1892, pp. 11–12; and D. D. Shamray, "K istorii tsenzurnogo rezhima Yekateriny II" (To the History of Catherine II's Censorial Methods), in *XVIII vek* (18th Century), Sb. 3., M.-L., 1958, pp. 187ff.

edict which ordered the surrender of all existing copies of the book and prohibited the translation of similar works in the future. Thus the translator became an apparently eager participant in the condemnation of his own work. [31]

Some manifestations of dissenting opinion can be found in various forms of "unofficial" and, of course, illegal literature such as the already mentioned *podmyotnyye pis'ma,* popular songs about prominent personalities or events, and, not least, the *lubochnyye kartinki,* a practically untranslatable term denoting prints, usually produced by a rather primitive woodcut technique by anonymous artists, which became popular from about the middle of the seventeenth century. Besides the traditional subjects of folklore, such as fables, legends of ancient and medieval heroes (some of them Western-European or Oriental in origin), popular tales, etc., they occasionally depicted important contemporary events viewed in a satirical light, i.e. performed the function of the modern political cartoon.

Probably the best known example of this particular art from the period with which we are now concerned is *The Mice are burying the Cat,* a pictorial parody of the funeral of Peter the Great, of which several variants have been preserved. [32] It is interesting from the point of view of our subject as an example of an expression of "subversive" opinion which must have achieved quite a wide circulation notwithstanding the extremely severe restraints in force at the time. Whether or not it originated at what might be termed "the lower social level" is uncertain; there seems to be little doubt that it was inspired by conservative circles, opposed to Peter's reforms.

From what has been said here it should be clear that the conditions in Russia in the first half of the eighteenth century did not favour either the appearance or growth of the idea that expression should be free. The interpretation of the *slovo i delo* which became the rule in the reign of Peter made anything approaching free speech quite unthinkable; the current legislation and practice had the same effect with regard to the written word. The literary output within the country was negligible as was the demand for printed matter of a secular character. The few printing presses that did exist were rigidly controlled by the state, and there were no popular assemblies or quasi-legislative bodies in which differing opinions might compete openly and freely. In general, the medieval out-

[31] Sukhomlinov, *Istoriya Rossiyskoy Akademii* (History of the Russian Academy), I, St. P., 1874, pp. 63f. Also Skabichevsky, p. 12.

[32] D. A. Rovinsky, *op.cit.*, V, p. 157.

look was still clearly apparent in the attitudes of society towards the new cultural phenomena. The first clear signs of impending changes in these attitudes, at the higher political level, appear in mid-century, in the relatively benevolent reign of Elizabeth. These will be indicated in the following chapter.

CHAPTER II

EROSION OF OLD ATTITUDES

In the course of Elizabeth's reign two hitherto non-existing factors begin to play an ever-increasing part: the softening of repressive measures resulting from the milder character of the regime, and increased Western-European, notably French, cultural influences. Although, as we have noted earlier, the intercourse with Europe did not cease after Peter's death, it was, especially in the reign of Anna, largely restricted to its German-speaking part. With the tide of revulsion from the rule of the German clique of Biron which had brought Elizabeth to the throne, came also the interest in France and things French, aided and abetted by the new empress herself and her immediate entourage. [1] Another important difference was that the carriers of Western-European influences were themselves, no longer, as in the early part of the century, predominantly "technicians" – carpenters, shipwrights, navigators, engineers, etc. – but often leading intellectuals, men of letters or creative artists. (Such were the foreign, mostly German, professors at the Academy of Sciences and, later, Moscow University; the organisers of and some participants in court theatricals, painters, sculptors, architects; the Russians sent to study at the universities abroad, of whom Tredyakovsky and Lomonosov are the most prominent examples). Their impact was consequently making itself felt in the realm of ideas rather than that of material things, and although it was confined to a very small group of people, these were the people whose influence was far in excess of their number. It was fortunate, if possibly fortuitous, coincidence that the type of the court favourite in Elizabeth's reign was considerably superior in most respects, not least intellectually, to that in the regimes immediately preceding.

Among the most prominent recipients of ideas coming from France,

[1] This does not appear to have been particularly affected by the fact that there was a break in diplomatic relations with France between 1748 and 1755. Close political ties were resumed towards the end of 1756.

within the circle close to the throne, were Count I. I. Shuvalov (1727-1797) who maintained a direct correspondence with Voltaire, Helvétius, and D'Alembert; Count M. P. Bestuzhev-Ryumin (1688-1760) at one time the Russian Ambassador in Paris and correspondent of Voltaire; Prince D. A. Golitsyn (1734-1803), Russian envoy in France and Holland, an exceptionally enlightened and cultured man who also corresponded with Voltaire, Diderot, Helvétius, and D'Alembert; Count K. G. Razumovsky (1728-1803) who corresponded with Voltaire and Rousseau; Count M. L. Vorontsov (1714-1767), and B. M. Saltykov (1723-1808) both correspondents of Voltaire. Between themselves, their relatives and close associates and, of course, Elizabeth herself, these people practically represented the government of Russia at the time. Elizabeth, notwithstanding her modest educational background and rather limited interests, was by no means excluded from this process. We know, for example, that a form of digest of the Western-European press used to be prepared for her, from references to it found in her correspondence with the Chancellor M. L. Vorontsov.[2] By the mid-century we already have evidence of French influences spreading beyond the court circles: Bolotov, who came from a noble family of moderate means, recounts in his memoirs how, in 1752, his French tutor made him copy articles from a Dictionary published by the French Academy.[3] The teaching of French as an optional subject began at the Army Cadet Corps already in the reign of Anna,[4] and the majority of nobles, even from less well-to-do families such as the Fonvizin brothers, of the generation educated during the 'fifties, appear to have been quite familiar with that language.

The impact of this cultural intercourse with France was so much the

[2] *Arkhiv kn. Vorontsova,* (Vorontsov Archives) III, M., 1871, p. 649. This contains a rather remarkable item in the form of a translation of an article from a newspaper published at Utrecht, in French, dated 8 February 1754. The article is in the form of a report from Russia which refers to the fact that Elizabeth had abolished the death penalty upon her accession. After commenting on the allegedly dire consequences of this act, such as the increased incidence of arson, the author of the article notes that "it has been decided to make representations to the Empress, in the strongest possible terms, to prevail upon her to renounce her vows [never to condemn anyone to death] both for the sake of the preservation of Faith in her Realm and of Good Order"; and that "some members of the Holy Synod have taken it upon themselves to explain to the Empress the urgent necessity for this change." Needless to say, the article looks very much as if it had been faked or, at least, inspired by someone in Russian government circles.

[3] *Zhizn' i priklyucheniya Andreya Bolotova,* (The Life and Adventures of Andrey Bolotov) I, M.-L., 1931. p. 174-5.

[4] Cf. N. Vasilenko, "Rost frantsuzskogo vliyaniya v Rossii do frantsuzskoy revolutsii" (The Growth of French Influence in Russia Before the French Revolution), *Otechestvennaya voyna i russkoye obschestvo 1812-1912,* (Te Patriotic War and Russian Society), M., 1911, p. 23.

greater as it coincided with the period when the activities of the leading figures of the Enlightenment had just about reached their peak.[5] Incidentally, French literature did not act exclusively as the carrier of French cultural and ideological influences; it was also helping to acquaint the Russian reader with the products of British thought: indirectly, as in the case of Montesquieu whose writings reflect some ideas of British political thinkers, or more directly as in the case of French translations of Addison, Steele, Swift, Samuel Richardson, Sterne, and others.

The general educational level of the Russian nobility began to rise with the establishment – mainly thanks to the efforts of the founder of the Moscow University I. I. Shuvalov – of new *gimnazyi* and military schools. The employment of foreign tutors, opening of private schools by rich nobles, and similar cultural phenomena assisted in this process and helped further the spread of Western influences. Poroshin's diary provides us with a good example of the effect of these new trends which were instrumental in moulding the outlook of young noblemen of the 'fifties and 'sixties: an outlook contrasting quite sharply with that of the previous generation.[6] Further vivid illustrations of this contrast can be found in the correspondence of the young brothers Vorontsov, Alexander and Semyon (brothers of Catherine Dashkova) with their father Roman.[7] A great number of people destined to achieve fame in the last part of the century spent their formative years in the newly established educational institutions during this period: Novikov, the Fonvizin brothers, Grigory Potyomkin – at Moscow University; Derzhavin at the Kazan' *gimnaziya* founded in 1758; Sumarokov, Kheraskov, Yelagin, and the brothers Orlov at the Army Cadet Corps.

[5] The effects of Voltaire's activities as a writer and a playwright had just about reached their climax. (Voltaire himself lived in Berlin between 1750 and 1753. His contacts with Russia gained in intensity after 1756, as a result of his having begun to work on the history of Peter the Great. The first volume of the *Encyclopaedia* came out in 1751. Montesquieu's *L'Esprit des Lois* was published in 1748 and *L'Esprit* by Helvétius ten years later in Amsterdam. Didérot's *Sur La Poésie Dramatique* appeared in 1757–58 (shortly before Rousseau's *Nouvelle Héloïse* (1761) and *Emile* (1762).

[6] *Semyona Poroshina zapiski* ..., (Memoirs of S.P.) St. P., 1844. Poroshin, born in 1741, was educated at the Army Cadet Corps and appears to have had a good knowledge of French and German. From 1762 until 1768 he was tutor is mathematics to Prince Paul (the future Paul I). In 1765 he quotes his following remark to the young Prince: "There are books which are indispensable for every person's education, among their number I count ... the works of Mr. Montesquieu and *L'Esprit* by Helvétius ..." (p. 217).

[7] Roman Larionovich Vorontsov (1707–1783), brother of the Chancellor Mikhail Larionovich. Alexander and Semyon were born in 1741 and 1744 respectively. The relevant correspondence dates from the period 1753–1783 and is to be found in *Arkhiv kn. Vorontsova,* (Vorontsov Archives) Vols. XVI (1880) and XXXI (1885).

The first decade of the second half of the century is marked by a substantial rise in the availability of media of expression. The number of printing presses is doubled,[8] the newly founded Moscow University provides unprecedented facilities for public debates in addition to its teaching function; there appear the first periodicals,[9] the first Russian-language permanent theatre and, the most important tool of expression, the language itself undergoes a process of rapid adjustment to the practical requirements of intellectual life.

The official government attitude towards freedom of expression remains unchanged. The *slovo i delo,* still in force, continues to inhibit free speech; other media remain, directly or indirectly, under the control of the government. No conscious formulation of theoretical principles of free expression, whether from the government's or the society's side, is forthcoming. Yet there appear certain purely practical phenomena which are interesting and ought to be recorded; their appearance is closely connected with the increased availability of the media of expression just noted. It may therefore be useful to look into the principal areas in which such phenomena occurred: the institutions of higher learning, the new periodical press, and publishing activities in general.

The Academy of Sciences in St. Petersburg was run on strictly conservative lines, leaving its members little latitude in the exercise of independent judgment. The Constitution of the Academy drawn up in 1747 made it quite clear that decisions in all matters involving publishing or publicising the achievements of members were the sole responsibility of the President or, in his absence, of the Chancellery (*Kantselyariya* – a central administrative office). This body maintained a rigid control over the academicians and their lives in the best tradition of Peter the Great: their attendance at the Academy was compulsory at set times, with penalties prescribed for absence, tardiness, or failure to observe any other regulations.[10] This

[8] The following printing presses opened during this period: in 1753 at the Metropolitan See at Kiev; in 1756 at Moscow University; in 1757 at the Army Cadet Corps; in 1759 at the School of Artillery and Fortification. In 1761 a second press was opened at the Senate, "for the printing of Books translated by Court Counsellor Volchkov."

[9] In 1755 the Academy of Sciences began to publish the first Russian semi-popular scientific and literary magazine *Yezhemesyachnye sochineniya* (Monthly Essays); from 1756 *Moskovskiye Vedomosti* (Moscow News) began to be published at the newly established University of Moscow press; in 1759 *Prazdnoye vremya v pol'zu upotreblyonnoye* (Leisure Usefully Employed), published at the Army Cadet Corps and *Trudolyubivaya pchela* (The Industrious Bee) edited by Sumarokov and printed at the Academy of Sciences, appeared at St. Petersburg.

[10] Cf. Pekarsky, *Istoriya Imperatorskoy Akademii Nauk v Peterburge,* (History of the Imperial Academy of Sciences at [St.] Petersburg), II, St. P., 1873, pp. XLI f. Schumacher

tight administrative control is perhaps the most typical feature of the internal life of the Academy during the forties and fifties of the eighteenth century.

From about 1748 the Academy of Sciences assumes, under the authority of its President, a function similar to that of censorship in respect of the output of its own printing press. It is important to appreciate the limitation inherent in this: it did not have the powers of "censorship" [11] over anything published or sold outside of its own jurisdiction.

Also from approximately 1748, following Elizabeth's (verbal) decree mentioned earlier inviting the members of the Academy to translate books on secular subjects, there is a noticeable increase in the output of translations of foreign authors. The translators were usually members or employees of the Academy itself. The Academy records show that such translations, when ready for print, used to be submitted "for examination". This was usually carried out by some members considered competent, [12] and the findings referred to the *Kantselariya* or to the President for the final approval. Both the *Kantselariya* and the President not infrequently acted independently of the "examiners" or of each other, with the higher authority overriding the lower. Furthermore, the Holy Synod in the exercise of its jurisdiction over subjects touching upon religion or metaphysics, often had to be consulted, if it did not interfere on its own accord. Under such conditions, in addition to the personal strife then prevailing between various members and factions within the Academy, there could of course be no question of a reasonably consistent policy or of set guiding principles in this process of examination of written works.

A sample of some of the standards used can be provided by the following report, by Tredyakovsky, dating from 10 October 1748:

"In accordance with the directive received from the Chancellery of the Academy I have read the newly composed tragedy called *Hamlet* [by Sumarokov]. This, according to my view, does not contain anything prejudicial to goodness, but, on the

and Teplov were the joint authors of the Constitution of the Academy of 1747. A typical example of the spirit in which it was written is Section 17: "A new invention, suitable for publication in the *Comentarii* of the Academy, must not be included without the permission of the President, since no Academician – and even less an Adjunct – is permitted to make any decisions on his own.' (The text of the Constitution is reproduced in Appendix 4 to *Istoriya Akademii Nauk SSSR,* (History of the USSR Academy of Sciences), I, M.–L., 1958, pp. 436–453.

[11] For the present purpose I understand "censorship" to mean a direct control with the power to pass or suppress, exercised by the government or its organs, over the contents of a written work.

[12] For example, the Minute of the *Kantselariya* of 16 January 1748 directs: "Two

contrary, it seems quite excellent. Indeed, the Author has corrected here the most important fault of his first Tragedy *Khorev* (in which evil had won and virtue had perished) and has seen to it that all evils have been destroyed – wherein lies the principal value of a tragedy – and virtues have received their just reward, much to the rejoicing of the Reader's heart." [13]

Thus Tredyakovsky's comments seem to resemble an opinion of a literary critic rather than that of a "censor" called upon to pronounce upon the suitability of a written work for publication. On the other hand, Lomonosov's submission in respect of the same tragedy and dated on the day following that of Tredyakovsky, has a different ring: "I have examined the Tragedy by Mr. Sumarokov called *Hamlet,* in my opinion it contains nothing that could be prejudicial to anyone and [thus] prevent its publication." [14]

Lomonosov also played a prominent role in the suppression of G. F. Mueller's (Miller's) dissertation *De origine plebis et nomine Russorum* in 1749-1750, an affair well known to students of Russian historiography as the first conspicuously recorded dispute between the "Normanists" and "anti-Normanists". Here Lomonosov listed his following objections:

"(1) It is to be feared that it may be considered a provocation of the Russian Orthodox Church that Mr. Mueller assumes the settlement of the Slavs along the Dnieper and at Novgorod as having taken place after the time of the Apostles: whereas the Russian Church commemorates each year the coming of St. Andrew...

(2) This view may attract undue criticism to the wise decision of Peter the Great to establish St. Andrew's Order of Chivalry.

(3) The derivation of the origin of first Russian Princes from nameless Scandinavians, contrary to Nestor's testimony who holds them to have been the descendants of Rus-Varangians, [the representation] of the origin of the name of Russians as not at all ancient, and, moreover, as derived from the *"Chukhontsy"* [a slightly derisive colloquial term for Finnish peasants living in the St. Petersburg area] in refutation of the clear testimony of Nestor's... are not only inadmissible in a dissertation of this kind..., but would bring shame upon the whole of Russia before other nations." [15]

books translated by Vassily Lebedev ... to be forwarded to Prof. Lomonosov, for examination..." (Sukhomlinov, *Materiyaly...*, (Source Materials), IX, p. 17). *Anson's Voyage Around the World* translated (from the German version) by the same Lebedev, was passed for publication in March 1750. (*Ibid.*, p. 320).

[13] Sukhomlinov, IX, p. 460.

[14] *Ibid.*, p. 461.

[15] Pekarsky, *Istoriya Imp. Akademii* ..., (History of the Imperial Academy ...), II, 1873, pp. 897ff.

Lomonosov's main argument is thus in effect that political or "ideological" reasons must prevail over scholarly objectivity. His submission was accepted as the basis for the final decision, written on behalf of the Academy by the Assessor Grigory Teplov, whereby Mueller's dissertation "was found to be so harmful that it was ordered to be kept under seal and not a single copy was to be allowed out."[16]

Much of the "censorship" by the Academy of Sciences during this period was affected by emotional factors, personal likes and dislikes etc., resulting in an overall picture which is far from coherent.[17] One discernible general tendency is to consider the acceptability of a manuscript in relation to both "ideological" and literary standards.

An example of censorial interference by the Holy Synod is provided by the case of the translation of Alexander Pope's *Essay on Man.* This was done by N. Popovsky, a pupil of Lomonosov and one of the first two native professors of Moscow University (the other one being Barsov) whilst still a student at the Academy of Sciences, in 1753. Popovsky, who did not know English, used a French translation of the *Essay* published in 1738 at Amsterdam.[18] It was submitted to I. Shuvalov, via Lomonosov, in March 1754, but its publication was held up by the Synodal censors who had found that "the Author of this book is basing his views entirely on natural principles, without any reference to the Holy Scripture or to the laws of our Orthodox Church mixing in also the system of Copernicus and ideas about the existence of many worlds, quite incompatible with the Holy Scripture."[19]

This was followed by a prolonged argument between Shuvalov, representing Popovsky, on one side and the Synod on the other. After some three years, in 1757, the book was finally passed for publication with some modifications and alterations made by Archbishop Ambrosius of Moscow who had been invited by Shuvalov to act as an arbiter. It is interesting to note that Popovsky showed some spirit of independence by causing the passages tampered with by the "censors" to stand out in bold print[20] and by noting in his foreword:

[16] *Ibid.*, p. 432.

[17] For further examples cf. the Minutes No. 303 of 16 Jan. 1750 (Sukhomlinov, Vol. IX, p. 243) and No. 311 of 19 January 1750, (*Ibid.*, p. 250). Also Skabichevsky, p. 32.

[18] *Essai sur l'homme par M. Pope. Traduit de l'anglois* [sic.], Amsterdam, 1738. The translator was one Silhouette. (N. S. Tikhonravov, "Istoria izdaniya " "Opyta o chelovveke" " v perevode Popovskogo", *Sochineniya,* (The Story of the Publication of the *Essay on Man in* Popovsky's Translation, in *Works*) II, M., 1898, p. 82. This article was originally published in *Russkiy Arkhiv, (Russian Archives),* VII, 1872, pp. 1311–1322.

[19] *Ibid.*, pp. 82–3.

"Since this is a delicate matter it may be possible that someone will find something doubtful from the point of view of our religion. However, the judicious reader will forgive me for two reasons: first, I am not a Theologian... second, I acted not as a critic, but as a translator; consequently even if I had found something wrong I had no right whatsoever to correct it." [21]

The next point to consider is the freedom of teaching. On 10 August 1750 were issued new regulations governing the functioning of the University and the *Gimnazya* attached to the Academy of Sciences. [22] These are written in the traditional spirit of tight control and reglamentation. The relevant Section 3 runs as follows:

"He [the Rector] shall watch diligently over the Professors in order to ensure that they conduct their lectures properly and in accordance with the plan approved by the *Kantselariya,* and that they do not teach anything that might be inimical to the Orthodox-Greek-Russian Faith, the form of Government, or Good Manners (*dobronraviye*)"[23]

This appears to be the first reasonably clear formulation of the principle on which censorship was later to be based, namely that the subject matter of a spoken or written utterance must not challenge: (a) the established Church, (b) the political system, and (c) the accepted standards of decency. It will subsequently be referred to as "the three-fold limiting clause". This principle was not, of course, new in the general European context, but its introduction in Russia represents a visible step in the process of "westernisation" of ideas in this particular field. Another Section (16) reads:

"The professor of History shall also take care to conduct the teaching of Civil History and Political Geography cautiously and in accordance with local religious and civil laws. In order to forestall any critical or hostile talks he shall submit all that he has taught and what he proposes to teach in the future, to the *Kantselariya,* in writing." [24]

Thus the professors were to be given no latitude whatever in preparing their lectures, and the attitude of the authors of the regulations toward freedom of expression – indeed any kind of academic freedom – is de-

[20] The book was printed at the Moscow University Press at the time when Popovsky was, in a sense, one of its supervisors.

[21] Tikhonravov, p. 86.

[22] In 1747 the University was officially separated from the Academy proper.

[23] Sukhomlinov, *Materialy* . . . , X, p. 518.

[24] *Ibid.*, p. 521.

cidedly negative. Perhaps it would be more correct to say that the problem does not yet arise, since the limitations imposed by the regulations just quoted are simply a reflection of the traditional principle of strict administrative control over any form of activity by the citizens – intellectual or otherwise.[25]

The Statute of the University of Moscow upon its establishment, embodied in the Edict of 12 January 1755, shows a similar attitude towards the teaching staff. In teaching his course, a professor was not permitted to follow his own system or an author chosen by himself: he was obliged to submit to the judgment of the Conference and of the Curator.[26] But the statute also contains certain significant innovations. Perhaps the most important of these from the point of view of our subject is the introduction of debates between students as a part of the curriculum. These were held on the last Saturday of each month and, from 1756, were also open to the public. In fact, the very first item published at the University Press was the *Invitation to all Friends of Learning* to a public meeting on the 26 April 1756, to celebrate the first anniversary of the University. The first *Catalogue of Public Lectures* was printed in the same year.[27] The professors were also allowed to deliver what was termed "private" lectures to members of the general public and this became the accepted practice.[28]

Thus in Moscow, unlike the other Capital, close links were established between local society and the institution of higher learning from its very inception. The subjects of debates were always advertised beforehand at

[25] E.g. professors who were late for their lectures were to be fined at the rate of one day's pay for one hour's absence. (*Ibid.*, p. 522).

[26] S. Shevyryov, *Istoriya Imperatorskogo Moskovskogo Universiteta 1755–1855,* (History of the Imperial University of Moscow) M., 1855, p. 13. The first Curators were I. I. Shuvalov (until his death in 1797) and Blumentrost. The Conference in 1756 consisted of six members appointed by Shuvalov: three Assessors and three Professors. By 1761 the proportion of the administrative to the academic element within the Conference changed in favour of the latter, its composition then being two Assessors, four Ordinary Professors, plus the Rector (Schaden) and a Secretary. (Cf. *Dokumenty i materialy po istorii Moskovskogo Universiteta vtoroy poloviny XVIII veka,* (Documents and Source Materials Relating to the History of Moscow University in the second half of the 18th Century), ed. by N. A. Penchko, I, (1756–1764), M., 1960.

[27] I. I. Melnikova, ed., *Izdaniya Moskovskogo Universiteta 1756–1779,* (Publications of Moscow University), M., 1955, p. 8.

[28] To avoid confusion of terms it is necessary to explain that the term "public lectures" referred to the lectures delivered before the students as a part of the ordinary curriculum, whereas "private" lectures, for which the professors were allowed to charge their own fees, were open to anyone interested outside the University. (Shevyryov, p. 15; Solov'yov, *Istoriya Rossii . . .* , (History of Russia), XXVI (Book XIII, M., 1965), p. 555; also cf. A. Kizevetter, "Moskovskiy Universitet", in *Moskovskiy Universitet 1755–1930,* (Moscow University 1755–1930), Paris, 1930, pp. 15, 43.

the University and, from 1756, in the newspaper *Moskovskiye vedomosti* (Moscow News) as were the topics of "private" courses and lectures. Some examples are quoted by Solov'yov: on 17 December 1758 a public debate was held on the subject of natural theology, with Professor Fromann in the chair. Professor Dilthey "shortly after his arrival in 1756 announced private lectures on natural law, in French, promising to complete the course within six months. In 1761 Dilthey conducted a course of lectures in natural law, heraldry, history, and geography; the fee for each course was 12 rubles, [but] no fees were collected from those who could not afford them." The University bookshop opened in March/April 1756 and the library which opened in July of the same year, were both accessible to the public, the library being opened for that purpose for three hours on three afternoons a week. The list of titles of books sold at the bookshop at its opening shows that about 90 percent of them were classical Latin texts.[29]

Another point of a more general significance was that the new University was, almost from the beginning, exempted from local administrative interference through being made, by the edict of 5 March 1756, responsible directly and exclusively to the Senate.[30]

There can be no doubt that all these previously unheard of activities and facilities contributed greatly to a change in traditional attitudes which can be observed from the seventeen-fifties onwards, and to the awakening of interest in the free expression of ideas within society. Some indication of the scope of these influences can be found in the fact that by the end of 1767, after seven years of its existence, Moscow University produced, according to Shuvalov's report, 1800 graduates, 300 of whom were non-noble (*raznochintsy*).[31]

Among the new instruments of expression which appear in the seventeen-fifties, the periodical press occupies a conspicuous position. The credit for the first popular-scientific periodical in Russia belongs to the Academy of Sciences where, in 1754, the idea was conceived to publish a monthly magazine *St. Petersburg Academic Commentaries,* shortly to be renamed *Monthly Essays: Useful and Amusing,* under which latter title it is generally known. The Academy Conference at its meeting in November 1754, when the publication was finally decided upon and the editorship of the journal entrusted to Mueller, admitted contributions from persons

[29] Shevyryov, pp. 23f.
[30] *P.S.Z.*, XIV, No. 10,515.
[31] Solov'yov, XXV (M., 1965), p. 193. The University library, according to the same report, consisted of about 5,000 volumes, not counting the text-books used by the students.

outside the Academy; at the same time it explicitly banned from the future journal all items pertaining to matters of faith as well as anything critical or potentially offensive to individuals: "Exilent quoque omnia scripta critica vel que aliquo modo famam alicujus laedere aut contra aliquem scripta videri possint." [32]

It may be noted here that Lomonosov suggested to the Conference that all contributions be examined at a plenary meeting of the members of the Academy before being published. This was opposed by Tredyakovsky on the grounds that it would cause unnecessary delays, and was eventually overruled by the President, K. Razumovsky. By a decision taken in December 1754 this "vetting" authority was entrusted to Mueller, without whose signature no contribution was to be accepted. [33]

The early history of the *Essays* is unfortunately marred by personal strife amongst the members of the Academy who may be considered to have formed its editorial body, i.e. principally Mueller, Lomonosov, and Tredyakovsky. Much of this was directly connected with the acceptability or otherwise of items intended for publication in the *Essays*. The following examples will serve to illustrate some of the attitudes displayed by those concerned and the criteria applied in the evaluation of contributions.

As soon as the first issue of the journal was ready, in January 1755, Lomonosov attacked Mueller criticising his introductory article. In the ensuing argument Tredyakovsky took Mueller's side, but their alliance was short-lived. It was in fact replaced, a few months later, by a bitter feud resulting from Mueller's refusal to accept contributions from Tredyakovsky for publication. In October 1755 Tredyakovsky denounced the playwright and poet Sumarokov to the Synod on account of the latter's "Spiritual Odes" printed in the September issue of the *Essays*. Tredyakovsky had found there an ode, purporting to be a translation of one of the psalms, where "he had noticed that from the eight to the eleventh verse inclusive [the author] speaks as himself and not as the psalmist about the infinity of the Universe and of many worlds as if they existed." [34] The Synod took no apparent action for over a year, but in late 1756 wrote to the Academy asking for an investigation. At the same time they submitted a report directly to the empress, asking her "first of all, to forbid anywhere in Russia to write anything about the multiplicity of worlds, and secondly to suppress both the *Monthly Essays* and the translation by Prince Kantemir of Fontenelle's work about the existence of many

[32] Pekarsky, *Redaktor, sotrudniki, etc.*, (The Editor of the Contributors to, etc.), p. 4.
[33] *Ibid.*, p. 5.
[34] *Ibid., p. 42.*

worlds." [35] The fact that there is no record of any action having ever followed this report may be considered as another indication of a certain relaxation of the government attitude towards matters of this kind.

Lomonosov became a member of the Academy *Kantselariya* on 1 March 1757, whereupon he lost no time in undertaking suppressive measures against the *Essays*. The immediate target of his attack was an article then being prepared for print, by Grigori Poletika, "On the Origins, Revival, and Growth of Learning and Schools in Russia and of their Present State", to which Lomonosov objected on the grounds that it did not mention the existence of schools in Russia during the period from the tenth to the seventeenth century. Mueller's argument to the effect that since no historical record exists of a school of any kind during that period, the author could hardly be expected to write about them, was overruled and Poletika's article was judged to be "full of improprieties" (*napolnena mnogimi nepristoynostyami*). At the same time, Mueller was reminded to adhere strictly to the directives received from the *Kantselariya* and, in particular, to abide by its ruling that all contribution to the *Monthly Essays* be submitted to it "for examination" *before* and not *after* they have been published. [36]

Another similar case is that of "grave political errors" found by Lomonosov in Mueller's article, published in May 1760 issue of the *Essays,* "Information on the Zaporozhian Cossacks". Before the article was published, one of the pages had been re-printed and "some words" had been removed. [37]

From 1759, the Academy printing press also published a new periodical, *The Industrious Bee,* edited by Sumarokov which together with *Leisure Usefully Employed* – of which more below – can claim the honour of being the first private undertaking of its kind in Russian history. Sumarokov's correspondence with I. I. Shuvalov in this connection throws some additional light on the concept of censorship practiced by the Academy. In his letter, written in 1758, negotiating for the use of the Academy's printing facilities, Sumarokov accepts its right of supervision over the *contents* of his periodical, but asks that no alterations be made to his *style,* and that he may be "protected from interference and difficulties

[35] *Ibid.*, p. 44. This refers to Bernard de Fontenelle's work *Entretiens sur la Pluralité des Mondes.*

[36] *Ibid.*, p. 47. Cf. also USSR Academy of Sciences, M.V. Lomonosov – *Polnoye sobraniye sochineniy* (Complete Collection of Works), X., M.–L., 1957, pp. 141ff.

[37] Pekarsky, *op. cit.*, pp. 51–52. For an account in English of the "historical" controversies within the Academy at the time see H. Rogger, *National Consciousness in Eighteenth-Century Russia,* Harvard U.P., 1960, chapter "The Uses of History".

in the process of publication." [38] The Academy appointed Adjunct N. I. Popov to act as the supervisor, instructing him "to peruse items to be published in this journal before they are printed. Should you find anything adverse in the subject matter, but not in style *(v dele a ne v sloge)*, you are to draw it to the attention of the Editor", (i.e. Sumarokov). [39]

In April 1759 Sumarokov complained to the Academy about Popov whom he accused of drunkeness and incompetence. This resulted in the appointment of Professor Kotel'nikov and Adjunct Rumovsky in Popov's place and, for a while, the relations between Sumarokov and his "censors" appeared to be relatively harmonious.

One incident of possible interest arose in connection with Sumarokov's article in praise of Peter the Great written for publication in the November issue of the *Bee*. Kotel'nikov refused to pass an opinion on this contribution on the grounds that this was an extremely important subject, beyond his capacity as a professional mathematician. The case was then referred to President Razumovsky who ruled that the article should be printed "in view of the author's insistence and in consideration of the fact that in earlier times, before the publication of this journal, many of his plays had been published without the Academy censorship." At the same time Sumarokov was to be told that he himself would be held responsible "if the Court or the Public show any signs of displeasure." [40]

[38] Ya. Grot, *Pis'ma Lomonosova i Sumarokova k I. I. Shuvalovu,* (Letters by Lomonosov and Sumarokov to I. I. Shuvalov), (Supp. to Vol. I of *Zapiski Imp. Akademii Nauk,* (Records of the Imp. Academy of Sciences), No. 1), St. P., 1862, p. 18.

[39] Letter from Taubert to Popov dated 7 January 1759, *Arkhiv Akademii Nauk SSSR,* (Archives of the USSR Academy of Sciences), No. 239, Fol. 33, quoted by D. D. Shamray and P. N. Berkov in "K tsenzurnoy istorii " "Trudolyubivoy pchely" " A. P. Sumarokova" (A Contribution to the History of Censorship of A. P. Sumarokov's *The Industrious Bee), XVIII Vek, Sb. 5,* M.–L., 1962, p. 400. The authors of this article use the quoted instruction to Popov as a premise for the assertion that the "censorship" exercised by the Academy was intended to deal with both the "ideological" and "formal" aspects of a written work. In this they overlook Sumarokov's letter applying for the use of the Academy's printing facilities from which I have just quoted. Since the distinction between the contents and the form of items to be published was first made by Sumarokov himself, Taubert's letter clearly amounts simply to an acceptance of his terms and cannot serve as a basis for a theory of principles of censorship as conceived by the Academy authorities. Berkov and Shamray also maintain a discreet silence around the rather unsavoury part played by Lomonosov in the "censorship" of the *Bee* and in its demise, producing instead the hypothesis that it may have been suppressed as a result of Sumarokov's article in praise of Peter the Great (see below).

[40] *Dela arkhiva Akademicheskoy Kantselarii,* (Files in the Archives of the Academy Chancellery), No. 239 (Report by Prof. Semyon Kotel'nikov of 4 October 1759 and the President's order of 7 October 1759), quoted by Sukhomlinov, *Istoriya Rossiyskoy Akademii,* (History of the Russian Academy), III, St. P., 1876, p. 52.

It was not long, however, before Lomonosov – apparently acting entirely on his own initiative – assumed the function of a chief "censor" of Sumarokov's periodical. The situation became quite farcical when, for example, Lomonosov censored the parodies of his own odes written by Sumarokov for publication in the *Industrious Bee*. Some idea of the extent of exasperation to which poor Sumarokov was brought by this state of affairs can be gathered from his letter to Shuvalov dated 15 November 1759:

"I am unable to publish any more issues, as Lomonosov keeps holding up their publication and forcing me into the situation where I have to ask several times for permission [to publish them]. He acts as both the plaintiff and the judge and is, as far as I am concerned, the greatest villain, afraid of my exposing his complete incompetence in the literary field; ... The Censors have been appointed I do not know for what purpose – neither does the President – and whatever they pass is scrutinised by Lomonosov, who has ordered the proof-reader to show him every page of my publications. Whatever he does not like he suppresses in the name of the *Kantselariya,* notwithstanding the fact that I am publishing in a private capacity and am paying money for it." [41]

The story of the *Industrious Bee* ends with its issue of December 1759 in which, on p. 768, Sumarokov wrote: "For a great many reasons I have come to detest the title and the rank of a writer... I bid farewell to the Muses for ever and will never write again."

Leisure Usefully Employed, a contemporary of the *Bee,* can likewise be regarded as a private periodical. It was published at the Army Cadet Corps in St. Petersburg by a group of teachers and pupils of that school, during the years 1759 and 1760. It was financed by the contributors each of whom had to pay the costs of printing his own work. It published predominantly translations, from French, Italian, German, and Danish, and it may be noted that among these were included some "second-hand" items from Addison's and Steele's *Spectator.* In 1760, after closing down of the *Industrious Bee,* Sumarokov also wrote for the *Leisure* which he seems to have used mainly as a platform for polemic with his adversaries at the Academy of Sciences. [42] In this case there is no record of editorial strife or suppression of contributions; as far as the "censorial" super-

[41] Grot, *op. cit.,* p. 42.

[42] Berkov, *Istoriya russkoy zhurnalistiki,* (The History of Russian Periodical Press), pp. 126–7. See also D. D. Shamray, "Tsenzurnyi nadzor nad tipografiyey Sukhoputnogo Shlyakhetnogo Kadetskogo Korpusa" (Censorial Supervision over the Printing Press at the Land [i.e. Army] Corps of Noble Cadets), in USSR Academy of Sciences, *XVIII vek,* Sb. 2., M.–L., 1940, pp. 303–308, for details indicating that the "censorship" at the Corps printing press (established in 1757) was analogous to that at the Academy.

vision was concerned, the principle that a government institution is capable of exercising this function in respect of its own published output was evidently accepted. There is no evidence of *Leisure* ever having been "censored" by the Academy or by any other outside branch of the administration.

The two other periodicals in existence at the time were both published at the University of Moscow. These were *The Moscow News (Moskovskiye vedomosti)* which began to appear in April 1756 and continued until the end of the century, and *Useful Recreation (Poleznoye uveseleniye),* which existed from 1760 until 1762 and was edited by a group of members of the University headed by Kheraskov.

We have already noted a slightly more liberal climate at the University of Moscow as compared with the St. Petersburg Academy. (One apparent reason for this phenomenon seems to be the physical distance from the seat of government in case of the former, the other main characteristics of the two institutions, such as administrative structure and ethnic composition of their staff, being very similar). This factor which, in a somewhat different form, assumed greater scope and significance in the reign of Catherine II, also affected the periodicals published in Moscow. Here the supervision over publications printed at the University Press was, from the beginning, entrusted to the University authorities who were, in turn, responsible, as we have seen, directly to the Senate. As far as the *Moscow News* was concerned its editorship was, from its inception, entrusted to Professor Barsov [43] whose authority in matters of grammar, style, and choice of material for publication does not appear to have been seriously challenged by anyone. [44] *Useful Recreation* which published satirical poems by Kheraskov, Rzhevsky, and some others, and was quite enthusiastic in its assurances of loyalty to Peter III, appears to have had a similarly uneventful existence under the aegis of the University.

One final point of practical nature which should be noted in connection with these periodicals is one which arises from the fact that items translated from foreign languages formed the major part of their contents. The choice of material for translation lay, as a rule, with the translators themselves and appears to have been dictated largely by the economic factor of anticipated demand. The same applies, of course, to the translations of books

[43] Anton Alexeyevich Barsov (1730–1791) studied at the Academy of Sciences under Lomonosov and Tredyakovsky. Transferred to Moscow University upon its opening in 1755, appointed Ordinary Professor of Rhetorics in 1761 in which post he remained until his death.

[44] *Cf. Dokumenty i materialy* . . . , (Documents and Source Materials . . .), N. A. Penchko, ed. I, *passim.*

where the translators' freedom of choice does not, likewise, seem to have been restricted in any way.[45] All this was a powerful factor in the flow of ideas into Russia from Western Europe. The increase in these influences was thus directly connected with the increase in the availability of the instruments of expression.

One other such instrument or medium which must be mentioned here is the first permanent Russian language theatre, originally the company formed at Yaroslavl' by Fyodor Volkov and associates. The theatre in which Volkov's company acted was, from 1756, placed under direct government control. This may indeed be regarded as an illustration of the typical attitude: anything new can normally be introduced only as a result of government initiative; if, as in this rather extraordinary case, it is independently conceived, it must be taken under the government sponsorship as soon as possible. During the early part of its existence this theatre served primarily as a vehicle for Sumarokov's plays. The important point is that, even if this particular medium did not produce any spectacular ideas during this period, it was nevertheless there, ready to be put to use by the Fonvizins, Knyazhnins, Kapnists, and Nikolevs of the coming generation.

Thus, while in the seventeen-fifties there is still no conscious or articulate concern with the idea of freedom of expression on either the government's or society's side, certain new elements come into play working towards the erosion of old concepts. One factor of a general nature involved here was the fact that the process of secularisation of culture that had been set in motion a generation or two earlier, was now producing visible effects. Other factors which came into prominence in the "fifties" were: the increase and changed character of European influences (by "changed character" I mean that they now came mainly from France, that they were generally carried by people of greater cultural significance, and that the prevailing attitudes towards freedom were now changing at their source), and the increase in the availability of media of expression. These were responsible for creating certain unprecedented situations; the practical manner of dealing with these reveals attitudes both old and new. Insofar as it is possible to discover any definite trends in this multitude of mostly *ad hoc* measures undertaken by the government and its administrative

[45] For example, an announcement which appeared in *St. Petersburg Vedomosti* in 1761 offered financial inducement to those who had in their possession books already translated and invited them to bring such books to the Academy for publication; it also offered a choice of books in foreign languages available at the Academy bookshop free of charge to potential translators. (Solov'yov, XXVI, p. 574).

organs, it may be claimed that there is a certain tendency towards relaxation of centralised control – and delegation of supervisory powers, as in the case of Moscow University.

The powers of supervision over printed matter were still technically vested in the Senate and the Synod. If the latter occasionally showed some signs of vigilance, it can almost be said of the former that it allowed its powers to lapse by default or, more accurately, that it tacitly delegated them to the institutions of higher learning. But it must be borne in mind that these institutions held such powers only in respect to their own output, in their capacity of government organs in actual control over printing presses, and that they were not the recognized instruments of censorship. We have seen that the character of their supervisory functions tended to be "editorial" rather than strictly "censorial" and that the fear of attracting criticism or adverse publicity to the institution concerned played a prominent part in the actual decisions.

It may be useful at this point to glance briefly at the situation with respect to censorship prevailing at about the same time in Western-European countries with political systems roughly comparable to the Russian. One very essential point affecting the validity of any comparison between, say, France, Prussia, or the German Empire on the one side, and Russia on the other, as far as the control over written matter is concerned, is the absence of privately-owned printing presses in the latter country. In the context of mid-eighteenth century absolute monarchies there existed a practical need for supervision, by powers spiritual and temporal, over the publication and dissemination of printed matter. This need would not, however, be apparent in the situation where the means of publication were under the direct control of the state. Moreover, in Russia the number of printing establishments was very small and their geographical location was close to the centres of administration, quite unlike France, for example.

This is why, in Russia, censorship in the juridical sense did not yet exist in mid-eighteenth century. The first censorship laws were not promulgated until after the private printing presses came into existence, in the latter part of the reign of Catherine II. Until then, appropriately enough, the relevant legislation shows some concern only with the secondary aspect of the problem, i.e. the dissemination and circulation of the written matter considered objectionable.

In France, the law of 1744 prohibited all printing and reprinting of books without the prior examination and approval by a censor appointed by the Chancellor. In practice there also existed a form of post-publication censorship: the book could still be suppressed, after appearing in print if it incurred the displeasure of the Sorbonne or the Parlement.[46] The ecclesiastical authorities were vigilant and sensitive to anything offensive to, or incompatible with the Catholic dogma. This last point, to an even greater extent, applies to Spain and Portugal. In Italy the situation varied from quite liberal, as in Tuscany or in Venice (where commercial considerations played an important part) to extremely repressive, as in Rome. In Austria, under Maria-Theresa, the ecclesiastical censorship was strict, and even forbade the circulation of the *Index* on the grounds that its perusal might excite unhealthy curiosity about the forbidden books.[47] In Protestant Prussia of Frederick II, according to Lessing's testimony, "...you can deliver yourself of any sort of nonsense about religion; but just put a finger into the political pie, and you will see how your so-called freedom will turn into serfdom."[48] In the Netherlands, the printing and publishing business was largely free and the Dutch presses did a brisk trade in literature that could not be published in the country of its origin, but could be brought back, without much difficulty, in the form of a finished product. Official censorship existed in Sweden and Denmark until its abolition, respectivelly, in 1766 and 1770.

Insofar as any comparison can be made with Russia of that period, the quasi-censorial actions within the Imperial Academy of Sciences seem to have been motivated by precepts not unlike those of the French guardians of the printed word, that is to say, principally by the fear of passing anything potentially offensive to the Court or to the Church authorities. What is quite apparent, however, is the gradually decreasing importance of the "ecclesiastical" factor, a process which accelerated noticeably in the reign of Catherine II. With her accession, the Russian government attitude towards freedom of the press tends to move closer to the Prussian model, as we shall see presently.

The short reign of Peter III is notable from the point of view of our subject for one conspicuous event: the abolition of the Secret Chancellery and of the *slovo i delo* type of offence.[49] The removal of this important restraint of free speech, even if it could not be expected to produce any immediately visible results, was significant as a clear indication of a change in attitude to these matters at the highest level.[50] The ground had

[46] J. Lough, *An Introduction to Eighteenth Century France*, Lond., 1960, p. 305.

[47] P. Hazard, *European Thought in the Eighteenth Century*, Cleveland, 1963, pp. 74ff.

[48] Hazard, *ibid.*

[49] By the Manifesto of 21 February 1762. (*P.S.Z.*, XV, No. 11, 445). It prescribed corporal punishment, without investigation, for those invoking *slovo i delo*.

[50] Samuel Bentham, younger brother of the famous Jeremy, describes a case of a practical application of this law some twenty years later. Among his unpublished diaries

thus been considerably softened for the new ideas which were to be planted in the following reign.

The first few years after the accession of Catherine II are characterised by the concern of the new regime to consolidate its political power achieved as the result of the *coup* of 28 June 1762. Its attention being thus focused on this domestic political problem, things are, in general, left as they were in other fields. The precise duration of the period in which this situation obtained is difficult to determine; it may, however, be suggested that it came to an end in late 1766, with the publication of the Manifesto calling into being the Commission for the Compilation of the New Code of Laws. This was the first open step in the direction of major reform, presumably meaning that the regime was now feeling strong enough to transfer its attention to problems other than the immediate task of self-preservation.

From the point of view of the history of free expression it is not a particularly eventful but nevertheless an interesting period. On the government side no clear statement of policy in this regard is as yet forthcoming; but the liberal views of the monarch which manifest themselves on various occasions, in private pronouncements as well as in practical administrative decisions, make it clear to a gradually increasing circle that a definite relaxation, if not a drastic change, in government attitude towards civil liberties is imminent.

In speaking of "government attitude" it is necessary to state at the outset to what extent the term "government" can be identified in this case with the person of the ruler. Without entering into a detailed discussion it can probably be safely maintained that these two terms, in relation to the whole of Catherine's reign, are practically interchangeable: during this time, in the words of a prominent Russian historian, "Russia was being governed, in the full sense of the word, by the Empress and the Senate" with the ultimate decision always reserved for the former, who "did not pass single a Senate report without [submitting it to] her careful criticism."[51] For the present purpose it would probably be fair to define the term

written during a trip to Siberia in 1781–1782 there is a note dated June 1781 about a man who had invoked *slovo i delo* in a quarrel with his brother: " ... the ukaze is to flog such a man directly without further inquiry, but as he [one Grigori Grigorievich, apparently a manager of a factory] does not chuse to be call'd a cruel person he would immediately send him in chains to Catherinburg, for the Governor to punish him". (British Museum, *Additional Manuscripts* – shown subsequently as B.M., *Add.Mss.* – 33,552, Fol. 190).

[51] N. D. Chechulin in *Istoriya Pravitel's tvuyushchego Senata za dvesti let 1711–1911*, (History of the Governing Senate for the Two Hundred Years 1711–1911), II, St. P., 1911, pp. 690–691 and 696.

"government" as meaning Catherine with the small circle of her immediate advisors at a given time.[52] It must be made clear that this does not include senior administrators who, at times, displayed attitudes or views diametrically opposite to those of the "government" thus conceived. Examples of this will be found below.

Catherine II came to the throne at the age of 33: mature enough to know what she wanted and to understand the main problems she was facing: at the same time youthful enough to be untouched by disillusionment and to accept the optimistic philosophy of her age, with its belief in the practically unlimited power of human reason and the new enlightened society "just around the corner". In becoming the Empress of Russia she was eagerly looking forward to a successful practical application of theoretical principles gleaned from her earlier studies. Many of these principles were as yet untried in real life; she considered herself in an unique and fascinating position being now able to put them to the test on a ground she believed to be virgin and unspoiled and therefore receptive and fertile.[53]

In the period of her reign with which we are now concerned Catherine's professed views can be considered quite liberal by the standards of the age; this is conceded even by her most hostile critics who merely question her honesty in this regard. The insurmountable difficulty with which she was faced from the outset – and which she consistently appeared to ignore – was the incompatibility of practical implementation of these views with the continued undisturbed maintenance of her own position within the political system which she had inherited and whose preservation alone guaranteed her the degree of power she considered indispensable. This paradoxical situation provides the most obvious general explanation for the ambivalence typical of Catherine's reign noted by practically all historians of the period which, naturally enough, became more and more apparent with the passage of time.

As far as she herself was concerned, Catherine did not see any need to liberalise the existing political system, and in this her practice was quite

[52] The Council of State established at the outbreak of the first Turkish war, in November 1768, was, for the remaining part of Catherine's reign, concerned almost exclusively with foreign affais, but it can be considered covered by this definition since its members were recruited from precisely this circle of immediate advisors.

[53] The following quotation taken from the draft of her letter to Voltaire, written in 1765, may serve as an illustration: "Je dois rendre justice à la nation; c'est un excellent terrain, sur lequel unne bonne graine prend bien vite; mais aussi il nous faut des axiomes incontestablement reconnus pour vrais." (*Sbornik Russkogo* (later *Imperatorskogo Russkogo) Istoricheskogo Obschestva* (The Collection of the Imperial Russian Historical Society), henceforth *Sb. R.I.O.*, X, p. 35).

consistent with theory. Her liberalism was concerned solely with civil rights, and here her ideas were far in advance of any demand raised by her subjects in this early period.

Since, as already pointed out, the accent in the first years of Catherine's reign was on the preservation and consolidation of her political power, no radical departures from the accepted practice can be expected during this period. As far as civil liberties in general and freedom of expression in particular are concerned, we have a number of administrative decisions unmistakably reflecting the humanity and the generally enlightened attitude of the new ruler, but no spectacular pronouncements or novel legislation. We also have a certain number of theoretical pronouncements and gestures which we shall now briefly examine.

A short time after her accession, Catherine took what in the context of time and place was an extraordinary step, in offering to sponsor the publishing of the *Encyclopaedia* within her realm.[54] While it cannot be denied that her principal aim here was, in all likelihood, to impress her Western-European pen-friends and other courts, there can be no doubt that it must have also served as a good indication of her attitude in these matters to those near her at home, and through them, to the wider circle of educated Russian society.

The fact that Catherine, in the first few months of her reign, reaffirmed the Manifesto of 21 February 1762 abolishing the Secret Chancellery and putting an end to *slovo i delo* prosecutions has already been mentioned. The investigation of suspected high treason and other offences against the Crown was, in Catherine's reign, the responsibility of a branch of the Senate called *Taynaya Ekspeditsiya.* Although this office took over the principal functions of the Chancellery and even some of its personnel,[55] its methods of operation were considerably softened, as a direct result of Catherine's instructions. Torture was still the lawful procedure in criminal investigation, but Catherine showed concern that its use be limited as far as possible, both as regards severity and frequency. Thus, in the edict of 25 December 1762, she directed that it may only be used "with extreme

[54] This offer was made on Catherine's behalf to Didérot by I. I. Shuvalov, via Voltaire. The latter wrote in this connection (to Didérot, on 25 September N.S., 1762): "... in what times do we live? France persecutes philosophers while the Scythians offer them protection." (M. F. Shugurov, *"Didro i ego othosheniya k Yekaterine II"* (Didérot and his Relations with Catherine II), in *Osmnadtsatyi Vek,* (The Eighteenth Century), ed. by P. Bartenev, M., 1868, p. 261). The *Encyclopaedia* was to be published at Riga.

[55] Among those was Sheshkovsky, later to acquire renown as the investigator of Radishchev and Novikov.

circumspection" and threatened "most severe penalties" for the use of torture unless absolutely necessary.[56]

Catherine always liked to stress the humane and tolerant character of her reign by contrasting it either – if speaking to Russians – with those of her predecessors, or, in case of foreigners, with conditions in Western Europe, notably France. For example, in a letter to D'Alembert, written in 1766, she says: "Vos climats doux et bénis délient l'esprit, le notre rude et engourdi ne saurait pousser si loin la pénétration: nous laissons les savants tout doucement s'occuper de leurs sciences et l'on ne brûle personne."[57]

Among Catherine's official pronouncements of this period may be noted the Charter of the Imperial Academy of Fine Arts, dated 4 November 1765.[58] This document is written in a very humane and enlightened spirit which is especially apparent in the part devoted to the upbringing and education of young pupils of the school attached to the Academy. One section authorises the establishment of a printing press "for printing not only of books concerning arts and crafts, but also other useful books, only taking care that, as it has often been the case until now, one printing press does not harm another" (i.e. does not engage in practices unfair to other presses). The Charter prescribes that the annual meetings of the Academy (on the 1st September each year) be open, apart from members, "also to other prominent persons" who would have the right of expressing their opinion on matters under discussion, and also that:

> "The Academy shall have a public library to which a competent Librarian shall be appointed from among the Academicians, permitting outsiders to visit it on appointed days and times, for the purpose not only of reading, but also of placing subscriptions for anything they might find of use to themselves or what would arouse their interest."

Thus the new trend which we have noted in the reign of Elizabeth with respect to Moscow University was being sustained and fostered by Catherine's regime. Unlike her predecessors – with the possible and only partial exception of Elizabeth – Catherine professed the view that humanity and tolerance bring better results than ruthlessness and suppression. In

[56] *P.S.Z.*, XVI, No. 11,717.

[57] *Sb. R.I.O.*, X, p. 133.

[58] *Privilegiya i ustav Imperatorskoy Akademii tryokh znatneyshikh khudozhestv, Zhivopisi, Skul'ptury i Arkhitektury s vospitatel'nym pri onoy Akademii uchilishchem*, (The Charter and Statute of the Imp. Academy of the Three Most Prominent Arts, Painting, Sculpture and Architecture With the Boarding School Attached to the Aforementioned Academy), St. P., 1765. This Academy was actually established already in the reign of Elizabeth, in 1758, but no legislative act concerning it was passed at the time.

1766 she wrote to Voltaire on the subject of "Old Believers" and other religious minorities: "La persécution irrite les esprits, la tolérance les adoucit et les rend moins obstinés: elle étouffe ces disputes contraires au repos de l'état et à l'union des citoyens." [59]

A rather spectacular move which undoubtedly helped further to establish Catherine's reputation as a liberal, both at home and abroad, was her undertaking to translate *Belisaire* by Jean François Marmontel during her trip on the Volga in the early summer of 1767. Marmontel had sent her a copy of his book, accompanied by a letter, on its publication in the spring of that year. [60] In his book he openly condemns absolute monarchy and favours a political system where the rule of law is supreme. In deciding to translate it into Russian, Catherine put to work various members of her entourage (A. Bibikov, G. Kozitsky, I. Yelagin, Grigori Orlov, and some others) dividing the book between them, while she herself took the most controversial chapter (IX) devoted to absolute monarchy. Having heard of this, Marmontel "refused to believe that the Empress herself had translated a whole chapter, above all one in which autocracy is subjected to merciless criticism...," [61] while the significance of this gesture could not have been lost on her Russian audience, coming, as it did, on the eve of the opening of the legislative Commission. The translation appears to have been completed in September 1768, and it was published in the same year at Moscow University Press, with a dedication by Catherine to the then Bishop of Tver', Gavriil. [62] According to Catherine's own statement, she endeavoured to publicise the translation "so that my subjects might understand the ties that bind us together." [63] All this is, of course, in perfect accord with the spirit of the "age of reason" and with Catherine's view of herself as an enlightened monarch; what is important here from the point of view of our subject is the fact that it showed plainly that the government no longer regarded the utterance of views critical of absolute monarchy as treasonable or even dangerous. Another gesture in the same

[59] Letter dated at St. Petersburg, 29 June/10 July 1766. *(Sb. R.I.O.*, X, St. P., 1872, p. 94).

[60] It was suppressed in Paris and the author confined to the Bastille, albeit for a short period.

[61] Sukhomlinov, *Istoriya Rossiyskoy Akademii,* (History of the Russian Academy), I, p. 121. The autograph draft of Marmontel's letter to Catherine is in the British Museum (Add.Mss. 21,514).

[62] Cf. *Sochineniya Imperatritsy Yekateriny II,* (Works of Empress Catherine II), ed. by A. N. Pypin, Vol. V, St. P., 1901, pp. 17f. Gavriil (Petrov) later Metropolitan of St. Petersburg, figured prominently in the work of the "Commission" (see also below, p. 97).

[63] Sukhomlinov, p. 122.

category was the translation into Russian of the *Encyclopaedia* – then banned in France – carried out by the same group of Catherine's associates, at about the same time. Three volumes of this translation were published at Moscow University Press in 1767.

In turning to the practical measures affecting the problem of free expression, undertaken by the government during this early period, I propose to look first at the relevant legislation and administrative orders. The first concern of a regime which had come to power through a *coup d'état* and whose legal claim to power was uncertain to say the least, was obviously the prevention of a counter-coup and the removal of the vestiges of the previous regime. That fears connected with the first of these points were well founded was soon confirmed by the Khrushchov-Guriyev plot and by the Mirovich affair; the second involved, among other things, the removal of books and other printed items with references to the deposed Peter III: a problem identical to that faced by Elizabeth some twenty years earlier although, as we shall see, it was dealt with rather differently. Appropriately enough, we have legislative acts relevant to each of these aspects during the first two years of Catherine's reign.

The first of these to be noted is the Manifesto of 4 July 1763,[64] issued to prevent threatening popular unrest in connection with the rumour that Catherine was to marry Grigori Orlov, and with the case of *Kammeryunker* Khitrovo who opposed the Orlovs, was in favour of Catherine marrying one of the brothers of Ivan VI, and spoke quite openly of the temporary character of her regime.[65] The text of this document is remarkable for its circumlocution:

> "... it is with extreme regret and displeasure that We hear that there appeared some people of such corrupt morals and thoughts who are not at all concerned with the common good and peace; but being themselves contaminated by strange arguments about matters that do not concern them in the least [and] about which they have no direct information, nevertheless try to contaminate other weak minds, and even go so far ... that in their talk they insolently touch upon not only the matters of Civil Rights, Government and Laws promulgated by Ourselves, but upon the very Divine Laws, without any thought of the prohibitions and dangers which surround such improper philosophising."

Bil'basov quotes some excerpts from despatches by foreign diplomats in Russia dated between November 1762 and May 1763 from which it is

[64] *P.S.Z.*, XVI, No. 11,843.

[65] Cf. V. A. Bil'basov, *Istoriya Yekateriny Vtoroy*, (History of Catherine the Second), II, Berlin, 1900, pp. 292ff. Catherine, in one of her notes, referred to this decree as "the Manifesto on Silence" *(o molchanii)*.

evident that the "improper philosophising" had reached quite serious proportions. If the method chosen to deal with it in this case resembles in its crudity some similar acts of earlier governments,[66] it differs from them in tone – which is decidedly milder, if possibly more obscure – and in the absence of severe sanctions.

Also in the course of 1763, the government issued directives aimed at preventing importation of books published abroad favourable to Peter III. This was caused by the publication in Germany, in French, of a book entitled *"Mémoires pour servir à l'Histoire de Pierre III, Empereur de Russie,* ... par Mr. D. G., Francfort et Leipsic, 1763." On 22 June of that year Catherine sent an urgent note to the Chancellor M. Vorontsov about this book, as a result of which appropriate instructions were sent to Customs offices at St. Petersburg, Riga, Revel, Narva, and Viborg.[67] This was followed on 6 September of the same year by a written administrative order the draft of which has been preserved in Catherine's own hand,[68] aimed at preventing further imports of this and other "undesirable" books, many of which appear already to have found their way into Russia. The order notes that books are currently on sale at the Academy of Sciences which are "against the Law, Good Manners, Ourselves, and the Russian Nation and are prohibited in the whole world as, for example, Rousseau's *Emile, Memoirs of Peter III,* Jewish Letters in the French Language, and many others like these." It assumes that such books are being sold on an even larger scale by private bookshops in the two Capitals "since they [the bookshops] are not under anybody's supervision." To put an end to these practices, the order directs private booksellers to submit annually to the Academy of Sciences, or to the University of Moscow, lists of "books which they propose to import, whereupon the two Institutions shall delete from these lists books which are contrary to law, Good Manners, and Ourselves." In the future, offenders were to be punished with forfeiture of their shops, the proceeds of their sale to go to the Orphans' Home. Details as to the best practical implementation of this order were left to the Senate.[69]

[66] For example, in 1757, during the Seven Years War, Elizabeth issued an edict ordering the immediate cessation of "discussions and arguments on various political matters". (*P.S.Z.*, XIV, No. 10,733).

[67] *Sb. R.I.O.*, XLVIII, p. 559, and the memorandum from the College of Foreign Affairs to the College of Commerce, dated 24 June 1763 and signed by M. Vorontsov and Prince Alexander Golitsyn. *(Arkhiv. kn. Vorontsova,* henceforth: *Vorontsov Archives,* VII, M., 1875, p. 605.)

[68] It was reproduced by Bartenev in *Vosmnadtsatyi Vek,* (The Eighteenth Century), Book 3, p. 392.

[69] *Sb. R.I.O.*, VII, p. 318.

This legislative item, strictly speaking, is not concerned with freedom of expression within the country, being directed exclusively at books imported from abroad. It is nevertheless of considerable interest because it outlines the two principles on which government policy in relation to printed matter was to be based for the whole of Catherine's reign. The first of these lists, albeit in this instance somewhat vaguely, the three points in relation to which the acceptability of a written work was to be judged – what I have called "the three-fold limiting clause,"[70] the second entrusts their actual interpretation to the institutions of higher learning.

The Senate delegated the task of working out the details of the implementation of the order of 6 September 1763 to the Academy of Sciences, which commissioned one of its Councillors, Taubert,[71] to prepare a report on the subject. Taubert proposed the establishment of censors' offices in ports and at border points after the example of other countries,[72] and thought it best to reserve for the Academy the exclusive right of selling foreign books, so as to facilitate supervision. He repeated, in a more precise form, Catherine's ruling as to what kind of books were to be prohibited, namely (a) those openly hostile to the principles on which the Christian faith and "civil society" were based; (b) offering temptation and damaging to private morals; and (c) libels or satirical writings prejudicial to the State, national honour, or to individuals; suggesting that a list of such books be compiled and kept at the ports of entry. The report concluded:

"Since nothing is more detrimental to the success of learning and to the enlightenment of the human mind than deprivation of freedom to read books of all kinds, it is the opinion of the *Kantselariya* of the Academy of Sciences that no definite prohibition of the importation of foreign books such as here mentioned... ought to be publicised any further. This instruction could best be kept secret without letting the public know anything about it so that no adverse comment is aroused, either here or abroad. Anyway, the principle can be accepted that people who are brought up in virtue and have the fear of God in their hearts would not be shaken in their virtue and their duty before the law and society if forbidden books should

[70] For the possible Western model cf. the French Royal Decree prescribing death penalty for "all those who shall be convicted of having composed, or caused to be composed and printed, writings intended to attack religion, to assail our authority, or to disturb the ordered tranquillity of our realm". (Quoted in Kingsley Martin, *French Liberal Thought in the Eighteenth Century*, N.Y. & Lond. 1962, p. 100.)

[71] Johann Kaspar (Ivan Andreyevich) Taubert (1717–1771), born in Russia of a German family, from 1758 member of the *Kantselariya* of the Academy (the other members at the time were Lomonosov and Staehlin).

[72] This advice was not to be followed until 1796.

fall into their hands, whereas those whose morals are bad will have a tendency towards evil deeds and corrupting thoughts also without reading such books." [73]

To what extent this report represented the genuine views of Taubert and his colleagues (of whom, incidentally, Lomonosov refused to sign it) and to what extent it can be considered a reflection of Catherine's known or presumed ideas, is a point on which it is impossible to offer any definite opinion. It might, however, be suggested that if Taubert had held such relatively liberal views on these matters during the earlier reigns he would not then have dared to put them into an official document. The report had no practical significance as none of its recommendations were implemented at the time.

It should be noted that while Catherine took steps to prevent influx of books favourable to Peter III from abroad [74] she, unlike Elizabeth, did not apparently bother to issue any directives against this type of literature already existing and circulating within the country. There is, however, some evidence indicating that, at the lower administrative level, officials trained under previous regimes sometimes acted on their own initiative as, for example, the manager of the Army Cadet Corps printing press, who wrote a note suggesting that the "remaining sixteen copies" of a French ode in honour of Peter III be converted into pulp. [75]

There are a few instances of direct "censorial" interference by Catherine herself during this period. Semennikov quotes the case of Sumarokov's ode in honour of the newly elected King of Poland, Stanislas August, written in 1764 which appears to have been suppressed on Catherine's orders. Although the records of the Academy of Sciences (entry dated 1 February 1765) show that this poem "had been destroyed, on special orders received from the court of Her Imperial Majesty," the effectiveness of this measure is very much in doubt since three hundred copies of the

[73] Pekarsky, *Istoriya Akademii Nauk,* (History of the Academy of Sciences), II, pp. 789–790.

[74] Another example of a book of this kind is *Anecdotes russes ou lettres d'un officier Allemand* published in London and also (in German), ostensibly at "Petersburg", in Holland, in 1764, with subsequent editions in 1765, 1766 and 1769. Its author, "C. F. S. de la Marche" was actually Christian Friedrich Schwann (1733–1815), a Prussian who had served in Russia as a proof-reader at the Academy of Sciences, and later on the staff of Prince Georg v. Holstein-Gottorp, between 1758 and 1762. *(Allgemeine Deutsche Biographie,* Vol. XXXIII, Leipzig, 1891). Bil'basov in referring to this book mistakenly states that the author "had never been to Russia" and speculates as to the sources of his information. (*Istoriya Yekateriny Vtoroy,* (History of Catherine the Second), XII, Berlin n.d., p. 30).

[75] Cf. D. Shamray, "Iz istorii tsenzurnogo rezhima Yekateriny II" (From the History of Catherine II's Censorship), *XVIII vek,* Sb. 3, M.–L., 1958, p. 188.

ode had been printed and collected by Sumarokov from the Academy press some five months earlier (in September 1764).[76]

Another instance, again involving Sumarokov, concerns his comedy *The Grafter* written for the anniversary of Catherine's coronation (22 September) in 1768. Catherine had read the manuscript before it was printed and corrected a few passages she considered capable of offending religious feelings or the accepted standards of decency. She also altered one sentence containing a reference to the Legislative Commission then in session, but since the alteration involved style and not the meaning, it is doubtful whether in doing this she was guided by political considerations as is suggested by some commentators.[77]

The fact that Catherine thus, in some instances, personally interfered in clearing manuscripts for printing can, under the then prevailing conditions, be considered a positive rather than negative factor. She was more enlightened than most of her administrators, was not involved in the network of petty animosities existing between various authors and others connected with publishing, and her authority was obviously final. It is indeed quite clear that, in this last case, Sumarokov's play would not have seen the light of day for a long time yet, if at all, had it not been for her interference.[78]

As an example of attitudes of some of Catherine's administrators can be quoted the case involving Count Pyotr Saltykov who, during the first decade of her reign, occupied the post of the Military Governor of Moscow. In 1764 there appeared in that city a satirical pamphlet, in Russian and in French, in the form of a "Catalogue" of titles of imaginary books by various well-known personalities, e.g. "*Encyclopaedia* by Mr. Panin", "*Triumph of Bacchus* by Mr. Buturlin", "*The History of Bygone Days* by Mr. Shuvalov", etc. Saltykov took an extremely serious view of this and, in reporting the matter to Catherine, asked for a permission to launch an investigation aimed at finding the author or authors of the *Catalogue* – whom he believed to be local young men – and punishing them "with appropriate severity". Were it to prove impossible to find the culprits,

[76] V. P. Semennikov, *Materialy dlya istorii russkoy literatury i dlya slovarya pisateley epokhi Yekateriny II*, (Source Materials for the History of Russian Literature and for the Dictionary of Writers of the Period of Catherine II), St. P., 1914, p. 96.

[77] E.g. Shamray, *op. cit.*, p. 191. For the actual wording of the original and the correction see *Sb. R.I.O.*, X, p. 274.

[78] Cf. *S. R.I.O.*, XIII, p. 13 for Catherine's note to I. P. Yelagin who, between 1766 and 1779 held the Post of the Director of Public Spectacles – assuring him that there are no objections to the performance of the comedy, and Semennikov, *op. cit.*, pp. 96ff. for other details of this incident.

he suggested that an official edict be issued condemning the *Catalogue* to be burnt by a public executioner.[79] Catherine acceded to this last suggestion and, on 25 November 1764, despatched an edict to the Senate in Moscow[80] to that effect, but did not encourage any further investigation.[81]

Another similar report sent in by Saltykov involved a popular ballad that used to be sung on the streets of Moscow in the first years of Catherine's reign, on the subject of her relationship with Peter III and the circumstances immediately preceding her accession.[82] In this case the empress directed Saltykov to take steps to have this song "relegated into oblivion", taking care not to make it known that this action emanated from "the higher level of Government". We do not know precisely what action was taken and how effective it was, except that there appears to be no record of any major prosecution or punishment arising from it.

To complete the survey of official policies towards free expression in the early years of Catherine's reign, it may be worthwhile to quote testimonies of some foreign observers. George Macartney, the British envoy at St. Petersburg at the time in question (later to achieve fame as the Ambassador to China), who by no means can be considered biased in Russia's or Catherine's favour, wrote in his book published shortly after his return to England: "... the administration of the present Empress ... has been extremely mild and gentle; perhaps too mild, too gentle for the rough nature of her subjects, whose manners are not yet sufficiently softened for them to receive a grateful impression of her lenity and moderation ...[83] And speaking of the non-Russian nationalities of the Empire he had this to say:

"All these enjoy ample security for their persons and property. While resident in

[79] *Sb. R.I.O.*, VII, pp. 292–3. Saltykov's report which is dated 17 November 1764, contains the following characteristic sentence: "The licence amongst these young men has now reached the point where, if allowed to go unpunished, they may well start writing about other things [as well]."

[80] Saltykov then headed the Department V of the Senate in Moscow. (From 1763 the Senate was divided into six Departments, four of which were located in St. Petersburg and two in Moscow).

[81] *P.S.Z.*, XVII, No. 12,313. That the authors of the *Catalogue* had no fear of any serious consequences, despite Saltykov's attitude, is evident from the fact that, as we learn from Poroshin's diary, Count Alexander Stroganov openly admitted its authorship a few months later, in the presence of the young Crown Prince Paul and several members of the latter's entourage. (Poroshin, p. 146).

[82] Its text was published by T. A. Martemyanov in "Iz istorii tsenzury russkoy narodnoy pesni" (To the history of the Censorship of Russian folk song), *Istoricheskiy Vestnik*, (The Historical Messenger), XCVIII, St. P., 1904, p. 685.

[83] G. Macartney, *An Account of Russia 1767*, London, 1768, p. 90.

this empire, they are permitted the free exercise of their religion, whether christian, pagan, or mahometan, every sect of which is now tolerated."[84]

This last point is repeatedly emphasised, e.g., "There is no country in the world where all religions are more freely tolerated than in Russia..."[85]

The French Ambassador, Marquis de Bausset in his despatch of 27 May (N.S.) 1766 describes the general intellectual atmosphere of St. Petersburg generated by Catherine's domestic policies and, in particular, by her decision to call the "Commission" (of which the St. Petersburg society was apparently already aware) in these words:

"Toute cette nation, les grands surtout, ne cessent de faire l'éloge de la liberté. Ils ont tenu les propos les plus singuliers à l'occasion du tumulte arrivé en dernier lieu à Madrid, et leurs idées à ce sujet vont bien au-delà de celles que les nations les plus libres se forment du pouvoir et de l'autorité d'un roi."[86]

This is, without doubt, an important first-hand testimony of the degree of freedom of speech available, at least to the educated nobles, barely four years after Catherine's accession. We only have to compare this to the situation prevailing under the earlier rulers to appreciate the extent of the change.

Finally, the renowned historian August Ludwig Schloezer who lived in Russia during the years 1761-1765 had the following to say of this very change (the quotation refers to early 1765):

"... from this time [Catherine's accession] there begins in Russia a new literary world which alone makes the reign of Catherine II epoch-making. If someone should accuse me of a wrongful conclusion, post hoc ergo propter hoc, I shall ask them to compare the following events: Before that time the fear of publicity (*Publizität's Scheu*) was unbelievably great and the fear of the printed word (*Furcht von der Presse*) simply childish. Almost anything that had to do with the State was considered a State secret... but then Catherine II appeared: she defined the concept of State secret, legalised the enormous difference between treasonable spying and learned research..."[87]

All this leads to the obvious conclusion that a very considerable liberalisation in the field of freedom of expression became apparent in Russia in the first years of the new reign. It can be said that Catherine was the

[84] *Ibid.*, p. 35.
[85] *Ibid.*, p. 228.
[86] *Sb. R.I.O.*, CXLI, p. 84.
[87] *August Ludwig Schloezer's öffentliches und privat-Leben von ihm selbst beschrieben*, Erstes Fragment, Goettingen, 1802, pp. 300f.

first ruler in Russian history who was conscious of the concept of freedom of expression and of its positive value. Another novel feature was her personal interest in literary matters resulting in her occasional direct intervention in cases which would formerly be dealt with by administrative organs or, at best, by the institutions of higher learning.

One event of this period which to some extent illustrates the changing attitude to forms of activity outside direct government control is the foundation of the Free Economic Society in 1765. The Constitution of the Society states in its opening paragraph that it is "based on a voluntary association of its members and shall be self governing under the chairmanship of a President elected by ballot every four months."[88] It also proclaims the complete equality of all members. It represented therefore a radical departure from the long-established principle that any new body or organisation must be fully controlled by the government. In practice, of course, it was under the empress' supervision, so that the real difference lay in the fact that this supervision did not extend to her executive or administrative organs. It is interesting to note that this partial independence was evidently appreciated and jealously guarded, as will be apparent from this incident:

> "On 13 December 1766 at the meeting of the Society, an edict was read sent in by ... the Senate, with which there was enclosed a box with "Siberian buckwheat for examination by Messrs. botanists." It was decided to ignore this edict, in accordance with the Constitution ... which conceives it [the Society] as independent of all Departments, being under the sole protection of Her Majesty."[89]

The Constitution in one of its sections (9) provided for the publication of Society's own periodical called *Works of the Free Economic Society for the Encouragement of Agriculture and Good Housekeeping in Russia.*[90] Another important departure from the earlier practice was the ruling that items to be published were to be approved by a majority vote of the members. We thus, for the first time, see here a journal which is exempt,

[88] A. I. Khodnev, *Istoriya Imperatorskogo Vol'nogo Ekonomicheskogo Obschestva s 1765 do 1865 goda,* (History of the Imperial Free Economic Society from 1765 to 1865), St. P., 1865, p. 4.

[89] *Ibid.*, p. 34.

[90] This was originally published three times a year in 1200 copies. From the following year (1766) the number of copies published was doubled. The rate of three issues a year was maintained until 1775, thirty volumes having appeared in all. The publication then ceased for some years. It was resumed in 1779 under the title *Continuation of the Works, etc.* and was published until 1794, inclusive, at the rate of one to two issues a year. In 1795 the title was changed to *New Continuation* ... of which only three issues appeared: in 1795, 1796, and 1798.

at least in theory, from administrative supervision and interference. Being under the direct control of the ruler it enjoyed, in this particular case, a considerable amount of freedom; but it must, of course, be remembered that this freedom was dependent on the attitude of the ruler and his, or her, views at a given time. Another point is that many members of the Society occupied high administrative positions in the government.

In this connection a reference ought to be made to one aspect of the incident involving the essay on the abolition of serfdom by Beardé de l'Abbaye. In 1766, under the auspices of the Free Economic Society, but on the direct initiative of Catherine – no doubt related to the calling of the "Commission" – a competition was announced for an essay on the subject: "What is more beneficial to society: for the peasant to own his land, or only his movable property, and what ought to be the extent of his rights in one or the other direction?"[91] Of 162 competing essays the first prize was awarded to one by a member of the Dijon Academy, Beardé de l'Abbaye, which unequivocally advocated complete – if gradual – liberation of serfs before granting them property rights over their land.[92] The proposal to translate this winning essay into Russian was defeated by an overwhelming majority[93] at the meeting of the Society on 16 July 1768, on the grounds that "the Russian people will not be able to read a book in a foreign language, but it will be quite a different matter if it is in Russian." Under the behind-the-scenes pressure from Catherine, several more ballots were taken at subsequent meetings, with the balance in favour of a translation gradually increasing. The outcome of this affair is quite remarkable: with the ballot standing at 12 votes for the translation and 16 against, a letter was received by the Society, signed by members of the Academy of Sciences Taubert, Klingstedt, and Staehlin, advancing the argument that since the question was political rather than economic, the votes of well-informed statesmen[94] ought to be given more weight than those of less knowledgeable members. This was accepted, and the balance of votes – without taking any further ballot – announced as 15 for and

[91] Macartney is writing about this competition in his *Account of Russia 1767* refers to the Free Economic Society as the "Society of Free Inquiry".

[92] For the full text of this essay see *Chteniya v Imp. Obshchestve Istorii i Drevnostey Rossiyskikh*, (Lectures at the Imp. Society of Russian History and Antiquities), M., 1862, Book 2. Five other essays were awarded secondary prizes, among them one by a Russian, Polenov. (Cf. also *Istoriya Akademii Nauk SSSR, I*, p. 405).

[93] By twelve votes to three, the latter being those of the German members of the Academy of Sciences (The Eulers – father and son, and, probably, Taubert) who obviously had no personal involvement in the matter.

[94] Such as Roman Vorontsov, Sivers, brothers Chernyshov, Mellisino, and Teplov who voted in favour of translation.

13 against. With Catherine's permission already available, the translation was immediately authorised for publication. [95]

It is indeed ironical that Catherine, in order to defeat a point of view which might be termed "reactionary", had to resort in this instance to a violation of the freedom she herself had granted to the Free Economic Society.

There is no spectacular increase in the availability of media of expression in the first years of the new reign. Two new printing presses were opened during that period: at the War Department and at the Holy Synod in St. Petersburg, opened in 1762 and 1763 respectively, both of them of a very limited significance as obviously destined to fulfil departmental needs. The press authorised in 1765, for the Academy of Fine Arts, did not apparently become operational until 1794. However, the output of the existing presses increased very considerably. According to the available statistics, the average number of books (titles) published per year during the decade 1761-1770 was more than three times that of the period 1741-1760. [96] This brought about the appearance of new private outlets for books and periodicals. The existence of private, unsupervised bookshops in both Capitals in 1763 is apparent from the text of Catherine's order of the 6 September that year, from which I have quoted earlier. Further evidence can be found in Bolotov's memoirs who notes with reference to August 1762: "I have found here [in Moscow] a shop almost in all respects like the one I had seen in Prussia, at Koenigsberg, in which large quantities of all kinds of German and French books, bound and unbound, were being sold." [97] And Semyon Vorontsov, the future Ambassador in London, writing to his father in June 1766 asks him to get some books which "in St. Petersburg can always be obtained at the Academy or at the Frenchmen's [shop]..." [98] We can therefore assume that the demand for printed matter has increased a great deal since the days, not so long ago, when a compulsory purchase of books by all members of certain social groups was being seriously suggested to clear the Academy bookshop of its accumulated stock.

[95] Khodnev, pp. 23ff. Cf. also USSR Academy of Sciences, *Istoriya russkoy literatury,* (History of Russian Literature), IV, Part 2, M.-L., 1947, p. 17.

[96] 105 titles per year as opposed to 30. (*Russkaya kniga ot nachala pis'mennosti do 1800 goda,* (Books in Russia from the Earliest Writings to 1800), ed. by V. Adaryukov and A. Sidorov, M., 1924, table on p. 346). P. Milyukov in *Ocherki po istorii russkoy kul'tury* (Studies in the History of Russian Culture), III, Paris, 1930, p. 396, quotes the figures: 105 titles per year for 1761–1770 and 23 per year for 1751–1760.

[97] *Zhizn' i priklyucheniya Andreya Bolotova, Russkaya Starina,* (The Life and Adventures of Andrey Bolotov, *The Russian Past),* III, St. P., 1871, p. 298.

In the field of the periodical press during this period there is little of interest from the point of view of our subject. Four new periodicals appeared between 1762 and 1764, none of them to last longer than one year.[99] One point possibly worth noting is that excerpts from Helvétius' *L'Esprit* appeared in *Innocent Pastime* in 1763. This shows that the principle, proclaimed by the government in the same year, that no writings inimical to the Christian religion must be imported into Russia was not, at least in this instance, being applied to items published within the country.

To conclude this account of the period ending with the calling of the Legislative Commission, it may be said that the "erosion" which we have noted with regard to the seventeen-fifties continues, at an accelerated rate, during the first five years of the reign of Catherine II. The main factor which distinguishes this last period from its immediate predecessor is the clearly different attitude of the new ruler towards freedom of expression. In both theory and practice Catherine undoubtedly appears more enlightened and liberal – one might say more progressive – than most of her entourage. She is also the first Russian ruler with a personal interest in literature from the standpoint of a writer. In a more general sense it can be said that to a large extent, the function of a carrier of contemporary Western-European ideas, performed in the days of Elizabeth by the circle of people close to the throne, has now been taken over by the monarch herself.

[98] *Vorontsov Archives*, XVI, M., 1880, p. 96.

[99] These were: *Svobodnyye chasy*, (Leisure Hours) – 1763, *Sobraniye luchshikh sochineniy*, (Collection of the Best Works), – 1762, *Nevinnoye uprazhneniye*, (Innocent Pastime), – 1763, and *Dobroye namereniye*, (Good Intention), – 1764. All were published in Moscow.

CHAPTER III

THE EMERGENCE OF THE IDEA: THE "GREAT COMMISSION" AND ITS SIGNIFICANCE

The importance of the "Great Commission" of 1767-68 from the point of view of the history of freedom of expression in Russia can hardly be over-emphasized.[1] Its transactions – using the word in its widest sense – provide us with clear written statements of the government attitude towards the problem, with the similarly recorded ideas of representatives of administrative organs, and enable us to assess the degree of interest in free expression displayed by society. The actual debates accord a good view of practical application of theoretical principles within this novel and in many ways unprecedented instrument.

Before proceeding any further it might be useful to recall some basic data about the 'Commission", its composition, and activities. The Great Commission for the Compilation of the Project of a New Code of Laws, to give it its full title, was called into being by Catherine's Manifesto of 14 December 1766. Elections of deputies throughout the Empire were held during February, March, and April of the following year, and the solemn opening session took place at the Moscow Kremlin on 30 July 1767. The Commission sat in Moscow until the 14 December 1767, but, as in due course it became apparent that it would be more convenient to have it transferred to St. Petersburg, it reassembled at the new Capital after the Christmas recess, on 18 February 1768. It continued there until its disbandment on 12 January 1769,[2] but approximately one hundred deputies remained to carry on the work of the various Committees, the last of these coming to an end as late as December 1774.[3] There were, in all, 203 consecutive plenary sessions between July 1767 and the end of 1768,

[1] Cf. also my "The Problem of Civil Liberties in the Records of the "Great Commission" ", *The Slavonic and East European Review,* XLII, No. 99, June 1964, which is based on the material used in this chapter.

[2] The last full session actually took place on 18 December 1768.

[3] The Senate Edict of 5 December 1774 suspending the last committee (not listed in the *P.S.Z.)* was published for the first time by M. A. Lipinsky in Novyye dannyye dlya

and the total number of deputies reached 564 at its maximum. The composition of the Commission by social groups (*sosloviya*) and the figures indicating the number of Instructions (*Nakazy*) and projects (*punkty*) submitted by each group in the course of the debates, may be conveniently shown in the form of a table:[4]

The above figures require a certain amount of qualification and explanation before any conclusions can be drawn from them. Thus, for example, it might appear at the first glance that the deputies of the nobility represented less than one-third of the whole; in actual fact, however, a certain number of deputies representing towns were also members of the noble class: such was the case, for example, with the two Capitals, (St. Petersburg and Moscow). The majority of deputies from government departments were, of course, also noblemen, so that the actual percentage of nobles in the assembly would appear to be certainly closer to 40 than to 30 percent. One interesting point, to which I shall return later, namely how vocal were the representatives of a given class or social group, cannot be judged either by the number of Instructions or by the number of "projects" submitted, since the table does not show the participation in actual debates. Nevertheless, it must be remembered that the "Great Commission" was representative of the free segments of society to an unprecedented extent; this is one important respect in which it differed from the bodies with a similar task called into being during earlier reigns.[5]

One thing that immediately strikes one upon looking at the table is the fact that while the deputies of all other groups came equipped with, roughly, one Instruction each, those of the group described as "Free Peasants and other Free Rural Dwellers", although amounting only to

istorii Yekaterininskoy Kommissii o sochineniyi proyekta novogo ulozheniya" ("New Data on the History of Catherine's Commission on the Compilation of New Code of Laws") *Zhurnal Ministerstva Narodnogo Prosveshcheniya,* (Journal of the Ministry of Popular Education), CCLI, 1887, p. 233.

[4] This table contains data compiled from the following: A. V. Florovsky, *Sostav zakonodatel'noy Kommissii 1967–1774 gg.* (Composition of the Legislative Commission), Odessa, 1915; *Sb. R.I.O., IV;* Solovyov, *Istoria Rossii, etc.* (History of Russia), XXVII; USSR Academy of Sciences, *Ocherki Istorii SSSR* (Studies in History of the USSR), M., 1956.

[5] This point is often conveniently ignored by historians intent on proving that Catherine, in calling the Commission, was merely following in the footsteps of her precedessors, and was really no more liberally-minded than Anne or Elizabeth. (e.g. A. A. Kizevetter, "Pervoye pyatiletiye pravleniya Yekateriny II" (The First five years of the reign of Catherine II), *Sbornik statey posvyashchonnykh P. N. Milyukovu* (Collection of Papers in Honour of P. N. Milyukov), Prague, 1929, p. 323; Georg Sacke, "Zur Charakteristik der gesetzgebenden Kommission Katharina's II von Russland", *Archiv fuer Kulturgeschichte,* XXI, Leipzig & Berlin, 1931).

Groups represented	Deputies		Number of Instructions	% of the whole	Number of Projects	% of the whole
	Maximum number	% of the whole				
Government Departments *) . .	28	approx. 5	28	approx. 2	21	21
Nobility	161	„ 30	161	„ 11	28	28
Towns and Cities **)	208	„ 39	210	„ 15	40	40
Free Peasants and other free rural dwellers ***)	167	„ 26	1066	„ 72	11	11
Total	564	100	1465	100	100	100

*) Including the only representative of the clergy, the deputy from the Holy Synod, Metropolitan Dimitri (Sechenov) of Novgorod.

**) With the exception of some noblemen among them, composed of members of the socalled "middle class", defined in Catherine's Instruction as those who "whilst enjoying freedom are neither noble nor tillers of land." (Art. 377).

***) This included representatives of military communities settled in borderlands (Cossacks), non-Russian indigenous nationalities, settled Tartars, etc. in the proportion: Free Peasants: 14 %; others: 12 % of the whole. It did not, of course, include the peasants in bondage (serfs) who were not represented.

about 26 percent of the total number of deputies, brought with them 72 percent of all Instructions or, on the average, six Instructions per Deputy. This is partly explained by the electoral system and by the administrative division of the Empire [6] but, at the same time, it can serve as an indication of the particularly pressing nature of the needs of this group – as well as of their eager response to the invitation to make these needs and grievances known to the government.

These Instructions, most of which never came under discussion at the plenary sessions of the "Great Commission", represent probably the most important, and certainly the most revealing part of its records. The other principal source of information in these records are the Minutes of the Daily Proceedings (*Dnevnaya zapiska*) edited in a somewhat abridged form under the direction of an official specially appointed for that purpose and styled Director of the Daily Minutes. The fact that they thus represent a précis rather than an accurate record of the proceedings which was, moreover, "edited" by the Director and finally vetted by Catherine herself, obviously detracts somewhat from their value as a historical source – possibly the more so because this is precisely what Catherine had intended them to be. [7]

After the inaugural meeting of 30 July 1767 there followed a number of sessions devoted to reading of the "Great Instruction" (*Bol'shoy Nakaz*) prepared by Catherine. On 20 August commenced the reading and discussion of deputies' Instructions, beginning – for some reason which is not clear – with those of the free peasants. This continued for fifteen sessions, until September 21st, during which the twelve Instructions ever to be read at the plenary sessions had been gone through. Whilst this was still in progress, on 11 September 1767, the Commission commenced the reading of the existing laws relating to the nobility. This evoked a particularly lively debate, and continued until October 2nd. The following 46

[6] The Empire was, at that time, divided into twenty Governments *(Gubernii)* which, in turn, were divided into Provinces (*Provintsyi*) and those into Districts (*Uyezdy*). One deputy was elected by the nobility from each District, one by each city or town, and one from each Province by the following: (a) *odnodvortsy*, (b) *pakhotnyye soldaty* (both these terms refer to land-owning peasants with certain military obligations), (c) *chernososhnyye krest'yane* (State peasants), and (d) *inorodtsy* (non-Russian indigenous nationalities), i.e. four such deputies from those Provinces where all four categories were present. The number of Cossack deputies was left to the discretion of their leaders.

[7] The appropriate section of the Rules of Procedure which were drawn up by Catherine herself, states that all Keepers of Daily Minutes, with the writers (or copyists) attached to them, come under the sole authority of the Director, and that the latter is responsible directly to the Empress. It also states plainly that the Minutes are intended to serve as a historical source for future generations. (*P.S.Z.*, XVIII, No. 12,948. Also cf. *Sb. R.I.O.*, X, p. 234).

sessions, until early December, were devoted to reading laws concerning the merchant class. Finally, the last nine sessions in Moscow consisted of reading laws and privileges relating to the Baltic provinces – the former Polish and Swedish dependencies Livonia and Estonia – up to the time of the adjournment for Christmas recess on 14 December 1767. The timetable for the following year, when the Commission sat in St. Petersburg, was as follows: 18 February until 1st July 1768: reading of the existing laws concerning judicial organs and jurisprudence. 10 July until 6 October: reading of the Project of the Nobles' Charter, October to 15 December: consideration of laws relating to the two existing forms of land-ownership (*pomestye* and *votchina*) by the nobility, 18 December 1768: the last full session. [8]

The principal source of information for ideas which had come to light in connection with the activities of the "Great Commission" are, as we have noted, the "Instructions": the so-called "Great Instruction" (*Bol'shoy Nakaz*) prepared by Catherine as an exposition of her views for the guidance of deputies, and the Instructions (*Nakazy*) brought with them by the latter on behalf of the electorate or, as in the case of the free peasants etc., of practically anyone within reach of their "constituencies" who was willing and able to produce one. The impression produced by closer acquaintance with these documents is that the only side concerned with the problem of human liberties in general and of freedom of expression in particular is, curiously enough, the government side – i.e. the potentially "giving" side – whereas there is practically no concern with such things, let alone any demand for them in the deputies' Instructions. I shall return to this important point later, but, for the time being, propose to devote some attention to Catherine's "Great Instruction".

The origins and history of this document have been thoroughly investigated and documented [9] and are not really relevant to our subject (with the exception of the period immediately preceding its publication, when its draft was "censored" by some members of Catherine's entourage, of which more below). To sum up the most important points concerning the origins and influences which shaped its preparation, it may be recalled that the earliest known reference to her having started working on

[8] *Sb. R.I.O.*, IV, pp. XIX ff.

[9] Probably the most authoritative analysis of the "Great Instruction" and of origins of the ideas contained therein is by N. D. Chechulin, *Nakaz Imperatritsy Yekateriny II-y* (Instruction by the Empress Catherine II), St. P., 1907.

[10] Marie-Thérèse Rodet Geoffrin (1699–1777) who maintained one of the best known Paris intellectual *salons* of that period.

this project is in Catherine's letter to Mme Geoffrin,[10] dated 28 March 1765 in which she says: "Il y a deux mois que je m'occupe trois heures tous les matins à travailler aux Lois de cet Empire."[11] We know that the Great Instruction showed little originality and that Catherine herself often mentioned this fact and never tried to pretend otherwise; Chechulin's analysis demonstrates that four-fifths of its contents were derived from works of others, mainly from Montesquieu for political philosophy and from Beccaria's *Dei Delitti e delle Pene* (On Crimes and Punishments) for ideas concerning criminal law.[12] From the point of view of the present discussion it is of no practical importance whose ideas they were originally, as long as Catherine accepted them as correct and valid principles.

As to the progress of her work on the "Great Instruction" and the fate of its first version, we learn from Catherine's own note, written some time in the latter part of 1779, that after working on the draft for approximately a year and a half, she began showing parts of it to various people, among others to Grigori Orlov and to Nikita Panin. This was the occasion when the latter according to the same note made his often-quoted comment: "*ce sont des axiomes à renverser des murailles*". Finally,

> "... I prepared the Manifesto calling up deputies from the whole Empire, in order that I might learn more about the situation in each area. They gathered in Moscow in 1767 where, ... I appointed various persons of very differing views to hear the Instruction prepared for the Commission. Here discussions arose about each article. I gave them the liberty to delete and cross out anything they wished. They deleted more than half of what I had written which left the Instruction for the Code in the form in which it was printed."[13]

Although Catherine's words cannot, of course, be accepted as objective and complete truth, we have no reason to disbelieve this account of the reaction to some of the ideas expressed in the earlier drafts of her Instruction. It is unfortunate that we know very little of these people "of very differing views" she mentions and what precisely was deleted by them;[14] the fraction of the draft which has been preserved concerns the peasants

[11] *Sb. R.I.O.*, I, p. 268.

[12] A useful recent analysis of Beccaria's influence on Catherine's views will be found in an article by T. Cizova, "Beccaria in Russia", *The Slavonic and East European Review*, XL, No. 95, London, 1962, pp. 384ff.

[13] *Sb. R.I.O.*, XXVI, p. 175.

[14] In fact, already several months earlier, in the beginning of 1767, Catherine wrote to D'Alembert with reference to the draft of her Instruction: "I crossed out, tore up, and burned more than half of it and God only knows what will happen to the remainder". (*Sb. R.I.O.*, X, p. 167).

in bondage. Its comparison with the published version of the Great Instruction [15] shows that the best part of this section of the draft, written in what can certainly be termed a liberal and humanitarian spirit, aimed at easing the peasants' lot and at preparing the ground for abolition of serfdom, was left out of the final version.

On the other hand, the opinions of some critics of the "Great Instruction" at the earlier stage, dating from between September 1765 and May 1766 have been preserved. [16] Among these are to be found, fortunately, the comments on the part of the Instruction directly relevant to our subject, made by three prominent churchmen: the future Metropolitan of St. Petersburg and Novgorod Gavriil (Petrov, 1730-1801), [17] Innokentiy, bishop of Pskov, and the then *ieromonakh* and later Metropolitan of Moscow Platon (Levshin, 1737-1812). Their comments were sent to Nikita Panin with a letter dated 29 April 1766 which, in contrast to the tenor of remarks by some lay critics of the *Nakaz*, hails it as a document in which "throughout shines the holy idea of granting to everyone their cherished natural freedom while preserving public peace, and of combining the punishment of evil with the rehabilitation of the evil-doer." [18] The comments themselves, however, suggest that, in the opinion of their authors, Catherine had gone a little too far in her liberal attitude towards some aspects of free expression. This, in particular, applies to her treatment of the crime of *lèse-Majesté* since:

> "... the security of the person of the Monarch is connected with the security of the whole State in the same way as a head is connected to the rest of the body, therefore even a minutest suspicion in this regard should not be left without a careful, if just, investigation." [19]

Likewise, with reference to Art. 484 of Catherine's Instruction dealing with "satirical writings", the three churchmen concerned felt that:

[15] The materials for comparison can be conveniently found in the following: *Sb. R.I.O.*, X, pp. 152ff, Chechulin, *op. cit.*, pp. XXXIV ff.; Reddaway, *Documents of Catherine the Great*, Cambridge, 1931, pp. 256–257; a ready if not very detailed comparison will be found in Solov'yov, XXVII, pp. 67ff.

[16] See *Sb. R.I.O.*, X, pp. 76–83.

[17] Successor to Dimitri (Sechenov), who had died in December 1767, and whose functions as a deputy to the Commission were also assumed by Gavriil.

[18] Snegiryov, I. M., *Zhizn' moskovskogo mitropolita Platona* (Life of Platon, Metropolitan of Moscow), M., 1856, Part I, p. 117. Cf. also Sukhomlinov, *Istoriya Rossiyskoy Akademii* (History of the Russian Academy), I, pp. 59ff.

[19] For the text of the relevant article of the "Great Instruction" (Art. 482) see below, p. 55.

"...although the freedom to write is indeed congenial to man and greatly helps in the spreading of knowledge, nevertheless since freedom [in general] has already been very wisely defined (*Instruction*, Art. 38) as the freedom of doing what the laws allow, this freedom would cease to exist if any citizen were free to do what is forbidden by laws. Therefore this freedom of writing ought to have its just limits which it would not be permitted to transgress." [20]

These remarks, in common with the overwhelming majority of known utterances by critics of Catherine's Instruction at this stage, are thus aimed at restraining rather than encouraging her liberal zeal. It is interesting to note, however, that unlike those parts of earlier drafts of the Instruction which were altered as the result of pressure from champions of serfdom, the part devoted to freedom of expression apparently remained unaffected by this preliminary criticism. It is true, of course, that the two are not exactly comparable as far as the relative weight of the two problems under the then prevailing conditions and the degree of the actual criticism are concerned; this fact can nevertheless serve as an indication that Catherine's views on the subject of freedom of expression were quite firm and definite at the time.

Turning to the discussion of passages relevant to freedom of expression in the final, printed, version of the Great Instruction, [21] it must be stated that their importance from our point of view lies in the fact that they amount to the first articulate statement of the principles of this aspect of freedom, conceived as one of the civil liberties, in the history of Russia. The principles themselves are not remarkable reflecting, as they do, the ideas then current in Western Europe; what is extraordinary about Catherine's pronouncement is that it should have originated from the government side, without any apparent pressure on the part of society.

Speaking of freedom in general, the Great Instruction sees it as the natural state of man which, however, cannot be absolute owing to the obvious limitations representing the price of living in a community. Thus (Art. 36): "General or political Liberty does not consist in that licentious Notion, *That a Man may do whatever he pleases*" since (Art. 37): "In a State or Assemblage of People that live together in a Community, where there are Laws, Liberty can only consist *in doing that which everyone ought to do and not to be constrained to do that which one ought not to do.*" This is summed up in Art. 38 (referred to by the three ecclesiastic

[20] Snegiryov, pp. 120f.

[21] The quotations which follow are from the 1767 English translation of the *Great Instruction* reproduced by Reddaway. The parts of quotations in italics are underlined in the original text.

"censors" of the "Great Instruction") which states: "Liberty is the right of doing whatsoever the Laws allow."

Articles 464 to 479 are devoted to the concept of the crime of high treason. Here, as in the Arts. 481 and 482 which are concerned with freedom of speech, Catherine is obviously referring to *slovo i delo* and is attempting to draw a clear dividing line between the *lèse-Majesté* and high treason proper. For example (Art. 467): "The Liberty of a Citizen is endangered by nothing so much as by judicial and oblique Accusations in general. How dangerous then would it be if this important Statute should remain *obscure?*" And: 469. "If the Crime of High-treason is laid down in the Laws in *vague indefinite* Terms, it will then be productive of an Infinity of different Abuses."

Arts. 480 to 485 deal with freedom of expression. The part concerned with free speech reads as follows:

"481 ... Words *spoken* in Conversation are subject to *arbitrary* Interpretations, and *so great* a Difference subsists between *Indiscretion* and *Malice* and so *little* between *indiscreet* and *malicious* Expressions, that the law can by no Means subject *Words* to capital Punishment; at least, without *expressly specifying* those *particular Words* which it declares treasonable.

482. And, consequently, *Words* do not form the *Essence* of a Crime; they frequently signify *nothing* of *themselves* but by the Tone of Voice they are pronounced with. Frequently a Repetition of the same Words does not give the *same Sense;* this Sense depends upon the Connexion with what *preceded* or *followed.* Sometimes *Silence* expresses *more* than *Words.* How then can so capital a Crime as *High-Treason* be made of *Words* and punished in the same *Manner* as the very *Action* itself? I mean not to lessen the Indignation which every one ought to have for *those,* who try to tarnish the Glory of their Sovereign; but will say this, that simple corrective Punishment will *suit better,* on these Occasions, than the Charge of *High-treason,* which is always terrible even to *Innocence* itself."

Catherine thus not only exposes the evils inherent in the interpretation of *slovo i delo* prevailing before 1762 and separates the concepts of high treason and *lèse-Majesté,* but regards the latter as a relatively unimportant offence. This is the point objected to by the three churchmen mentioned earlier in their comments on the preliminary draft of the "Instruction".

Catherine's attitude towards written matter is similar:

"483. Writings contain Things which are more durable than Words; but if they do not *lead* to the Crime of *High Treason,* they cannot, of themselves, constitute the *Essence* of High Treason."

484. Satirical writings are prohibited in Monarchies;[22] but they make them a

[22] The term used for "satirical" writings in the original French text is *"trop satiriques",*

Misdemeanor subject to the *Police* of the Town and *not a Crime;* and great Care ought to be taken in the examination of *these Libels,* how we *extend it farther;* representing to ourselves, that Danger of *debasing* the human Mind by *Restraint and Oppression;* which can be productive of nothing but Ignorance and must *cramp* and *depress* the *rising Efforts* of Genius, and destroy the *very Will* for writing."

We may thus say that the "Great Instruction" lays down the following broad principles in connection with freedom of expression: Firstly, it regards it as one of the freedoms – or civil liberties – to which the citizen has a natural right, at the same time making it clear that it is important that this right should be preserved. Secondly, it points to the direct relationship between the degree of freedom of expression available and the advancement of learning and literature. Lastly, it downgrades the offences against laws limiting this freedom from the category of high treason to a simple "misdemeanour" while stressing the need to exercise great circumspection in the enforcement of such laws.

Catherine's tolerance is religious matters, already mentioned in the preceding chapter, is reflected in the appropriate section of the Great Instruction. This is headed "*Rules necessary, and of Great Importance*" and its opening words have a certain ring of practical expediency:

"494. In such a State as Ours, which extends its Sovereignty over so many different Nations, to forbid, or not to allow them to profess *different Modes* of Religion, would greatly endanger the Peace and Security of its Citizens";

and again, in Art. 486:

"The human Mind is irritated by Persecution, but the permission *to believe* according to *one's Opinion,* softens even the most *obdurate Hearts . . .*"

Although these passages contain no direct reference to the freedom of religious expression, i.e. the freedom to write and publish or otherwise proclaim principles of faith other than Greek-Orthodox, it may be assumed that this is covered by the phrase "profess different modes of religion." That this was in fact so is confirmed by the practice of subsequent years. For example, in 1776, the Catholic bishop of Byelorussia was given an official permission to print religious books, in Russian as well as in Latin characters, at the printing press administered by him. (*P.S.Z.*, XX, No. 14,520). In 1790 Catherine ordered the establishment of a printing press

in Russian "*proizvedeniya ochen' yazvitel'nyye*". For "Monarchies" the Russian text has "*samoderzhavnyye gosudarstva*".

in the Mogilev Government for printing Jewish religious books. (*P.S.Z.*, XXIII, No. 16,877).

Before leaving the subject of the Great Instruction, it may be useful to refer to a point often stressed by historians hostile to Catherine, namely to the Senate Edict of 24 September 1767 [23] about the distribution of copies of the Instruction to government departments and courts of law, which allegedly denied access to it to practically anybody with the exception of high-ranking officials. [24] This supposedly proves that Catherine never intended the liberal principles of the Instruction to become widely known within Russia, still less to be applied in practice. It must be remembered, however, that this edict, although presumably approved by Catherine, was not written by her and is of a narrow, purely administrative character. What is more important, it was followed, on 28 April 1768, [25] by another one obviously intended to amplify it and explain the restrictions of access to the Great Instruction. This rules that *at least* three times a year, on Saturdays, the text of the Instruction shall be read in all judicial establishments (*sudebnyye mesta*) in the presence of court secretaries and recorders "only". Thus, in effect, only those court employees who were illiterate were banned from studying the "Instruction" while others were actually encouraged to do so. The fact that a four-language edition of the Great Instruction (published in 1770) was circulating freely and being advertised for sale at 70 kop. per copy in late 1783 is well known. [26] Finally, it may be mentioned that, at a fairly superficial glance, it is possible to note eight legislative acts appearing in the *P.S.Z.* between 1772 and 1790 – and two more in the reign of Alexander I – with specific references to the "Great Instruction". [27]

[23] *P.S.Z.*, XVIII, No. 12,977.

[24] The relevant part of the Edict states: "... these [copies of the Great Instruction] shall be kept only for the information of these judicial establishments, and shall not be issued to any office employees of lower rank nor to any outsiders, not only for copying, but even for reading".

[25] *P.S.Z.*, XVIII, No. 13,107.

[26] Cf. D. D. Shamray, "Iz istorii tsenzurnogo rezhima, etc." (From the History of Catherine II's Censorship), p. 198. The four languages were Russian, Latin, French, and German. Mme Shamray does not appear to be aware of the Edict of 28 April 1768. Sopikov lists the following 18th century editions (in addition to the French original kept at the Academy of Sciences): (1) in 1767, with German translation (Sopikov's No. 6454). (2) In 1768, Russian edition, with supplements (No. 6455). (3) In 1770, the four-language edition (No. 6456). (4) In 1771, with translation into modern Greek (No. 6457). (5) In 1776, in Russian only (No. 6458). (6) In 1796, in Russian, with the Rules of Procedure for the Commission. (No. 6549). There is also a number of foreign editions and translations dating from the same period.

[27] For details and further evidence to the effect that the Great Instruction was not meant to be forgotten cf. Chechulin, *Nakaz* . . ., p. CLII.

Among the Instructions of administrative organs (*prisudstvennyye mesta*) to which we shall now direct our attention, the Instruction of the Academy of Sciences is concerned, in part, with freedom of expression in some of its practical aspects. The pertinent part reads as follows:

"6. The Academy considers it advisable to submit suggestions as to the manner in which examination of books ought to be conducted here, that is to say, which books to release and which to prohibit. In France, specially appointed persons are stationed at various places, without whose permission no book may be printed. In England, anyone is free to print whatever they wish, without answering to anyone; however, such a liberty cannot endure without serious abuses. It seems that is could be done here in this way, that each place, especially the Academy and the University, be made responsible for books they print on their premises. When private printing-presses come into being, the University located in Moscow, and in St. Petersburg – the Academy, might issue permits for whatever books would be printed there. The same could be done at other places where printing presses will be established and where there will be Academies and Universities." [28]

This principle, to the effect that if there is to be censorship, it ought to be exercised by people who are best qualified for such duties, i.e. those who are best educated, was, in fact, accepted by Catherine's government in 1796 when censor's offices were officially established, and continued by that of Paul I. In general, the spirit of the passage just quoted is close to that of the "Great Instruction" and can almost be regarded as a suggestion for practical implementation of Catherine's view that "great Care ought to be taken in the examination of these Libels", the more so since the Instruction of the Academy is dated some three weeks *after* the opening of the Great Commission,[29] i.e. at the time when Catherine's Instruction was already publicly known.

A radically different view of the subject is taken by the Instruction of the Main Police Administration, a remarkable document of quite formidable length. One of its opening paragraphs shows some awareness of the changed climate since Catherine's accession:

"8. The Chiefs of Police always ought to strive to grasp the intentions of Her Imperial Majesty, and to conduct their affairs accordingly, having this in mind." [30]

[28] *Sb. R.I.O.*, XLIII, p. 373.

[29] 24 August 1767. An earlier draft of the Academy Instruction, considerably more conservative in spirit (based on the practice prevailing at the Academy since 1748), does, in fact, exist. It was found in the Academy Archives and published by D. D. Shamray in *XVIII vek*, Sb. 2., M. -L., 1940, p. 308.

[30] *Sb. R.I.O.*, XLIII, p. 297ff.

and:

"10. The Police are aware that H.I.M. notwithstanding Her exalted position and the important affairs of State, demanding Her constant attention, deigns, not infrequently, to direct Her eye onto the Police, including the most minute details of their activities, the Police therefore now request... permission for the Chief of Police to report to H.I.M. on all matters which appear doubtful to him."

How this is to work in practice becomes clear from the section devoted to what the Great Instruction calls "satirical writings":

"40. The Police shall not suffer libellous writings or any writings or books creating temptation to human morals or life, whenever these are found they shall be seized under penalty to those who fail to report [them] and destroyed, after having been referred to the Supreme Authority, and their authors shall not escape punishment in accordance with the circumstances and the degree [of their offence]."

The abysmal gap between this traditional attitude and Catherine's views on the same subject is obvious, while it is interesting to note, in the last quoted passage, that the offending material is not to be disposed of without reference to the Empress herself. In a similar vein, the Police Instruction shows little regard for the freedom of the spoken word. Thus, for example, no open criticism by priests, in churches, of errant police officials is to be permitted:

"... preachers dare not mention in their sermons anything that might be detrimental to the Police or to its Officials, but instead shall, having duly noted the harmful occurrence, get in touch with the Chief of Police, or inform him, if contrary to expectations, he should happen to be still unaware of it."

On their part, the police are quite prepared to assist the church authorities in maintaining proper order amongst the faithful:

"34. The Police request the right, also in the Lord's Temples to supervise citizens who enter for the purpose of prayer, so that they may maintain proper decency whilst thus engaged."

The Instruction also reserves for the Police the censorship functions over theatrical performances or "Comedies" as it calls them:

"... performance of Free [i.e. performed by private companies, as opposed to State-controlled theatre] Comedies, irrespective of who directs them, not to commence without a report being made to the Chief of Police on the nature of the

Play to be performed, this report to be made on the preceding day, who [the Chief of Police] shall judge whether this Comedy contains any kind of temptation to the Citizens, and if their chaste ears will be offended by rude words [pronounced] in Theatres."

In general, it may be said of the Police Instruction that while it shows some vague awareness of the changed climate of Catherine's reign it does not attempt to understand the nature of this change and is, in fact, written in a spirit directly contrary to that of the Great Instruction. The significance of this fact becomes the more poignant when we consider that this was the branch of the administration specifically and directly concerned in implementing Catherine's internal policies, not least those concerning freedom of expression.

This is the extent of references to matters having a bearing on our subject in the Instructions of administrative departments. In turning to those of the three remaining main groups of deputies, for which I propose to use the term "local Instructions", it may be worthwhile to touch briefly upon a point which is fairly important, if not directly relevant. This is the question of how truly representative were these Instructions of the actual state of affairs in the "constituencies" and of the demands of the "electorate", and whether or not there is any evidence of administrative interference or of pressure "from above" in their preparation. This subject was rather thoroughly investigated by Florovsky whose findings are that there is no evidence of such interference in the preparations of the Instructions at any level.[31] There are a few isolated examples of high-handed action by local administrative organs in organising the elections of deputies, but, on the whole, these elections can be considered to have been free and unhindered. Likewise, according to all available evidence, there has been no outside interference in the preparation of local Instructions and we can assume that their authors availed themselves of this opportunity to list their needs and grievances to the full extent.[32]

[31] Florovsky, *op. cit.*, pp. 488-492. For a recent work in English treating of this and related matters see P. Dukes, *Catherine the Great and the Russian Nobility*, esp. pp. 57ff.

[32] A first-hand testimony in this respect is provided by the merchant-scholar Vasily Krestinin who, writing about the preparation of the Instruction of the City of Archangel, notes that it was drawn up by "citizen Alexander Fomin, son of our champion of citizens' rights Ivan Fomin" and that "all the best Citizens of Archangel participated in the drafting of the needs of this community presented in the Instruction". (V. Krestinin, *Kratkaya istoriya o gorode Arkhangel'skom* (A Short History of the City of Archangel), St. P., 1792, p. 32. Cf. also A. Kizevetter, "Proiskhozhdeniye gorodskikh deputatskikh nakazov v Yekaterininskuyu kommissiyu 1767 g." (The Origin of the Instructions of Townsmen's Deputies), *Istoricheskiye ocherki* (Historical Studies), Moscow, 1912, p. 211. The report of the *General-Politseymeyster* Chicherin (the chief signatory of the Police Instruction from which I

On the whole, there is very little, if anything, in local Instructions which might be interpreted as a concern with freedom of expression or indeed any other form of civil liberty. With a few exceptions [33] there is not much that distinguishes the Instructions of one social group from another: most of the demands they put forward are of a very narrow character dictated by local conditions. Insofar as it is possible to generalise it can be said that the bulk of the local Instructions was really concerned with two things: the economic well-being of its own social group, and the desire for the establishment of the rule of law. The picture they give of the actual state of affairs in the provinces is quite incompatible with interest in any more or less abstract ideas, while the practical opportunity of openly listing their needs thus accorded to society at large appears to fully satisfy any latent demand for freedom of expression which might have existed at the time.

We must also remember that the local Instructions were being prepared at the time when the overwhelming majority of people engaged on this task had only the vaguest idea of their purpose and of what the calling of the "Great Commission" involved. This became a little clearer after the first few sessions devoted to the reading of the "Great Instruction" which came as a complete surprise to the majority of the deputies. Another surprise was the spirit of free discussion introduced by Catherine and relatively well maintained throughout by the Marshal (Speaker) Bibikov in the course of the subsequent debates. The first point to be considered in relation to these debates is, again, the degree of their freedom from restraining government interference.

In any assembly such as the "Great Commission" there are two principal limiting factors affecting the freedom of speech which might be called the "subject" factor and the "procedural" factor. The first has to do with the freedom of choice of the subject on which to speak; the second with the chances of any given individual to speak whenever and for as long as he likes. The first, even in cases where no subject is banned from discussion, will be affected by the agenda; the second by the rules of procedure.

have quoted), published in the Supplement to No. 6 of *St. Petersburgskiye Vedomosti* of 19 January 1767, described the election of the deputy from the City of St. Petersburg. It states that "the most prominent persons of rank ... sat among citizens of diverse calling and, in order to fit better in this assembly, they came without any insignia of orders, so that for someone not familiar [with them] it was difficult to distinguish them from artisans and working people". (Sukhomlinov, *Istoriya Ross. Akademii* (History of the Russian Academy), I, p. 59).

[33] Even these exceptions, found among the Instructions of the nobility, tend to reflect the higher educational level of their authors rather than any concern with more abstract ideas or with the welfare of the country as a whole.

The definition of the purpose for which the Commission was being called, as stated in the Manifesto of 14 December 1766, was sufficiently broad to permit discussion on practically any subject concerning the conditions existing in Russia at the time. The evidence available in the Daily Minutes indicates no interference with this particular freedom and, indeed, shows many instances of deputies speaking on matters of little or no relevance to the subject under discussion. One possible instance of interference "from behind the scenes" could conceivably have occurred in the case of deputy Korob'in which is mentioned below. The limitations imposed by the agenda affected this "subject factor" probably to a somewhat greater extent,[34] but, on the other hand, the deputies were free to submit their ideas in writing, for consideration by the appropriate committee. As shown in the table on page 49, one hundred such "projects" were produced in the Commission's lifetime. It can thus be said that any limitations of freedom of expression of the deputies imposed by this "subject factor" can be considered relatively insignificant.

The "procedural factor" was governed by the rules of procedure laid down in an Edict dated 30 July 1767[35] and supplemented by a few additions and amendments sent in by Catherine at various times during the subsequent proceedings. The first draft of the Rules of Procedure was prepared, on Catherine's instructions, by her then secretary Grigori Kozitsky.[36] Its comparison with the published version shows that certain passages of the draft written in the traditional spirit of tight government control over all activities of its subjects have been modified or removed. The final version can be considered quite liberal, even by Western-European standards of the time, and contains nothing that could seriously interfere with the freedom of the deputies to express their views on any reasonable subject.[37] Bibikov's son, in his biography of his father, provides

[34] For example, the mere fact that the Great Instruction was read and discussed at plenary sessions during the period 31 July–20 August 1767, and that this was repeated at the beginning of every month, curtailed the time which could be devoted to other subjects. The agenda for the first few sessions was prescribed in detail by the Edict of 30 July 1767, later it was largely left to the discretion of the Marshal, Bibikov, whose lack of experience in such matters was only too evident.

[35] *P.S.Z.*, XVIII, No. 12,948.

[36] In connection with the Great Commission Kozitsky prepared drafts of the following: (a) Project of Elections of Deputies of Townsmen and Professional Guilds; (b) Rules of Procedure; (c) Edict to Governors on the electoral procedure; and (d) Edict calling up deputies to assemble in Moscow. The final versions of (a) and (b) differ considerably from his draft, but (c) and (d) very little.

[37] The operative clause states that "everyone shall speak briefly and in a lucid manner", no one to be allowed to speak in the assembly for longer than half an hour, but if more time was required, the remaining portion of the submission had to be made in writing. It

examples of Catherine's concern to uphold this freedom and quotes his father as saying that "the Empress's greatest and continuous care is to deal with an assembly which is free in thought and in speech." [38] Her note, scribbled in pencil evidently during an actual debate and sent to Bibokov when the latter tried to hurry the assembled deputies into accepting some suggestion of his, reads: "For God's sake, do not rush ... or they will say that you are forcing them."

The fact that the general level of debates in the Commission was surprisingly high is evident from the Daily Minutes and from the testimonies of some contemporary foreign observers. Thus the British Ambassador, Lord Cathcart, who attended one session in the summer of 1768, was impressed by the orderliness of the proceedings, good manners of the deputies, and the spirit of tolerant controversy prevailing in the assembly. He also noted that "... the Instructions of the members are open to them all ... which all together creates as much information as possible." [39] It is only fair to mention, however, that one of his aides, William Richardson, recorded a different impression: "I have heard that freedom of extratemporaneous speaking was allowed in some of the first meetings of this assembly; but being likely to occasion too much disorder it was discontinued ... Indeed, this assembly has no pretentions whatever to freedom of debate ..." [40] Apart from the fact that Richardson's account is secondhand and contains a number of obvious inaccuracies, there may be some truth in his assertion that the degree of freedom of the actual debates tended to diminish somewhat as the time progressed. This can be inferred from the fact that, almost exactly at the same time, Catherine was taking steps to remedy such a situation. Her instructions to Bibikov, dating from July 1768, open with at reference to the necessity to remove "any hateful restraints of free speech" in the Commission, and direct him „to see to it that each deputy speaks rather than submits his opinion in writing." The stress throughout this document is on encouraging controversy, in order that "the pros and contras of each section of the project be thoroughly and adequately debated." [41]

became a common practice for a deputy to state that he had a submission to make on a subject currently under discussion, and to provide it in writing at a subsequent session, where it would be read before the whole assembly.

[38] A. A. Bibikov, *Zapiski o zhizni i sluzhbe Aleksandra Il'yicha Bibikova* (Memoirs on the Private and Service Life of A. I. Bibikov), St. P., 1817, p. 107f.

[39] Cathcart's despatch to Lord Weymouth dated 19/30 August 1768, *Sb. R.I.O.*, XII, pp. 355f.

[40] W. Richardson, *Anecdotes of the Russian Empire ...*, Lond., 1784, p. 30.

[41] Bibikov, pp. 109–112.

There can thus be little doubt as to the basic soundness of Catherine's Rules of Procedure both in theory and in practice. Indeed, the importance of these rules and of the manner in which they were being implemented must be strongly emphasized as second only to that of the "Great Instruction". If the latter laid down the theory of principles of free expression, the former through its practical application, showed some of these principles operating successfully in real life. For example, during the debate on the Instruction of free peasants of Kargopol' District (the first local Instruction read in the assembly), on 31 August 1767, the noble deputy Glazov submitted a twenty-three page written reply to an earlier submission by the peasant deputy Davydov in which, according to the Daily Minutes "it was difficult to find an orderly sentence – all thoughts are confused and obscure, almost every expression abusive". In language full of invective, Glazov cursed all State Peasants and accused his opponent of "corruptive views". The reading of Glazov's submission was halted by the Marshal on the grounds that such offensive language was against the Rules of Procedure. The motion by one of the deputies to have Glazov excluded from the Commission was then put to vote and defeated, by 323 votes to 105, in favour of a motion to have him pay a fine and apologise before the whole assembly to those offended by his remarks.[42]

Thus as a result of a clash in the assembly between a nobleman and a peasant, the former was publicly humiliated having been made to apologise to his opponent for displaying the kind of attitude which would then be considered perfectly normal outside the Commission's precincts. In the context of Russian social structure and conditions prevailing at the time, this was an unprecedented and exiting occurrence, no doubt disturbing to many, but encouraging to others.

We have thus seen that the degree of freedom of expression accorded the deputies to the Great Commission was, by current Russian standards, extraordinarily high. It now remains to see if it produced any ideas relevant to our subject in the course of the Commission's proceedings.

The minutes of early meetings show that the debates evoked by reading of the Great Instruction consisted mainly of obsequiously panegyrical comments on Catherine's wisdom with an added measure of probably genuine amazement at the liberal generosity of her ideas. A considerable time was spent in preparing an address to the Empress asking her to accept the title of "Catherine the Great the Wise Mother of the Fatherland". She declined to accept this and appeared somewhat irritated and

[42] *Sb. R.I.O.*, IV, pp. 108ff.

frustrated by the waste of time involved in these proceedings, as witness the exasperated tone of her note to Bibikov dating from that period.[43]

In view of what has been said earlier with regard to the local Instructions and of this rather inauspicious start, it is not surprising that no ideas showing a conscious concern with freedom of expression were produced in the course of the Commission's debates. The importance of these debates from the point of view of our subject lies in their having provided an unprecedented opportunity for a public and relatively unrestrained exchange of differing and often challenging opinions.

In this connection it may be worthwhile to mention the incident involving the deputy from the nobility of Kozlov District, Grigory Korob'in which took place during the debates on the Project of the Nobles' Rights in September 1768. Korob'in was not himself elected as a deputy, but took over from one Captain Murav'yov, in late 1767 or early 1768. He was quite vocal in his criticisms of the system of serfdom which, however, he did not propose to abolish altogether but to reform. The main point of this proposed reform was granting the land-ownership to the peasants whilst retaining their obligations to the noble landowners. The rather obvious contradiction inherent in this was eagerly seized upon by his opponents of whom the most prominent was Prince M. M. Shcherbatov. Although a considerable proportion of deputies – at least tacitly – sympathised with Korob'in and he was believed to have had some encouragement from the highest quarters,[44] his projects were, of course, doomed to defeat. Of interest is the following quotation from the Daily Minutes for 17 September 1768, the last day on which Korob'in publicly defended his views:

> "The Kozlov deputy of the Nobility [Korob'in] was saying: "...the name of freedom is not in the least harmful. I could prove it to you at some other place, or if I could say it in whisper." At this the Marshal declared to Deputy Korob'in that "you can tell us all your proofs openly without hiding anything, for there should not be anything here that would have to be said secretly or covertly, but everything ought to be discussed openly in an orderly manner." "[45]

Korob'in then continued for some time, more or less reiterating his position, but without saying anything spectacular. After this session he

[43] "I told them to make laws for the Russian Empire, but they are spending their time singing praises to my qualities". (*Sb. R.I.O.*, X, p. 271).

[44] There was some speculation to the effect that Korobin's actions had been directly inspired by Catherine, but as there does not appear to be any clear evidence of this, it must remain a matter of conjecture. See also *Sb. R.I.O.*, XXXII, pp. iii and 56.

[45] *Sb. R.I.O.*, XXXVI, p. 27.

disappears from the scene, the only further mention of his name in the Commission records occuring a little over a month later, when he handed over his seat "temporarily" to one Vasily Rodionov. Nothing certain is known of his subsequent life and activities.

The quoted extract from the Daily Minutes thus provides an account of a situation when the principle of free expression within the terms of reference of the Commission was officially upheld. On the other hand, it seems quite likely that some amount of behind-the-scenes pressure, whether actual or implied, was being exerted upon Korob'in by circles interested in preserving and consolidating the *status quo*. This last factor, however, in the sense of pressures of powerful economic interests making themselves felt in a legislative body, is by no means something particular to Russia or to the "Great Commission".

One other point that may be usefully mentioned in connection with the debates of the Commission is the degree of participation in them by deputies representing different social groups. The rather obvious fact that the deputies who were best educated were also most vocal is reflected, in part, in the table shown on page 49 which indicates that the number of "points" or projects submitted by the group referred to as "free peasants and other free rural dwellers" was proportionally smaller. Education was, of course, not the only factor here: the experience in public affairs was clearly another, as can be seen in the case of deputies from government departments who, whilst amounting only to five percent of the total number, producted twenty-one percent of the "points"; finally, the social position of a deputy must have unquestionably played its part. For example, in the discussion of the first local Instruction read at a plenary session of the Commission, that of the State Peasants (*chernososhnyye krest'yane*) of the Kargopol' District, a total of twenty-five opinions (*mneniya*) have been recorded. Fifteen of these were from the deputies of the nobility, six from representatives of government departments – of whom at least two were noblemen – and two each from townsmen and peasants. If we consider that the subject under discussion was of direct concern to this last group, these figures are most certainly striking. Nor is this an isolated instance: approximately one month later and immediately after the Glazov-Davydov incident described earlier, the Instruction of State Peasants of Saratov was read and discussed. Of the participants in this case twelve were noblemen, five townsmen, and one peasant, the total being eighteen.[46]

[46] *Sb. R.I.O.*, IV, *passim.*

Thus, as it may have been expected, the participation in debates diminishes towards the lower end of the social scale. The main reasons for this phenomenon are too obvious to be recounted here; at the most, it may be worthwhile to mention the traditional reluctance to voice one's views openly combined with a certain mistrust of the authorities' intentions, so characteristic of the broad masses of the Russian people, and the complete unpreparedness for their task of the majority of deputies, but especially of those of lower social orders.

We have a reference to the Commission in a contemporary folk ballad known as *The Serfs' Lament (Plach kholopov)* preserved in a manuscript form and published in 1895 by the Moscow Society of Lovers of Russian Literature. This contains a passage complaining of the fact that peasants in bondage could not be elected as deputies and asking, with irony, "what could the serfs be expected to speak about there?" This could be interpreted as evidence of interest in the Commission's proceedings among the under-privileged, and of the same desire to make their needs and complaints known to the powers-that-be which is so pronounced in the Instructions of their more fortunate brethren. Considering the disproportionally large number of Instructions brought with them by the State peasants, mentioned earlier, and the unquestionable community of interests in many areas between the two groups, it would not be too far fetched to assume that many of the serfs' problems must have been presented to the Commission at least in this indirect, if far from satisfactory way.

While the Commission was sitting at St. Petersburg, in 1768, there appeared a book by the Secretary of the Senate, Counsellor Yakov Kozel'sky [47] under the title *Philosophical Sentences,* the first work in Russian, by a native author, devoted, in part, to the evaluation of contemporary European political theories. Kozel'sky approaches his subject with some caution – as, for example, when he notes, at the outset, that his views are only tentative since "it is generally held that the discussion of political subjects is a matter reserved exclusively for the Ministers, whereas other people have not the ability to indulge in it" [48] but nevertheless

[47] Ya. P. Kozel'sky (1728–1793), a writer and thinker of Ukrainian origin. In the early 1760s taught mathematics and mechanics at the School of Artillery and Engineering. From 1766 to 1770, Secretary of one of the departments of the Senate, later member of the *Malorossiyskaya kollegiya* (Ukrainian College). There was also Ya. P. Kozelsky who was Deputy to the "Commission"; some doubt exists as to whether the two were identical or were brothers of the same Christian name. (Cf. S. V. Paparigopulo, "O dvukh Ya. P. Kozel'skikh" (Two Ya. P. Kozel'skys), *Voprosy istorii* (Problems of History), 1954, No. 8, pp. 109–112.

[48] This and subsequent quotations are taken from the text reproduced by I. Ya. Shchi-

discusses and quotes the ideas of a number of thinkers, notably of Montesquieu, Rousseau, Bielfeld, Helvétius, and Voltaire. His own thoughts on freedom generally reflect some of their ideas as, for example, when he states that "a man loses his natural freedom and unlimited rights upon making a contract with society... and [instead] acquires civil liberty and property rights." Referring to Voltaire in connection with the latter's enthusiastic praise of the freedom of public opinion in England where "the simplest burgher reads newspapers and discusses political matters and the [various forms of] government," Kozel'sky argues that such freedom is really meaningless since insignificant common people can neither understand these matters properly nor can they, by their discussions, influence the course of political events. Then, in his comments on Montesquieu's theories, we come across this rather remarkable thought:

> "...Mr. Montesquieu writes that it is difficult, if not impossible, for people to be virtuous where the government is autocratic: I consider that it is better to think this within oneself rather than to speak out for all to hear, and that it is preferable to assert publicly that people can be virtuous under any form of government..."

This remark should presumably be interpreted as meaning that ideas of this kind ought to be considered only by those qualified to do so and are not for general public consumption, a view related to the theory that it is futile for ordinary people to take interest in politics since their opinions can have no influence on the course of events.

Although not too much should be read into Kozel'sky's statements, in view of the ecletic character of his work and of his rather guarded approach, this attitude as well as precisely this guarded approach are interesting as examples of treatment of the current Western ideas by someone brought up under Russian conditions. In these conditions the value of public opinion appears as naught and public utterance of unorthodox or novel ideas as inadvisable. This, probably the first voice of its kind appearing in print on matters related to free expression, provides another illustration of the wide gap between the attitude of the "progressive" monarch – a foreigner in Russia in more ways than one – and those of her subjects at that particular historical moment.

Returning to the "Great Commission", we might say that it can legitimately be viewed not only as an important landmark in the history of

panov in *Izbrannyye proizvedeniya russkikh mysliteley vtoroy poloviny XVIII veka* (Selected Works of Russian Thinkers of the Second Half of the 18th Century), M., 1952, pp. 523ff.

freedom of expression in Russia, but as the actual starting point of this history in an articulate form: here we see for the first time a statement of the significance of this freedom and of the principles on which it ought to be based. The most remarkable and unusual thing about this statement in relation to the development of similar ideas in other European countries is the side on which it originated: the fact that it should have come from the supreme governing authority on its own initiative, instead of as a result of a demand by society, as it happened elsewhere.

This difference is brought home forcibly if we look at what was occurring in England at almost precisely the same time. Here the conflict between the State represented by the King and his party, and the offended sensibilities of the liberty-conscious populace personified in John Wilkes, leads to a consolidation and extension of civil freedoms. When – to reduce the issue to the simplest terms – an attempt, or at least a visible tendency by the State to arrest and possibly reverse the trend towards gradual extension of the rights of its citizens becomes apparent, the intensity of the resulting popular resentment forces the State to retreat and thus to restore the trend. As a result of this confrontation, organised public opinion, notwithstanding some of the excesses and crudities of the "Wilkite movement", established itself as a formidable force in the British system of political relationships. This would not have been possible without some essential pre-requisites, such as widespread literacy among the lower and middle classes, availability of adequate press facilities, a well-developed concept of freedom and sensitivity to its abuses, and a political system affording practical possibilities for bringing this kind of a dispute into the open. It was a result of a long historical process entirely different to that of Russia and its Muscovite antecedent.

The rather paradoxical situation created by Catherine's concessions, not to the *vox populi,* but to the spirit of the intellectual *milieu* of which she considered herself a member, did not bid well for the future of the freedom so suddenly revealed to her subjects. First of all, an absolute ruler who is at one time prepared to yield a part of his powers in the name of some more or less abstract idea, can just as easily revoke the concession – his successor is even more likely to do so; secondly, the previouly dormant appetite for civil liberties aroused within society as a result, is bound in one way or another to lead to a demand for political freedoms incompatible with the existing form of government – a point succinctly expressed by the then French Consul at St. Petersburg, Rossignol, when he wrote in his despatch to the Duc de Choiseul on 14 June 1768: "...on ne sait si Catherine aura lieu de s'applaudir ou de se repentir d'avoir fourni à sa nation, accoutumée à une soumision aveugle, l'occasion de penser et de réfléchir sur ses intérêts."[49] Thus, in this interesting and apparently encouraging episode it is already possible to see the seeds of the future conflict.

[49] *Sb. R.I.O.*, CXLI, p. 435.

CHAPTER IV

THE PERIOD OF GROWTH – THEORY

The two decades between the disbandment of the "Great Commission" and the beginning of the French Revolution are of particular interest. The reason for this, stated in simplest terms, is that the idea of freedom of expression introduced by the government in the Commission now has a chance to take root and develop in a generally propitious climate. Bearing in mind that this freedom was not to be absolute and that the "Great Instruction", while laying down the general principles, did not define its limits in a way which could have much practical significance, we might reasonably expect that the main feature of its development would be a process of trial and error aimed at finding these limits. It is possible to see this process in terms of a dialogue between the "givers" and the "users" of freedom, i.e. the government and society.

The present chapter will be devoted to the theoretical aspect of this process. The term "theoretical" must be, of course, elastic since it is often impossible or impracticable to draw a clear dividing line between theory and practice in a study of this kind. For example, a theoretical literary controversy acquires a practical character at the moment one side applies extraneous restrictive measures against the other. An additional complication is presented by Catherine's dual capacity, as a ruler and as a writer. Unlike the earlier Russian monarchs who used only official decrees and proclamations to make their views known,[1] Catherine had at her disposal also the "unofficial" means such as belles-lettres, theatre, and periodical press.

To deal first with the official plane, it can be said that the theoretical

[1] Such decrees at times amounted to quite detailed expositions of the monarch's views and explanations of the course of action taken. This was particularly noticeable in the reign of Peter I. It is, in fact, possible to regard his decrees as an important contribution to the 'publicist' literature characteristic of the period. (This view is taken for example, by the well-known Soviet historian B. B. Kafengauz).

principles of freedom of expression outlined by Catherine in her Instruction remained unchanged as far as she was concerned for the next twenty years. At the end of this period they were unequivocally re-affirmed in her personal edict (against duelling) of 21 April 1787 in which she wrote:

"We ourselves had removed from the most important law of lèse-Majesté the then existing confusion between words and the offence itself and we felt proud and honoured to be able to tell our Nation, in Art. 482 of the Instruction to the... Commission: 'Words do not form the essence of the offence: they often have no meaning by themselves since this depends on the tone of voice in which they were uttered; frequently a repetition of the same words does not produce identical meaning; this meaning depends on their connection with other things. Sometimes silence tells more thans any amount of talk.' There is nothing that contains more ambiguity than these things." [2]

Approximately ten years earlier we have a similar re-assertion of the same principles at the unofficial level. This is contained in Catherine's *Apofegmat* (Apophthegm) published in 1777 which amounts to a repetition of the main principles of the Great Instruction. Passages on liberty ("which consists in doing what the laws permit") amount to direct quotations from that document. [3]

One point that must again be emphasised here is that Catherine's liberalism never extended beyond the sphere of *civil* liberties. None of her written pronouncements suggest that it might have been otherwise; on the contrary, the Great Instruction made it quite plain that the existing political system must remain inviolate. Consequently, the development of civil liberties could be fostered – and tolerated – only as long as it did not infringe on the political sphere. In the context of freedom of expression this meant that neither an open criticism of the existing system of government nor an advocacy of any change in this field could be tolerated.

For the remainder of this chapter we shall, in effect, be examining the development of the idea of freedom of expression within society. A considerable proportion of this is reflected in the periodical press of that time – a subject on which much has been written. [4] This being so, I shall attempt to limit myself to these aspects of it which I consider relevant and to some less well known details.

The satirical journals of 1769-1774 form an important chapter in the

[2] *P. S. Z.*, I, No. 16,535.

[3] Cf. Makogonenko, *Nikolay Novikov i russkoye prosveshcheniye* XVIII *veka* (Nikolay Novikov and the Russian Enlightenment of the 18th Century), M.-L., 1951, p. 279.

[4] The best account in English is probably still by E. J. Simmons in *English Literature and Culture in Russia (1553-1840)*, Harvard, 1935.

history of Russian periodical press. In all, fifteen new periodicals (not all of them, strictly speaking, satirical) appeared during that period, eight of them in the first year (1769).

We may begin by making the assumption, supported by most authorities, that the appearance of these journals in 1769 was due entirely to Catherine's initiative. [5] A general agreement also exists as to the principal reasons for this initiative. With the closing of the "Great Commission" [6] a most important medium of expression had ceased to exist, in the shape of a public platform for discussion. In a sense, therefore, the satirical journals were to be its direct continuation. (Their predominantly satirical character bears little relation to this, and is simply a reflection of the trend prevailing in Europe at the time).

Since Catherine had called them into being we must assume that she wanted the public exchange of views to continue; another safe assumption that can be made is that she wanted it to be on her own terms. There can be little doubt that she regarded the satirical journals as her creation in the same way as she regarded the Commission which she had called into being, directed and dissolved as she saw fit. In both cases her positive contribution to freedom of expression and to the formation of public opinion through the very fact of creation of these instruments far outweighs any negative factor involved in their liquidation. [7]

In dealing with the satirical journals of the 1769-1774 I do not propose to enter into an analysis of the controversies between them, especially of the polemics between *All Sorts of Things* and other publications, notably *Drone* edited by N. I. Novikov. In the discussion of any kind of polemic we must first ask two obvious questions: who were the participants? and: – were they themselves aware of the identities of their opponents? In this case there is no satisfactory answer to either. The authorship of a large proportion of contributions to these periodicals remains to this day an open question. For example, as shown by Semennikov, a number of items, in *Drone* usually attributed to Novikov may have come from the pens

[5] E. g. Pekarsky, '*Materialy dlya istorii zhurnalnoy i literaturnoy deyateiinosti Yekateriny II* (Source Materials for the History of Catherine II's journalistic and literary activities), St. P., 1863; V. P. Semennikov, *Russkiye satiricheskiye zhurnaly 1769-1774 g.g.* (Russian Satirical Journals of 1769-1774), St. P., 1914, p. 4; *Satiricheskiye zhurnaly N. I. Novikova* (N. I. Novikov's Satirical Journals), P. N. Berkov ed., M.-L., 1951, pp. 16f.; and Berkov, *Istoriya russkoy zhurnalistiki* (The History of Russian Periodical Press), M., 1952, pp. 161 ff.

[6] The appearance of *Vsyakaya Vsyachina* (All Sorts of Things) on 2 January 1769 was practically simultaneous with the disbandment of the Commission.

[7] In the case of the satirical journals, Catherine's part in this 'liquidation' was by no means as simple or straightforward as with the Commission.

of Mikhail Popov and Emin. Semennikov also advanced the not implausible suggestion that the series "Letters to Falaley" in Novikov's *Painter* may have been written by the same Popov.[8] It has been proven that a proportion of contributions to *All Sorts of Things* were either direct translations or slightly modified versions of items from Addison's and Steele's *Spectator*. Among those are the articles on the purpose and limits of satire, the main subject of controversy between *All Sorts of Things* and *Drone* which, having been taken bodily from the *Spectator*, cannot be attributed to Catherine.[9] Another example of the complexity of this problem is that while I. Yelagin is believed to have been one of the principal contributors to *All Sorts of Things*, Denis Fonvizin and Lukin were then serving on his staff (the former until December 1769) and, being themselves men of letters, may well have participated in this. The controversy about the authorship of "A Fragment of the Journey to I... T..." published in 1772 in Novikov's *Painter* still continues.

There is also good evidence to the effect that the anonymity of contributors, and even editors, was in most cases successfully preserved at the time – of which more below. In view of all this is surely not possible to base any serious discussion of the 1769-1774 journals on sweeping generalisations, such as the assumption that *All Sorts of Things* represented the government and *Drone* the "progressive" elements of contemporary Russian society. This, of course, is not to deny that Catherine was an important contributor to *All Sorts of Things* or that Novikov was responsible for most of the interesting material in *Drone*.

It is therefore not the opinions expressed on the pages of these periodicals that I refer to in speaking of a "dialogue" within the framework of the satirical journals. I rather see it in the process of trial and error directed at finding practical limits of free expression for which the theoretical terms of reference have been outlined in Catherine's Great Instruction.

Catherine not only provided the initial stimulus but also took steps to create especially favourable conditions for the journals by removing the

[8] *Russkiye satiricheskiye zhurnaly*... (Russian Satirical Journals), p. 43f.

[9] Cf. V. F. Solntsev, '"Vsyakaya vsyachina" i "Spektator"' (*All Sorts of Things* and *The Spectator*), *Zhurnal Ministerstva Narodnogo Prosveshcheniya* (Journal of the Ministry of Public Education), Part 279, St. P., 1892, pp. 125-156. Also V. Lazursky, '"Le Spectateur" i "Vsyakaya vsyachina"' *Russkiy Bibliofil* (Russian Bibliophile), 1914, No. 8., pp. 23-27. See also Simmons, *op. cit.* An excellent recent essay on journalistic links between Russia and England in the 18th Century, which is likely to remain the definitive work on this subject for a long time, is Yu. D. Levin's "Angliyskaya Prosvetitel'skaya zhurnalistika v russkoy literature XVIII veka" (English Periodical Press of the Enlightenment in Russian 18th Century Literature), USSR Academy of Sciences, *Epokha Prosveshcheniya*, (Age of Enlightenment) L., 1967.

existing "censorship" restraints. Of the eight periodicals which appeared in 1769, five[10] were published at the press of the Academy of Sciences. The analysis of official entries from that period carried out by Semennikov shows that, contrary to accepted practice, the Academy did not ask for the names of persons involved in the publishing of satirical journals.[11] Furthermore, the supervision exercised by the Academy over its printing press, whereby anything published there had to be examined by some responsible person, appears to have been allowed to lapse in the first half of 1769.

While the editors thus found themselves in exceptionally favourable conditions they did not necessarily regard their freedom as unlimited. For example, the inaugural article to *Drone* – which can be safely attributed to Novikov – makes an appeal to its readers for contributions, all of which will be published, "with the exception of those aimed against God, the government, common decency, or common sense. Of such I hope there will be none, since no one who has a spark of understanding, will, in our age, write anything against the first two, while the sense of propriety will, no doubt, restrain them in case of the other two."[12] Novikov thus accepted the theoretical limitations in practically the same terms as those used in Catherine's pronouncements.

It was not long, however, before the restraints had to be re-imposed. The actual item which brought this about was a letter published in No. 17 of *Medley* which amounted to a very outspoken attack on the Russian clergy. This caused the then Director of the Academy Vladimir Orlov to issue an order requiring the manuscripts of the periodicals to be submitted for examination by a responsible official (in this case a translator named Bashilov) *before* being printed.[13]

Thus a form of censorship, affecting at least some of the journals, can be assumed to have operated from the second half of 1769. We must

[10] *Vs. Vsyachina; Ni to ni syo* (Neither This nor That); *Podyonshina* (Daily); *Smes'* (Medley); and *Truten'* (Drone).

[11] Semennikov, pp. 4f. Some editors signed applications for printing with the word "Anonime" and the resulting minute of the Academy Commission (a new name for the Kantselyariya) would read: '[name of the journal] submitted by one Anonime (*ot nekotorogo Anonima)* to be printed in ... [No. of copies]'.

[12] *Satir, zhurnaly N. I. Novikova* (N. I. Novikov's Satirical Journals), p. 47 footnote.

[13] *Arkhiv Konferentsii Akademii Nauk,* Zhurnaly Akademicheskoy Kommissii 1769 g. (Archives of the Conference of the Academy of Sciences, Records of the Academic Committee), No. 478, of 27 July, quoted by Semennikov, *op. cit.,* p. 7. See also, by the same author, 'K istorii tsenzury v yekaterininskuyu epokhu' (A Contribution to the History of Censorship in Catherine's Reign), *Russkiy Bibliofil,* 1913, No. 1, p. 57, for the text of the offending item.

note, however, that Novikov's *Drone,* generally considered to have been the boldest of all, was not alloted a specific supervisor until 18 January 1770.[14] We know virtually nothing of the standards applied by the "censors" and what, if anything, they prevented from being published. Judging by what *was* published we must assume these standards to have been liberal and it would be difficult not to conclude that the satirical journals enjoyed a high degree of freedom throughout their existence.

The bulk of contributions to the journals of 1769 was devoted to controversies between various editors and writers. The view which tends to see this as, essentially, a dialogue between Catherine speaking through *All Sorts of Things* on one side, and the "progressive forces" on the other is, as we have noted, oversimplified and inaccurate. In fact these polemics amounted to a free-for-all where much of the argument was carried on a personal plane, often involving rather a crude satirisation of the opponents, including their physical characteristics.

This can be assumed to have been one feature of the discussion which Catherine would disapprove of and therefore tend to correct.[15] It appears possible that some kind of pressure, most likely through the supervisors at the printing presses, was exerted on the editors since there is a noticeable moderation in both the tone and personal character of their satire towards the end of 1769 and, most certainly, by 1770. Of possible significance here may be an article in the October 1769 issue of *Drone* which, whilst affirming that satire ought to be aimed at individuals, at the same time prescribes that the targets must not be identifiable to anyone except themselves.[16]

The other weapon available to Catherine in controlling the satirical journals was, of course, suppression. Of the eight periodicals which began in 1769 only *All Sorts of Things* and *Drone* survived into the next year, but their publication also ceased by 1st May 1770. *All Sorts of Things* –

[14] In the person of Academician S. K. Kotel'nikov already mentioned earlier. It may be interesting to note that another periodical attributed to Novikov, *Pustomelya* (Prattler) which came out in 1770, received a different and less high-ranking supervisor: translator Samson Volkov. (Semennikov, *Russkiye* . . ., pp. 83-85).

[15] To quote A. N. Neustroyev: '. . . [the editors] instead of arguments, began to apply open abuse *(rugatel'stva).* No wonder that this war between periodicals was not to the empress's liking . . .' *(Istoricheskoye razyskaniye o russkikh povremennykh izdaniyakh i sbornikakh za 1703-1802 g.g.* (Historical Investigation of Russian Periodicals and Collections of Articles for the years 1703-1802), St. P., 1874, p. 148.

[16] *Truten',* XXV, 13 October 1769.

[17] Pekarsky, *Materialy dlya istorii zhurnalnoy i literaturnoy deyatelnosti Yekateriny II* (Source Materials for the History of Catherine II's Journalistic and Literary Activities), p. 8ff; Nezelyonov, *N. I. Novikov izdatel' zhurnalov 1769-1785 g.* (N. I. Novikov - Editor of Periodicals), St. P., 1875, p. 169f.

whose life-span was in any case pre-determined at the outset – need not concern us here, but a few words should be said about *Drone* and the rest.

The only available item of evidence suggesting suppression of *Drone* is the draft of a letter in Catherine's hand found among her papers by Pekarsky and now generally believed to have been addressed to Novikov,[17] beginning with the words: „Mr. Editor, I have been patient with you until now . . ." On the basis of this and of some pointed remarks in *Drone* (e.g. No. XIV, 6 April 1770, No. XVII, 27 April 1770) it may be deemed probable that this journal's demise is attributable directly to Catherine. I am not aware of any such evidence as far as the remaining periodicals are concerned, although the possibility of some similar action cannot be ruled out, at least in some cases. There does not seem to be a satisfactory answer to the question why precisely these suppressions had taken place. In the case of *Drone* it was not on account of audacious remarks about Catherine, nor because of its attacks on serfdom or gallomania: in all these areas Novikov went even further in his *Painter* some two years later, without incurring any vissible displeasure. For example: P. N. Berkov, in his *History of Russian Periodical Press in the 18th Century,* refers to the parody in *Drone* (Sheet XX) of a piece in *All Sorts of Things* (No. 103), attributing the former to the pen of Novikov and the latter to that of Catherine.[18] Assuming Berkov's interpretation of this exchange and his argument concerning the authorship of these items to be valid, Novikov, in this personal sally against Catherine, probably his boldest in *Drone,* accuses her of undue egotism. Against this we have a "letter" published in the *Painter,* purportedly from a "debauched maiden already in her forties" (Catherine was 43 at the time), who takes pride in the fact that no one can tell her any more "to live with one man and to love one man [only]." The letter is signed with the initials "R. G." which could conceivably stand for *"Rossiyskaya Gosudarinya"* (The Russian Sovereign).[19] *Painter* also published some scathing satire on serfdom and its abuses by noble landowners, in a series of letters under the headings "Fragments of the Journey to I . . . T . . ." (attributed by some scholars to Alexander Radischchev), and "Letters to Falaley" (similarly attributed to Denis Fonvizin).

One feature that is virtually absent in *Painter* are satirical sallies aimed at easily recognisable persons other than Catherine.[20] Thus reasonable grounds exist for the suggestion that Catherine had in this case set the

[18] Berkov, *Istoriya* . . . (History of Russian Periodicals . . .), p. 176-7.
[19] *Ibid.*, p. 180.
[20] Cf. *Ibid.*, pp. 284-5.

limit in that she would not permit the satirical journals to become offensive to individuals. This was established through a process of trial and error, with suppression being used as a warning rather than as a final silencing measure.[21]

Another reason for the short life-span of most journals must be sought in the simple economic factor.[22] The relatively large number of these periodicals suddenly springing up from nowhere bore no relation to the potential demand. It was, for all practical intents and purposes, a new commodity offered in a large quantity – there simply could not have been enough demand to sustain them all. The numbers of the reading public were small and its tastes generally crude: in fact, what it liked best was precisely the personal abuse which was curbed by Catherine's interference. This is very well reflected in the, sales of *Drone*: it was at first published in the amount of about 600 copies. At the end of 1769 this figure rose to 1240, whereas by 1770 it dropped to 750 and even of that number many appear to have remained unsold.[23]

Novikov's *Painter (Zhivopisets)* which appeared as a periodical during 1772 and 1773 and was subsequently re-published five times in a book form during the remainder of the eighteenth century[24] contains some interesting remarks showing his early tendency towards independence in the realm of literary and allied activities. In reply to a published letter from a reader writing ostensibly from Yaroslavl' and signed "Lyubomudrov" (i.e. "a Lover of Wisdom")[25] which refers approvingly to the recently founded "Society for Book Publishing",[26] Novikov states that the empress has already done "all that a sovereign can do to educate his subjects, to

[21] An indication that this was understood may be found in Chulkov's second periodical, *Parnasskiy Shchepetil'nik* (Peddler of Parnassus) which appeared in 1770. The opening editorial announces that the journal 'will avoid all that might sound unpleasant to delicate ears' and will endeavour 'not to appear suspicious to anyone' in the sense of not offending personal sensibilities. (Cf. Berkov, *Istoriya* . . ., pp. 266-7). Novikov's *Pustomelya* (Prattler) shows a similar attitude.

[22] It should be remembered that the journals were financed by their editors, even if published at government establishments. (Semennikov, *Russkiye* . . ., p. 6).

[23] Semennikov, *op. cit.*, pp. 82f.; *Satiricheskiye zhurnaly* . . ., (Satirical Journals . . .), pp. 246f.: Cf. also Novikov's own remarks addressed to his readers in No. XV of *Drone*, for 1770.

[24] The last of these editions came out in 1793 (already *after* Novikov's arrest and imprisonment) in the amount of 1200 copies. (Semennikov, *op. cit.*, pp. 86 f., Berkov, *Istoriya* p. 289). The third edition is reprinted in *Russkaya Proza XVIII veka* (Russian Prose of the 18th Century), (Makogonenko and Zapadov, eds.), Part. I., M., 1950.

[25] Semennikov advances the plausibly argued suggestion that this letter was sent in by Catherine herself. (*op. cit.*, p. 52 f.). If this was so, and if Novikov knew it at the time, then the significance of his reply would become even greater.

purify their hearts and minds, and to eradicate from them all kinds of abominable faults and prejudices; it is now up to us... to co-operate with her plans and to fulfil her wishes for our own happiness... And: "where there is duty there is also compulsion; but learning likes freedom and spreads better [in places] where people are able to think more freely." It is now up to society to take the initiative in developing the publishing and bookselling trades.[27]

This view, even if acceptable to Catherine personally, was quite incompatible with the principles on which her realm was being administered. The idea that a novel, growing, and politically sensitive field of endeavour should be left undirected and uncontrolled by the state, was clearly alien to a system which, although modernised in some respects, still largely operated on principles and usages inherited from the not very distant past.

The main points which emerge from the "dialogue" between Catherine and the editors of the satirical journals of 1769-1774, could be summed up as follows: it began on Catherine's initiative and remained generally under her supervision.[28] Restrictive measures, insofar as they occur, are a symptom of this supervision; their intended character is didactic rather than prohibitive. The object of these measures is personally-oriented satire and, at least in one identifiable case, an item offensive to the Church (and, probably, to the religious feelings of the majority of readers). At the same time there appear the first signs of a discordant tendency of whose significance neither side is probably yet aware: this tendency, personified in Novikov, no longer finds satisfaction in activities sponsored and super-

[26] *Obshchestvo starayushcheyesya o pechatanii knig'* (Society for Book Publishing) was established by Novikov in 1773 and closed in 1774 (or 1775) for lack of funds. Two other bodies with similar aims – both of which can be considered government-sponsored – existing during this period were: *Sobraniye starayushcheyesya o perevode inostrannykh knig na rossiyskiy yazyk* (Society for translation of foreign books into the Russian) established on Catherine's initiative on 4 November 1768 (cf. announcement in *St. Petersburgskiye Vedomosti* No. 89, 28 Oct. 1768, quoted by Sukhomlinov, *Istoriya Rossiyskoy Akademii* (History of the Russian Academy), I, St. P. 1874, pp. 5 f). It became defunct on the establisment of the Russian Academy in 1783. The other was *Vol'noye Rossiyskoye Sobraniye pri Moskovskom Universitete* (Free Russian Society at the University of Moscow) which was established in 1771 'for publishing [original] works and translations especially such as are needed for the edification of youth'. (*Opyt trudov Vol'nogo Rossiyskogo Sobraniya* (Transactions of the F.R.S., 1774, part. I). It also ceased to exist in 1783, for the same reason.

[27] Novikov, N. I., *Izbrannyye sochineniya,* (Collected Works), M. 1951, pp. 173ff.

[28] An evidence of this supervision in 1774 can be seen, for example, in the following extract from Novikov's note to G. V. Kozitsky: '...I enclose herewith the third issue of *Koshelyok* (Purse) and beg to be informed if it is acceptable to Her Majesty'. (Makogonenko, *Nikolay Novikov i russkoye prosveshcheniye XVIII veka)* (Nikolay Novikov and the Russian Enlightenment of the 18th Century), M.-L., 1951, p. 225, footnote).

vised by the government and begins to strive for full independence. Indeed, it is possible to see here one of the reasons for the cessation of the satirical journals by 1774. In the present chapter we are only concerned with the manifestations of this independent trend in the literary field.

As far as Novikov was concerned, his conscious realisation of the desire for independent expression probably dates from the period between 1775 when he joined the masonic movement, and 1779 when he transferred his activities to Moscow. A few remarks on the significance of each of these events may be useful.

The first masonic lodges in Russia appeared in the early 1730s, but the movement achieved its peak – with regard to both membership and influence – in the reign of Catherine, in the 1780s.[29] There is no doubt that in the 1770s and 1780s Russian free-masonry provided a natural haven for liberal trends within society which were seeking independence from the government. N. A. Pypin, to whom we owe one of the most comprehensive studies of this subject, sees in the masonic movement "the first experiments with independent thought,... the first example of social initiative on whose development depended the whole future of society."[30]

Catherine never made any secret of her strong disapproval of free-masonry, but up to 1785, her open expressions of dislike were kept mainly on the literary plane.[31] In the specific case of Novikov she registered her displeasure by withdrawing her co-operation and sponsorship from his journalistic and other ventures.[32]

[29] Samuel Bentham, who went to Russia in search of fortune in 1780, considered it opportune to become a freemason upon entering the empire. In a letter to Jeremy dated at Mittau, 21 January (NS) 1780, he apprised him of this fact adding: 'This is a circumstance which will be very useful to me in Russia'. (BM, *Add. MSS.* 33,539, Fol. 8).

[30] N. A. Pypin, *Russkoye masonstvo* (Russian Masonic Movement) Petrograd, 1916, p. 9. For a recent survey in English of the masonic movement in 18th century Russia see J. Billington, *The Icon & The Axe*, 1966, pp. 242ff.

[31] There is, however, one legislative item, namely a section of the *Ustav Blagochiniya* (Police Statute) of 1782, of a clearly antimasonic character which makes no secret of the government's preparedness to suppress the movement at any time it sees fit. The relevant clause states that any 'society, company or brotherhood' which is approved by the Government is assured of its protection. On the other hand, 'should there be a society, company, brotherhood, or some such association which causes loss or damage to the general well-being, or one which is useless, it shall be subject to liquidation and prohibition' (*P.S.Z.*, XXI, No. 15,379).

[32] While up to 1775 she had been helping Novikov, both financially and through written contributions, in the publication of his *Rossiyskaya Bibliofika* (Russian Library), she now ignored his *Sanktpeterburgskiye uchonyye vedomosti* (Learned News of St. Petersburg), and *Utrennyy Svet* (Morning Light) both of which date from 1777, in spite of panegyrical invocations to her published by Novikov in both these journals. (Cf.Nezelyonov, *N. I. Novikov, etc.*, pp. 233 & 266. She also refused to sponsor or participate in the

Thus it can be said that from this time Novikov consciously abandons his quest for expression within the official sphere and embarks upon his own independent course. The fact that he chose Moscow for the scene of his new activities is also of considerable significance. The old capital represented in the 1770s and 1780s a focal point of trends indifferent or hostile to Catherine's regime. She herself knew about it but, until approximately the last decade of her reign, took no steps to remedy the situation. As a result of her inaction and of the generally liberal climate of the regime, coupled with a concurrent rise in educational standards, Moscow became a centre of intellectual life largely independent of fashions dictated by St. Petersburg.[33]

During the period 1779-1789 Novikov was involved, as an editor and a publisher, in the production of at least ten periodicals. They were all of a more or less serious character[34] and concerned themselves for the most part with religious, philosophical, and educational matters, naturally betraying a strong masonic bent. However, two or three of them[35] occasionally ventured into the more sensitive field of politics, and it is here that we have to look for significant material.

An outstanding example of such material is the article which appeared in *Moscow Monthly Edition* in April 1781 (Part I, pp. 281-287) entitled:

opening of two St. Petersburg schools (Yekaterininskoye and Alexandrovskoye uchilishcha) established through the efforts of Novikov and his masonic friends in 1777 and 1778 respectively.

[33] An interesting testimony is provided by a Frenchman in the service of the Polish confederates (of Bar), one Thesby de Belcour who was taken prisoner by the Russians, spent three years in Siberia and, after being released, visited Moscow in 1774. He was told there by his compatriots that 'Moscow seems to be an independent City within the empire and people living there enjoy the same freedom as they would in a republic'. (Thesby de Belcour, F. A., *Tagebuch eines Französischen Offiziers . . .*, Amsterdam, 1776, p. 216). Prince de Ligne in his account of Catherine's journey to the Crimea in 1787 wrote: '. . . the greatest seigneurs of the Empire tired of the court, are living here, [in Moscow] finding fault and growling at their ease. The empress only knows about this in bulk and does not want to hear of it in detail; she does not like the police and their system of domestic spying'. (*The Prince de Ligne, His Memoirs etc.* selected and translated by Katharine Prescott Wormeley, Vol. II, London, 1899, p. 41). The French Ambassador, Count L.-P. de Segur called Moscow 'the capital of the discontented' with reference to the same period. (Count L.-P. de Segur, *Memoirs & Recollections*, London, 1825, II, p. 219).

[34] Even though some of them as *Gorodskaya i derevenskaya biblioteka* (Town and Country Library) published in 1782-1786, or *Pokoyushchiysya Trudolubets* (Industrious Man at Rest, 1784-1785) displayed certain satirical tendencies.

[35] *Moskovskiye Vedomosti* (Moscow News) which Novikov published during his tenure of Moscow University Press (1779-1789), *Moskovskoye yezhemesyachnoye izdaniye* (Moscow Monthly Edition – 1781), and *Pribavleniya k Moskovskim Vedomostyam* (Supplement to *Moscow News*) – 1783-1784. Students of Moscow University formed the bulk of contributors to the last two.

"On the principal causes of development of arts and sciences."[36] Its authorship is not definitely established, but the fact of its publication by Novikov is, in itself, of considerable importance. The main theme of this article is that intellectual freedom is the mainspring of learning, but, more important, such freedom is of little value in the long run, unless it is extended into the political sphere. A long-established political liberty is considered by the author to be the only guarantor of civil liberties, including freedom of expression, without which, in turn, learning cannot develop. Using historical examples, the article clearly refers to the contemporary Russian scene in making the point that even under such enlightened absolute monarchs as Charlemagne and King Alfred where "learning flourished in the shadow of the throne," it nevertheless withered away after their deaths. In such cases, learning grows together with the liberal regime which is temporary: "they both grow together and fall together." In the ancient Roman republic "freedom had been the soul of rhetorics," but when "base slavery followed under the emperors, this noble flame became extinguished and the wisdom of Romans was buried together with their freedom on the plains of Pharsalus." And: "The English have shown great achievements in philosophy. I believe the reason for it to be the proud liberty of their thought and writing which ought to be held as an example to the whole world."

This shows that by the early seventeen-eighties the school of thought represented by Novikov recognised the interdependence between the political and civil liberties and that, where freedom of expression was concerned, it saw little value in cultivating it "in the shadow of the throne", preferring to gain it through their own efforts. The realisation that liberty, in order to endure, must be won by active demand "from below" rather than be offered as a gift "from above" was obviously crucial in this process. As far as Novikov himself was concerned, it represented a point of no return in relation to Catherine.

The last periodical personally edited by Novikov, *The Industrious Man At Rest* which was published in 1784-1785, apart from some contributions of political character which could be construed as critical of Catherine's government, contains some thoughts on freedom of the press. An essay entitled "Bielfeld's Dissertation on Superfluous Arts and Sciences"[37] ex-

[36] This article was recently reprinted in *N. I. Novikov-izbrannyye sochineniya* (N. I. Novikov-Selected Works), G. Makogonenko, ed., M.-L., 1951, pp. 414-416, and in USSR Academy of Sciences, *N. I. Novikov i ego sovremenniki* (N.I. Novikov and his Contemporaries), M., 1961, pp. 213-215.

[37] *Industrious Man at Rest*, Part II, pp. 94-96.

pounds the principle that any repressive action against printed matter (in cases of violation of the "threefold limiting clause" which is accepted by the author as valid) is permissible only as a result of criminal proceedings in a court of justice. The "philosophical" (i.e. masonic) writings, even if they should contain some false principles, do not violate the "limiting clause". Any restrictive action against them undertaken by the government would bring more harm than good since it would "kill freedom of thought quicker than anything else." The publication of this item by Novikov can be interpreted as his response to the suppression of his "History of the Jesuit Order" in the autumn of 1784 which will be discussed in the next chapter.

This suppression was the first action against Novikov undertaken by Catherine on the official level. On the literary plane she had clearly expressed her disapproval of the Freemasons already in 1780.[38] This she repeated in 1785-86 in her three "anti-masonic" comedies the appearance of which was synchronised with the official investigation of Novikov and his publishing activities. Two of these, *Deceiver* and *The Deceived One* were written in 1785, and the third, *Siberian Shaman,* in 1786. All three were staged in St. Petersburg (but not in Moscow) in that latter year.[39] In *The Deceiver* – where the main character is Cagliostro (who had visited St. Petersburg in 1779-80) – and in *Shaman,* the pervading idea is that the freemansonry is simply an imported superstition "of which we already have enough at home." In both these plays it is only the educated people who fall victim to the impostors, whereas simple people take a sober, down-to-earth view and are not deceived. In *The Deceived One* the author suggests that anyone who wants to perform charitable deeds can do so openly, without recourse to secret societies.[40]

This completes the account of what we have called the theoretical "dialogue" between Catherine and Novikov. Another interesting figure in the same field is D. I. Fonvizin who, at least until approximately the mid-

[38] In her pamphlet *Tayna protivo-nelepogo obshchestva (Anti-absurde)* (Secrets of the Anti-absurd Society), published anonymously in that year (though marked 1759).

[39] N. P. Rumyantsev, the Russian envoy at Frankfurt, wrote to Semyon R. Vorontsov in London on 9/20 February 1786: 'On me mande de Pétersbourg que les *martinistes,* appelés en Russie *bogomudrtsy* y sont fort a la mode; le gouvernement, au lieu de persécuter ou traverser ces sectaires, s'est plu a les traduire au théatre. On m'a envoye la comédie ou on les tourne en ridicule. Vous devinez sans peine que l'auteur est celui de la comédie de Chubikhina [one of the principal characters in Catherine's comedy *O Vremya!*].' (*Vorontsov Archives, XXVII, p. 126.)*

[40] Cf. *Sochineniya Imp. Ekateriny II* (The Works of Empress Catherine II), ed. by I. A. Vvedensky, St. P., 1893; Nezelyonov, 'Literaturnyye napravleniya . . .' (Literary Trends . . .), p. 490.

seventeen-eighties, can be considered as working "in the shadow of the throne". His well-known comedies *Brigadier* and *The Minor* are in themselves a fair illustration of the degree of freedom then available, since their satire was aimed at weaknesses common to many members of the circles close to Catherine and at the existing social (but not political) system. But the most spectacular example of a conscious practical test of free expression are the remarkable "Questions" submitted anonymously by Fonvizin to the editors of *Sobesednik Lyubiteley Rossiyskogo Slova* (Companion of Lovers of Russian Letters) in 1783.

The *Companion* was published in St. Petersburg in 1783-1784 by a group headed by Princess Catherine Dashkova and O. P. Kozodavlev,[41] and including Fonvizin. Catherine herself was a principal contributor, her "Notes referring to Russian History" amounting to nearly half of the total contents of the journal. Her other regular feature was "Facts and Fancies". Dashkova had made it clear from the outset that the editors would encourage a free and unrestricted exchange of views by contributors.[42]

A few months after the journal's inception its editors received a contribution in the form of a questionnaire consisting of twenty-one points obviously addressed to the empress herself. It was accompanied by a letter in which the author stated that since the editors of *Sobesednik* "do not fear opening the door to admit the thruth", he was taking the liberty of sending the attached questions. "If they are published, a further instalment will follow. The public will then conclude... that if it is permissible to ask questions frankly it is also possible to answer them in all sincerity." The whole will help to bring forth the truth "which is so beloved by our Monarch."[43]

Fonvizin – although his authorship was not known until well after

[41] Osip Petrovich K. (1754-1819). Educated at Leipzig University (attended approx, 1769-1774), in 1783 appointed Assistant to the Director of the Academy of Sciences (i.e. Dashkova): Apart from *Sobesednik* was also, concurrently, editor of Lomonosov's *Collected Works*. Between 1784 and 1797 member of the Committee for Popular Education (Sukhomlinov, *Ist. Ross, Ak.* (History of the Russian Academy), VI, p. 53). See also below, p. 109.

[42] The introduction to the first issue stated that 'anyone wishing to offer criticism of any item appearing in this collection [i.e. publication] must not seek other printing presses in which to publish such critical or satirical remarks, but should send them directly to the Editors of this [journal] ... who will positively have them printed therein without any slightest alteration'.

[43] *Sochineniya, pis'ma i izbrannyye perevody Denisa Ivanovicha Fon-Vizina* (Works, Letters and Selected Translations by D. I. Fonvizin), P. A. Yefremov ed., St. P., 1866, P. 203. Also D. I. Fonvizin, *Sobraniye Sochineniy* (Collected Works), ed. by G. P. Makogonenko, II, M.-L., 1959, pp. 271ff.

Catherine had supplied her answers – thus clearly challenged Catherine's tolerance. His questions may therefore be regarded as another practical test of limits of free expression. It must be noted that the question No. 14 which the author presumably considered most audacious of all appeared in two different versions.[44]

The questionnaire was duly submitted for Catherine's personal censorship. She offered the following comments to Dashkova (the exact date of her note is not known, but it must have been written before 28 July 1783, the date on which Book III of *Sobesednik* appeared in print):

"I have in the meantime read carefully the article known to you and feel less strongly than I did before about leaving it unanswered. If it were possible to publish it together with answers, the satire would be rendered harmless... [The questions] originate undoubtedly from the Chamberlain as a revenge for the portrait of the indecisive man in the second part... [a blank space in the original]. I invite your attention to the fact that the question No. 14 is duplicated, possibly so that one of them could be excluded without affecting the total. Is not this caution, deplorable in itself, very much like the Chamberlain who in all his actions takes one step forward and one backward?"[45]

Although the "questionnaire" was published apparently in full, Catherine's anwers which appeared alongside left no doubt as to her disapproval. She returned to the subject in the next issue of the journal[46] in which she contrasted her own liberalism and leniency with the policies of her predecessors, under whom people used to "run away from such subjects with tails between their legs." At the same time she implied that she considered the satire to be improper principally in that it attacked easily recognisable persons *other* than herself.[47]

Fonvizin's "confession" was published, again anonymously, in Book V of the *Sobesednik.* It was addressed to the author of "Facts and Fancies", i.e. to Catherine, and noted that the author will refrain from sending in any further questions, not so much for fear of being unjustly accused of

[44] (a) 'Since our Monarch is an honest person what would prevent [her] from accepting for a guiding principle that her favours should be earned according to merit instead of being sought through deception and intrigue?'.
(b) 'Why, in the earlier days, clowns, buffoons, and jesters held no ranks whereas now they hold them and high ones at that?'

[45] Pekarsky, *Materialy dlya istorii etc.* (Source-materials to the History...), pp. 13/14. Catherine thought I. I. Shuvalov to have been the author, and his enemy, the Master of the Horse L. A. Naryshkin the target of question 14 (b).

[46] *Sobesednik...,* Book IV, 1783, pp. 157-172.

[47] This is reflected in her undue concern with Question 14 (b) and in the fact that she attributed it to simple envy and personal spite. (*Ibid.,* pp. 167-8).

"looseness of the tongue" (*svobodoyazychiye* – the term used by Catherine in her answers) but "so as not to set a bad example to others."

It is interesting that the whole affair was witnessed as it were "from the inside" by the already mentioned Samuel Bentham and described in some detail in letters to his brother Jeremy. Samuel had by that time been in Russia for about three years and, as is evident from his correspondence, had a fair knowledge of the language. He was close to Dashkova[48] through his friendship with her son Paul and, at least indirectly, in touch with Catherine herself who took sympathetic interest in his unlucky love-affair then at its height.[49]

In October 1783 Samuel Bentham wrote to his brother with reference to *Sobesednik:*

> "2 or 3 months ago there was published in this work a paper containing about 20 questions relating to the government which would astonish you by their freedom – one of them was "why are not trials in courts of justice printed?" another was "why do men of merit quit the service?"
>
> Princess Dashkoff shewed this paper to the Empress before she dared permit it to be printed. Leave however was obtained. Now in this same work one might in the way of dialogue cooked up into a tale introduce all your striking observations on jurisprudence. And in short through this channel we might exhibit all our remarks and criticisms wherever they do not attack the Empress herself more than that question of: "Why do men of merit quit the service?"
>
> We certainly could shew off in this work and at present while it is still new the Empress sees every thing that is in it." [50]

Bentham thus clearly saw Fonvizin's "questionnaire" as a yardstick by which to judge the practical limits of free expression. His scheme for using *Sobesednik* to propagate his brother's ideas is interesting. It is conceivable that it might have materialised had the journal not ceased its publication in the following year.

[48] Although he did not have too high an opinion of her, calling her in one of his letters 'mean, avaricious, and vain'. (BM, *Add. Mss., 33.539,* Fol. 424). For a time he was put to work by Dashkova alongside her daughter, translating articles from *Sobesednik.*

[49] For details see M. S. Anderson, 'Samuel Bentham in Russia 1779-1791', *American Slavic and E. E. Review,* XV, 2, 1956, pp. 157-172. For other aspects of Samuel Bentham's activities in Russia see also Walther Kirchner, "Samuel Bentham and Siberia", *The Slavonic and East European Review,* XXXVI, 87, 1958, pp. 471-480, K. A. Papmehl, 'The Regimental School Established in Siberia by Samuel Bentham', *Canadian Slavonic Papers,* VIII, 1966, pp. 153-168, and Ian R. Christie, 'Samuel Bentham and the Western Colony at Krichev, 1784-1787' *The S.E.E.R.,* XLVIII, 111, 1970, pp. 232-247.

[50] BM. *Add.Mss. 33,539,* Fol. 455. For additional details of this incident see K. A. Papmehl, 'Samuel Bentham and the *Sobesednik*' (1783), *The Slavonic and East European Review,* XLVI, 1968.

In his next letter with which he sent the translation of "Questions" and Catherine's answers – "which will serve to give you a better idea of what may be published there than anything I could tell you" – Bentham tells the story of how he had been shown the "Questions" by Dashkova –

> "... before she shewed them to the Empress and I had been I believe a good deal Instrumental in persuading her to soften one or two Expressions and to leave out entire Question which was too insolent.
>
> It is said "The Questions received from an unknown hand" but I know the Author and I believe other people know him, he is a Man of Fortune but not of the best Character. –
>
> You will learn by the Questions the manner of thinking and speaking of such of the Nation in general as pique themselves on their Understandings." [51]

We thus learn of the rather fascinating possibility that Fonvizin's questions might have been "censored" by an Englishman!

Bentham's version cannot, of course, be considered fully reliable as he can be assumed to exaggerate his own role in the affair. It is, nevertheless, interesting and certainly cannot be ignored.

Within the "officially sponsored" literary circles the degree of freedom of expression was thus undoubtedly high by any standards. One aspect of the incident just described which must be borne in mind is that the questions were published and answered when the identity of their author was not known – either to the editors or to the monarch who was directly involved. Surely it must be agreed that Catherine showed here the most remarkable tolerance and respect for public opinion. The limitations of freedom indicated as a result seem reasonable and are consistent both with the principles she professed and with the practice of earlier years.

The preserved drafts of articles by Fonvizin prepared for publication in his *Friend of Honest People or Starodum* – the last being the name of one of the principal characters in *The Minor* – also deserve to be mentioned. The introductory "Letter to Starodum", dated January 1788, contains hymns of praise to Catherine's tolerance and shows the very marked tendency to contrast it with the allegedly "reactionary" attitudes of her advisors. The following is probably a good illustration:

> "... the age of Catherine the Second is characterised by granting the Russians freedom to think and to speak. ... It is true that even now there are some persons who try to oppress talent and to prevent from appearing [in print] anything that is likely to reveal their ignorance and faults ..." And: "... thanks be to God we live

[51] Samuel Bentham to Jeremy Bentham, St. P., October 15, 1783, B. M. *Add.Mss. 33.557*, Fol. 279.

in an age when an honest person can express his toughts without fear... She [Catherine], by opening the road to education released writers from their chains... Should some slavish soul abiding in the body of a prominent magnate turn against you [the writers] out of fear... your pen can boldly expose them before the throne, before the fatherland, and before the whole world... I believe that such freedom to write as is now enjoyed by the Russians puts a talented man into a position of a guardian of common good." [52]

"General Court Dictionary" prepared for inclusion in the journal left no doubt that it is precisely these advisers and courtiers who were to be principal targets of Fonvizin's satire. But what must have appeared least acceptable of all to Catherine was his expressed belief that "a talented man can, with a pen in hand and without leaving his own room, become a useful counsellor to the sovereign and perhaps even a saviour of his country and of his fellow-citizens."

Fonvizin was not allowed to publish his *Friend of Honest People,* [53] and it is easy to see at least two good reasons why: firstly because Catherine could not permit what might have easily become an organ of political opposition – particularly in view of Fonvizin's known connections with the group close to Crown Prince Paul – and secondly, because it was highly likely that the journal would indulge in the kind of personal satire she was not prepared to tolerate. In addition, her experience with Novikov – the lessons of which were clear to her by that time – would tend to restrain her from encouraging a similar kind of independent publicistic activity.

In a sense, it can thus be said that Fonvizin, like Novikov before him, having first tested the practical limits of freedom of expression, turns away from literary activities carried on "in the shadow of the throne", in search of complete independence. In doing this both these writers show an appreciation of the fact that literature can only be truly free if it is divorced from government sponsorship, however benevolent the latter may be.

In addition to the trends already discussed, mention should be made of the continued existence of one other school of thought. This is the "traditional" school of administrators typified by attitudes such as that shown in the "Police Instruction" at the time of the "Great Commission",

[52] Fonvizin, *op. cit.*, pp. 229-230.

[53] In his letter to P. I. Panin dated at St. Petersburg, 4 April 1788, Fonvizin wrote: 'The local police forbade the publication of *Starodum* so that it is not my fault that it will not appear.' (*Ibid.*, p. 356). It appears highly probable that the matter had been referred to the empress and that the decision was hers.

and by the actions of people such as Saltykov, Bruce, Prozorovsky, and many others. While its main significance was, of course, practical, its theory is typically reflected in one literary work of the period, namely the *Puteshestviye v zemlyu Ofirskuyu* (Journey to the Land of Ophiria) by Prince M. M. Shcherbatov. The ideal political and social system described by the author as existing in his utopian kingdom[54] contains features characteristic of a "police-state" with the most rigid control of thought and its expression.[55] If the theoretical aspect of this trend evolved little, if at all, it undoubtedly acted as a form of a catalyst on the others in that it would naturally tend to inhibit both Catherine's liberal tendencies and the practical utilisation of the available media of expression by society.

[54] Basically a rule by the aristocracy with the powers of the monarch strictly limited.

[55] Cf. N. D. Chechulin, *Russkiy sotsiyal'nyi roman XVIII veka* (Puteshestviye v zemlyu Ofirskuyu knyazya M. M. Shcherbatova) (Russian Social Novel of the 18th Century – Prince M. M. Shcherbatov's *Journey to the Land of Ophiria),* St. P., 1900, esp. pp. 44f. Also A. A. Kizevetter, 'Russkaya Utopia XVIII stoletiya', *Istoricheskiye ocherki* (The Russian 18th Century Utopia, Historical Studies), M., 1912. A possible – admittedly tenuous – bearing on the affinity between Shcherbatov's ideas and those expressed in the Police *Nakaz* may be seen in his apparent friendship with N. I. Chicherin, the main author of the latter. (Cf. Shcherbatov's remarks on the allegedly unfair treatment of Chicherin by Catherine in 'O povrezhdeniyi nravov v Rossii' (On the Corruption of Morals in Russia), *Russkaya Starina* (The Russian Past), III, p. 686.

CHAPTER V

THE PERIOD OF GROWTH – PRACTICE

The practical aspect of the development of freedom of expression during the period 1769-1788 will be dealt with under the following main headings: (a) printing and publishing; (b) free speech; (c) theatre; and (d) educational institutions.

The whole period is characterised by the rapid growth of media of expression; nowhere is this process more conspicuous than in the realm of publishing. The government practice with regard to printing presses is liberal, culminating in the edict of 1783 which opened this field to private initiative. Society shows an eager response with a large measure of the same tendency towards independence which we have noted in the last chapter.

In early 1771 authorisation was given for the opening of the first printing press by "Foreigner Hartung" (Johann Michael H., then a newcomer to Russia) as a result of his petition to the Senate. The pertinent edict[1] permitted Hartung to print books in all languages *except the Russian.*[2] It also allowed him to manufacture type, Russian as well as "foreign", for sale exclusively to the government-controlled printing establishments.

The edict contained what I have called the "three-fold limiting clause" in that it explicitly forbade the printing of anything prejudicial to the Christian religion, the government, or common decency. The practical implementation of this clause was to be achieved by having Hartung submit all material for publication, whether brought in by his customers or purchased abroad, for examination by the Academy of Sciences prior to being printed.

[1] Senate Edict of 1 March 1771, *P.S.Z.*, XIX, No. 13,572.

[2] The edict made it plain that the purpose of this exemption was to protect the government monopoly in this field. Whether or not this was the reason is, of course, open to argument.

Hartung was also permitted to print advertisements of all kinds subject to their being passed by the police. The edict made it clear that he was not being granted a monopoly, on the contrary, anyone else was free to apply for a similar permit under analogous conditions.

In March 1776 Catherine approved an application for the opening of another private press, in this case by the St. Petersburg firm of booksellers Weitbrecht & Schnorr. The Senate edict which followed is dated 22 August of that year.[3] It differs from the charter given to Hartung in that it authorises the new press to print "books and other works" *in Russian* as well as in foreign languages. The manufacture of type was also permitted, for sale not only to government-controlled establishments, but also to other authorised private printing presses. The edict showed a particular concern that "Russian characters of any kind whatsoever should not be sold to private individuals under any circumstances" and that their manufacture be carried out exclusively on the approved premises. Censorship arrangements were the same as in the case of Hartung, with the added stipulation that books on religious matters were made subject to examination by the Holy Synod.[4] An additional safeguard was introduced in having the owners of the press issue a catalogue listing all books printed there as well as those imported from abroad. Finally, the edict introduced a form of a copyright clause which forbade unauthorised re-printing of books published at other presses.

In 1779 "Foreigner Schnorr", one of the partners involved in the last quoted edict, was granted the permission to open a private press at Tver'.[5] The regulations prescribed in this case were similar to those just mentioned, with the difference that the censorship functions in their respective fields were to be performed by officials especially appointed by the Synod and by the local branch of the Governor's office.

This process of gradual extension of the participation of private enterprise in the field of printing reached its apogee in Catherine's personal

[3] *P.S.Z.*, XX, No. 14,495.

[4] It is evident from the Senate Edict of 31 May 1780 (*P.S.Z.*, XX, No. 15,019) that this point was neither observed nor enforced in practice: all kinds of theological treatises had been published in the meantime, both at private and at government presses, without synodal censorship. The edict reminds everyone of the existing law and directs that henceforth it must be strictly observed. It appears doubtful if even this reminder had any practical effect: Novikov published at Moscow University Press between 1780 and 1783 a number of translations of books, by non-Orthodox writers, of clearly religious character (including Milton's *Paradise Lost* which was subsequently banned in 1795), without any apparent interference. (Longinov, *Novikov* ... pp. 129; 135; 186f.)

[5] By Senate Edict dated 3 October 1779, *P.S.Z.*, XX, No. 14,927.

edict of 15 January 1783, "On the Permission to establish printing Presses and to print Books in Russian as well as in Foreign Languages in all Towns and Capital Cities..." [6]

The significant principle on which this act was based was stated in its opening sentence which declared that, as far as the government was concerned, there was no difference between printing presses and any other "workshops or factories". Consequently, anyone was free to open a press in any town within the empire without any special permission, the only stipulation being that the local police were to be informed. The enforcement of the "three-fold limiting clause" – which was reiterated – was entrusted to the police, who were "to examine Books about to be published and prohibit those which are found to contravene this Our Regulation; and in cases of unauthorised printing of such provocative books, not only to confiscate them, but to report offenders to the appropriate authority so that they may be punished... according to law."

It is undeniable that this edict was of a paramount importance and may be regarded as the turning point in the history of the freedom of the press in the reign of Catherine II, in the sense that it marked the extreme point of liberalisation and therefore also the beginning of the reverse trend. [7] One point that becomes apparent upon reading the text of the edict is that, in the context of time, place, and the existing political system, it offered the opportunity for a radical increase in publishing facilities without really providing any adequate means of control. That there were to be limitations to what was permissible to print was explicitly stated; but it was done in such a vague, not to say casual manner, as to have little practical significance. The supervision over the output of private printing presses was entrusted to the police – seemingly a departure from the principle that this was to be exercised, in their respective areas, by the Church and the institutions of higher learning. It must be remembered that the edict did not, at the same time, alter the existing situation as far as the state-owned

[6] *P.S.Z.*, XXI, No. 15,634.

[7] Skabichevsky (*op. cit.*, pp. 37f.) discussing the edict of 15 January 1783 emphasises its 'ambivalence' claiming that, by subjecting the private presses to police control, it took away as it were with one hand what it gave with the other. In this, and in suggesting that this 'ambivalence' was something peculiar to Catherine's regime, he seems to be losing sight of the obvious fact that any legislative act granting some kind of freedom must, at the same time, define its limits. In any case, the police supervision proved in practice to be quite ineffective. A son of a contemporary printer, Selivanovsky, testifies with reference to late 1780-s: '... books used to be examined at the police headquarters (*pri Uprave*) or by the Chiefs of Police which meant that they would be produced there, but would not be read...' ('Zapiski Selivanovskogo' (Selivanovsky's Memoirs), *Bibliograficheskiye Zapiski*, (Bibliographical Notes), St. P., 1858, No. 17, p. 518).

presses were concerned so that, for example, Moscow University Press, then under lease to Novikov,[8] was technically subject to supervision by the University authorities and quite immune from police interference. The fact that local police organs were, on the whole, completely unsuited to this new task can presumably be taken for granted; they could hardly be seriously expected to assess each written work submitted to them in relation to the three points of the "limiting clause". It could rather be assumed that they would tend to show either great restrictive zeal or indifference, depending on the general policy from above. In this case it turned out to be the latter.[9] The general effect of the edict of 1783 was that the government lost control over publishing activities, something no authoritarian government can afford.

We shall now look at some examples of how the censorship operated in practice after 1783. As already pointed out, the Edict of 15 January 1783 while placing the output of free (i.e. private) presses under the supervision of the police, did not alter the existing situation where the government-controlled establishments were concerned. An interesting example of how the "censorship" in the latter worked is provided by Bolotov. In his memoirs he recounts how he had visited Novikov, in the latter part of 1783, with the view of having one of his books[10] published at the University press. Novikov advised him to take the manuscript to Professor Barsov,[11] the University "censor". Bolotov agreed somewhat reluctantly since, as he puts it, he "did not know Mr. Barsov from Adam." However:

> "This learned man surprised me not only by his gracious and polite manner, but also [by the fact that] upon being shown my book, he declared that there was nothing to be censored, that my works were known to everybody and, since he could not imagine that there could be something adverse in them, he would pass them without any further ado. And thus, seizing a pen, he there and then wrote his approval to the effect that they might be printed."[12]

The list of books found at the University press and bookshop and temporarily impounded in 1785[13] shows the names of "censors" against

[8] From 1779 to 1789.

[9] During the whole time this edict was in force (15 January 1783 to 16 September 1796) there is not a single recorded case of a prosecution arising from it instituted by the police.

[10] *On Prosperity* (O blagopoluchii).

[11] See above p. 27. Among his numerous functions were those of Inspector of Students, Editor of *Moscow News*, and examiner of books printed at the University Press.

[12] Zhizn' i priklucheniya A. T. Bolotova... (The Life and Adventures of A. T. Bolotov...), III, Part XXI, Letter 213, (*Russkaya Starina*, VI, p. 1087).

[13] Cf. below, p. 98.

the titles. The fact that in many instances the former read: "University" or "At. St. Petersburg" indicates that in such cases the precise identities of the "censors" could not be established. The name of Barsov occurs most frequently along with "University", otherwise we find there the names of Professor Chebotaryov, G. Kozitsky, Archbishop Platon and a few other members of the church hierarchy. It is clear from these entries[14] that the examination of books at the Moscow University press was not carried out according to some established system and that, insofar as it existed, it tended to be haphazard and perfunctory. As far as the Church censorship was concerned, Longinov tells us that after the edict of 1783 the "spiritual censors" often simply refused to examine books submitted for their perusal.

Society responded eagerly to the opportunities thus created. Here again the scene is dominated by the activities of N. I. Novikov. In view of the extensive literature existing on this subject I shall recall here only the most essential points of these activities.

Novikov, as it will be remembered, moved to Moscow in 1779 and, from May of that year, took over the lease of the University press and its bookshop. Together with Johann Schwarz ("Ivan Grigorievich" S., 1751-1784), a prominent mason and, from 1779 until 1782 Professor of German at Moscow University, he became – in fact if not in name – the leader of a masonic circle comprising many of the richest and most prominent residents of the ancient Capital.[15] With them he founded the "Learned Society of Friends", opened publicly in 1782 with the official approval of the Military Governor of Moscow Z. G. Chernyshov and with the blessing of Metropolitan Platon.

Novikov's publishing activities at the University press had assumed unprecedented proportions already from the beginning,[16] but their most spectacular expansion occurred as a direct result of the edict of 15 January

[14] Reproduced by Longinov, *op. cit.*, pp. 019f. (Supplement).

[15] The principal members of this circle were: I. P. Turgenev, brothers N. and Yu. N. Trubetskoy, M. M. Kheraskov, A. A. Cherkassky, P. A. Tatishchev, Engalychev, Prof. Kh. A. Chebotaryov, A. F. Ladyzhensky, O. A. Pozdeyev, V. V. Chulkov, and A. M. Kutuzov. (Longinov, *op. cit.*, pp. 136f)

[16] While in his 'St. Petersburg period' (1766-1779) Novikov had accounted for 53 published titles, including periodicals, he published 308 such titles during his first three years in Moscow – i.e. 1779-1782 incl. (Semennikov, *Knigoizdatel'skaya deyatel'nost' N. I. Novikova i tipograficheskoy kompanii* (The Publishing Activities of N. I. Novikov and of the Printing Company), Petersburg, 1921, pp. 9ff.) During the first three years of his tenure of University press it published more books than in the 24 years since its establishment. (V. O. Klyuchevsky, *Sochineniya* (Works), VII, M., 1959, p. 247). Bolotov speaking of Novikov's tenure of Moscow U.P. says: 'From that time [since N. took it over] it was as if it [the literature] was born anew, and it grew so much with each year that,

1783. Already in that year the "Learned Society" opened two printing presses (registered officially in the names of Novikov and P. Lopukhin and located in their respective houses) and a secret "Rosicrucian" press.[17] The year 1784 saw the establishment of the Printing Company founded by a group of fifteen freemasons, including Novikov. It was the first case in Russia of a private commercial enterprise based on a voluntary contract by shareholders of equal status. Its printing shop was exceptionally large and well equipped, consisting of 20 presses.[18]

Nothing gives a better idea of the effects of the edict of 1783 in the realm of publishing than the fact that the output of printed matter during the decade following it almost doubled in relation to the preceding one.[19]

In the publishing activities of Novikov and the circle of Moscow masons we can see the practical application of the tendency towards independence of government sponsorship which we have observed in the last chapter. The unusually large scale of operation of their enterprises and the fact that they were conducted under the auspices of a secret society – openly disapproved by the government – were the obvious potential bones of contention as far as the latter was concerned.

During the period the edict of 1783 was in force, i.e. from January 1783 to September 1796, thirteen private printing presses were opened in St. Petersburg, and about the same number in Moscow.[20] In the provinces the corresponding figure was about eleven, most of them established under the auspices of local *gubernia* authorities. In the 1790s there existed also at least two private presses operated by landowners on their estates (J. G. Rakhmaninov's at Kazinka near Tambov, originally established at St. Petersburg in 1788, but transferred to Kazinka in 1791, and I. E. Struysky's at Ruzayevka, Kozlov District, Government of Penza).[21]

after a short time, it became quite different;' ('Iz neizdanogo literaturnogo naslediya Bolotova: "Sovremennik ili zapiski dlya potomstva", 1795' (From Bolotov's Unpublished Literary Heritage: 'The Contemporary or Memoirs for Posterity', 1795), *Literaturnoye Nasledstvo* (Literary Heritage), 9-10, M., 1933, p. 176.

[17] This was located in Schwartz's house and employed exclusively Germans. Lopukhin did the proof-reading and dealt with the police 'censors'. During the time this press was in operation (1783-1786) it printed a number of translations of masonic books without indicating the place of publication. (Longinov, *op. cit.*, p. 206).

[18] *Ibid.*, p. 219.

[19] According to the figures quoted by P. N. Milyukov, the total number of titles published, excluding liturgical books and periodicals, was 363 for the decade 1776-1785. It rose to 665 in the period 1786-1795. (*Ocherki po istorii russkoy kul'tury, III,* (Studies in the History of Russian Culture), Paris, 1930, pp. 396-7.)

[20] *Svodnyi katalog russkoy knigi grazhdanskoy pechati XVIII veka* (Union Catalogue of Russian 18th Century Books in Secular Type), V. M., 1967, pp. 280ff.

Derzhavin gives the following account in his memoirs (written between 1802 and 1812) of the printing press at Tambov which he claims to have been instrumental in founding (in 1787):

"... [the press] printed many books translated by the local Nobility, especially by Ye. K. Nilova.[22] It also printed [official] publications and edicts in order to expedite matters... also *gubernia* newspapers which contained information on prominent people or troops passing through, and on prices of goods, especially grain..." [23]

It appears from this that the press at Tambov being thus under the personal sponsorship and, no doubt, close supervision of the Governor, resembled the government-controlled presses in the capitals rather than the truly "free" ones such as those operated by Novikov and associates. It seems likely that this may have also been true of some other "private" presses in the provinces.

The first indications of a change in government policy in the publishing sphere[24] date from the year following that in which the edict on free printing presses was promulgated. In the summer of 1784 Novikov began to publish in the Supplement to *Moscow News* instalments of a "History of the Jesuit Order".[25] Although apparently written in moderate and objective terms, the "History" fell foul of Catherine who announced that she would not permit anyone to offend the Jesuits whom she had taken under her personal protection. Accordingly, she ordered the then acting Military Governor of Moscow, N. P. Arkharov, on 23 September 1784, to prohibit its further publication. Arkharov reported one week later that this had been done and the copies of the *Supplement* already printed had been confiscated.[26] There can be little doubt that Catherine's action in this case was to be interpreted as a sign of her displeasure and a warning addressed to Novikov.

Almost simultaneously with this incident came a Senate Edict[27] accus-

[21] *Ibid.*, p. 289f.

[22] Two such translations by Ye. K. Nilova: *Graf Bal'mont ili zabluzhdeniya razsudka* (Count Bal'mont or the Errors of Reason), from the French, and *Priklyucheniya Edvarda Val'sona* (Adventures of Edward Walson), from the German, were actually published at Tambov. Cf. also E. Likhacheva, *Materialy dlya istorii zhenskogo obrazovaniya v Rossii* (Source Materials for the History of Women's Education in Russia), I, St. P., 1890, p. 268.

[23] *Zapiski Gavriila Romanovicha Derzhavina 1743-1812* (Memoirs of Gavriil Romanovich Derzhavin), ed. by P. I. Bartenev, M. 1860, p. 269.

[24] Although, as we shall see, these measures were directed specifically against the Moscow masons and not at the publishing activities in general.

[25] Nos. 69, 70 and 71 of the *Supplement*.

[26] Longinov, *op. cit.*, p. 231.

[27] 1 November 1784, *P.S.Z.*, XXII, No. 16,086.

ing Novikov personally of having infringed the "copyright" through having reprinted ,at the University press, some textbooks published for the Commission for Popular Education (established in 1782) under a government contract, by the firm of Breitkopf. The edict warned Novikov to refrain from such unfair business practices in the future.[28] Copies of the textbooks concerned which had been found at the University bookshops were confiscated and Novikov was ordered to reimburse Breitkopf for those already sold.

The subsequent developments are well known, and I shall limit myself here to a chronological account of the most important events. One point that has to be made is that the government's actions against Novikov and associates from the late 1785 onwards were really a reflection of its anti-masonic policy. It so happened that the activities of Moscow "martinists" were, thanks to the personal qualities and talents of Novikov, most prominent in the field of publishing. Consequently it was this field which became immediately affected by Catherine's anti-masonic campaign.

It appears highly likely that this campaign was precipitated by the events in Bavaria involving the Order of the Illuminati. In 1785 the Kurfuerst Karl-Theodor suppressed the order and seized their achives which allegedly exposed a revolutionary plot on a European scale. Although the Moscow masons had kept aloof from the Illuminati the developments in Bavaria obviously served to increase the already existing suspicions against them.[29]

On 23 December 1785 Catherine issued a personal edict addressed to the Military Governor of Moscow, Count Ya. A. Bruce[30] which, whilst clearly directed against Novikov's masonic circle, for the first time showed a practical concern with enforcing control over the output of private printing presses prescribed in the edict of 1783. It ordered an immediate examination of books published at the free presses in Moscow, to be

[28] The government-controlled presses themselves sometimes indulged in such practices. Thus the press of the School of Artillery and Engineering (*Artileriyskiy i Inzhenernyi Korpus)* had been found in 1780 re-printing and selling on its own account calendars published at the Academy of Sciences. (Senate Edict of 20 February 1780 forbidding all printing presses to publish calendars and other books printed at the Academy – ***P.S.Z.***, XX, No. 14,985).

[29] The Russian government was not alone in these suspicions. In the young republic of the United States it was officially believed 'that, during the era of the French Revolution, a vast international order, known as the Society of the Illuminati, for which Masonry was probably a "front", owed allegiance to a foreign power (France), [and] engaged in secret activities looking towards the capture of the government (Jefferson was suspect)'... (H. M. Jones, ed., *Primer of Intellectual Freedom,* Harvard U. P., Cambridge, Mass., 1949, p. xiv).

[30] ***P.S.Z.***, XXII, No. 16,301. For Catherine's draft note outlining the main points of this edict cf. ***Sb. R.I.O.***, XXVII, p. 359.

carried out under the direction of Bruce and the Metropolitan Platon whom it also directed to ensure that books published at Novikov's and other free presses should, in future, be "properly censored". For this purpose "one or two learned and enlightened" members of the clergy were to be appointed. Their task, together with two laymen to be appointed at the same time, was to examine such books in order to prevent "schisms, nonsense, and all kinds of absurd interpretations" from finding their way into print. In addition, the Metropolitan was to examine Novikov in the principles of the Orthodox faith and report his findings.[31]

One month later, on 23 January 1786, Catherine signed an order to the Civil Governor of Moscow, P. V. Lopukhin,[32] instructing him to interview Novikov making it clear that the "establishment of printing presses is usually assumed to be for the production of useful books needed by society, and certainly not for promoting the publication of works filled with the new schism, aimed at deceiving the ignorant and catching them into their net." Lopukhin sent his report already on 30 January, whereupon he received another order, dated 11 February 1786, telling him to place under seal all books published by Novikov which had not yet been seen by the Metropolitan and to forbid their sale pending further instructions.[33] As a result 461 titles were temporarily impounded, but the sale of books at the University bookshop appears to have continued throughout without impediment.[34]

In the meantime, the censors appointed in Moscow in the persons of the Abbot Moisey and Archimandrite Serapion on the ecclesiastical, and Professor Barsov and the Police Chief Godein on the lay side, went on with their work, while Novikov passed his examination in catechism with flying colours. One slightly ironical touch of Platon's report which was submitted in March, is that of the books examined he condemned the

[31] Platon, unlike Bruce, approached his task with little enthusiasm. In a letter dated 7 January 1786 to the Archbishop of Kazan' Ambrosius (Podobedov) he wrote: 'Ab Imperatrice mihi praescriptum est, ut omnes libri Novicovii subirent examen meum et ipse examinetur in Religione et ut censores simul cum saecularibus a me assignarentur pro imprimendis libris. Multas hisce praevideo pro me difficultates . . . et pericula; nihil vero quod erigat animum'. (S. Smirnov, 'Tsensurnaya vedomost' 1786-1788 godov' (Censorship Report of the Years 1786-1788), *Os'madtsatyi vek* (The Eighteenth Century), ed. by P. Bartenev, M., 1868, Book I, p. 426).

[32] On the same date she also sent him an order to investigate the hospital established by the Moscow masonic circle and to find out if there were any schools operated by them. (*Sb. R. I. O.*, XXVII, p. 363, for both items). Thus the anti-masonic campaign was clearly not limited to the publishing sphere.

[33] *Sb. R. I. O.*, XXVII, p. 364. Cf. also *Chteniya v Imp. Obshchestve istorii* . . . (Lectures at the Imperial Society of Russian History . . .), M., 1867, Book IV, pp. 46, 51f, and 55.

[34] Longinov, *op cit.*, p. 254.

works of the encyclopaedists while refraining from passing judgment on the masonic literature. The resulting Personal Edict addressed to Bruce and dated 27 March 1786 [35] lists six books [36] which were to remain under seal, their sale forbidden until further notice; all others were to be immediately released, with no restrictions as to their disposal. But, the edict went on, "at the same time, you shall impress in the strictest terms upon the said Novikov and all other operators of free printing presses in Moscow that they must take care not to publish books filled with similar strange philosophies... under the pain not only of forfeiting the books involved, but also of losing the permit to operate a printing press and a bookshop, and of legal proceedings [against them]'.'

It is thus clear that the character of the government action just described was anti-masonic rather than anti-free press. Although the warning to Novikov could hardly have been made more explicit, it unfortunately went unheeded. The copies of the six books listed in the edict were removed by the authorities from the University bookshop, but a number of them were left at Novikov's book depot, where no search had been made. Novikov not only did not report their existence, but some time later, with the knowledge of his associates, gave them to one of the Moscow booksellers (Kol'chugin) "for safe keeping". The latter proceeded to sell them in Moscow and at various country fairs. Although the authorities took no action at the time, it is not surprising that this blatant contravention of Catherine's orders was held against Novikov after his arrest in 1792.

One other item worth mentioning in this series of decrees arising from the investigation of Novikov and associates, is the Synodal Edict of 17 March 1786 [37] which directed all diocesan authorities to submit a list of private presses existing in their areas and report any new ones as they appear. A possibly interesting point is that it refers to Catherine's edict of 23 December 1785 as the one which had established censorship. In fact, of course, the same form of "censorship" had been prescribed already in 1783. The text of the synodal edict and the fact that until then the Church authorities obviously did not even keep records of private printing presses, are another proof that, at least as far as the "spiritual censorship" was concerned, it had not been enforced in practice until then.

[35] *P.S.Z.*, XXII, No. 16,362.

[36] Their titles: (1) *On Error and Truth;* (2) *An Apology or Defence of Free Masons;* (3) *Brotherly Announcement;* (4) *Chrisomander: an Allegorical and Satirical Story;* (5) *Pocket Book;* (6) *Chemical Paracelsis, Psalter.* The first of these was the work of the French mystic St.-Martin from whose name the term 'martinists', generally applied to Moscow masons at the time, was derived.

[37] *P.S.Z.*, XXII, No. 16,352.

The question arising from this whole affair is whether or not the measures undertaken by the government in this instance can be regarded as retrogressive in relation to the edict of 15 January 1783. Although at a first glance the answer might appear to be in the affirmative – which is the view generally taken by writers on this subject whether pre-revolutionary or of the Soviet school – it need not necessarily be so. The whole issue is confused by the masonic factor. Insofar as it is possible to separate it from that of the freedom of the press, it is clear that the government did not take anything away from what it had granted in 1783; it merely attempted to correct undesirable tendencies and to regain the degree of control which was reserved for it under the act of 1783, but which it had lost in practice.

Evidence in support of this assertion can be seen in the fact that the growth of printing and publishing continued unhindered. The output of books in fact reached its peak in the period 1786-1790,[38] and about eleven new printing presses opened between 1786 and September 1796 (when the edict of 1783 was repealed).[39] The censorship continued to be ineffective, perhaps the best example being the passing for publication of Radishchev's manuscript of his *Journey from Petersburg to Moscow* by the St. Petersburg Chief of Police N. I. Ryleyev. The censorship as conceived by the edict of 1783 simply did not work – subsequent restrictive actions in this field again had to be initiated at the highest governmental level.

However, the masonic aspect of the activities of Novikov's group did suffer somewhat, even if to a probably lesser degree than Catherine had intended.[40] One further sequel to the events of 1785/86 was Catherine's edict to the Synod given on 27 July 1787, shortly after her return from a trip to the Crimea, forbidding lay printing presses and bookshops to deal in liturgical books and in any kind of literature pertaining to the Orthodox

[38] 366 titles as compared with 197 between 1781 and 1785, and 299 in 1791-1795. (Milyukov, *op. cit.*, p. 396). Cf. also Semennikov, 'Literaturnaya i knigopechatnaya deyatel'nost' etc., (Literary and Publishing Activities...), pp. 15-18.

[39] The reports received from bishops as the result of the synodal edict of 17 March 1786, show the existence of 8 private printing presses in St. Petersburg, 5 in Moscow, and one at Yaroslavl' (Semennikov, *op. cit.*, p. 22), the total being 14.

[40] The 'Learned Society of Friends' appears to have become defunct in the course of 1786. Novikov's private press was absorbed by that of the Company while the secret press continued for some months, eventually closing on its own accord, in the latter part of 1786. (Longinov, *op. cit.*, pp. 270ff.) All this in no way slowed down the output of Novikov's publishing enterprises, as is clear from what had already been said. The following year, 1787, saw the masonic circle effectively combating the famine through free distribution of grain on an unheard of scale, while te government looked on unable to deal with the situation.

faith.[41] It was obviously aimed at checking the spread of masonic propaganda. As a result, 313 books were seized in Moscow and handed over to the Metropolitan Platon, among them copies of his own works. The effects of this edict in St. Petersburg are not known, while in the provinces, judging by the example of Kaluga where not a single book of this category was found, they appear to have been negligible.[42]

Before leaving the subject of publishing, a mention must be made of the other, older form of the same method of expression, namely the manuscript literature. It is difficult to make anything approaching a reasonably accurate assessment of its scope and significance. Much of it in Russia, as indeed elsewhere at the time, consisted of manuscript copies of printed books or parts thereof. During the period with which we are concerned it co-existed with printed literature: there are some preserved samples of manuscript satire which, because of its strongly personal character or unprintable language, could not be officially published.[43] A recent Soviet author takes the view that the edict of 1783 caused the decline of manuscript literature by giving society a new weapon for its struggle against the government: the old one could therefore be discarded.[44] While things were certainly not that simple, there can be no doubt that the increased availability of printed books in the last two decades of the century did play some part. The point that can be made is that there are no known instances of legislation or administrative action against manuscript literature during this period.[45] We may therefore conclude that it did not present anything like a serious problem from the government's point of view.

As far as free speech is concerned, the absence of some specific instrument such as the "Great Commission" makes it rather difficult to assess its development. Admittedly, the very fact that the Commission was not convoked again can, and has been interpreted as indicating that the government was reluctant to repeat the experiment. There is, of course, no doubt that Catherine was disillusioned in this matter and also, that her

[41] *P.S.Z.*, XXII, No. 16,556, Cf. also Senate Edict of 17 August 1787, *P.S.Z.*, XXII, No. 16,564. Also Khrapovitsky, p. 42. (Entry for 25 July).

[42] Longinov, p. 285.

[43] Such were, for example, 'poems' on Catherine's love-life. Cf. G. Gukovsky and V. Orlov, 'Podpol'naya poeziya 1770-kh-1800-kh godov' (Underground Poetry of the Years 1770-1800), *Literaturnoye Nasledstvo* (Literary Heritage), 9-10, M., 1933, pp. 6 ff.

[44] S. L. Peshtich, *Russkaya istoriografia XVIII veka* (Russian Historiography of the 18th Century), Part I, L'grad, 1961, p. 14.

[45] Unless we include such 'borderline cases' as the edict reminding everyone that only the *printed* government announcements are to be recognised as valid. (*P.S.Z.*, XXI, No. 15,718).

views had evolved since 1769.[46] But this is only a part of the picture. During the period 1769-1788 the government created new instruments of expression favouring free speech at the provincial and local levels, through legislative acts such as the Decree on Gubernias of 1775, the Nobles' Charter, and the Townsmen's Charter of 1785. The last of these[47] is perhaps especially interesting since it established Town Councils the members of which were to be elected on the same principle as the townsmen's deputies to the "Great Commission", i.e. by free permanent residents, irrespective of social status (*sosloviye*). Consequently the elected Councils were of a mixed social character consisting of noblemen alongside merchants, artisans, etc.[48] Thus the government, in a sense, continued to encourage the public exchange of opinions among the various strata of society.

Another legislative act which, to some extent, shows the government's attitude towards free speech is the already mentioned Police Statute of 1782. This allows popular gatherings, such as games, spectacles, etc., provided they are kept within the prescribed legal bounds and do not lead to the utterance of "words or deeds injurious to some particular person or offending public decency." It does not permit swearing in the presence of nobility, "superiors", or women. It also forbids arguments against the Orthodox religion. The sanctions are not particularly severe: e.g. three days confinement on bread and water for staging a theatrical performance or some other public entertainment without police permission, while 24 hours of similar punishment is prescribed for drunkeness.[49]

We have at least one recorded statement of Catherine's concerning free exchange of opinions, dating from 9 August 1773. At one of the meetings of the Council of State, after an argument with G. Orlov, Catherine declared that she wanted everybody "always not only to state their views openly, but also to argue against her own, since only in this way is it possible to get at the truth."[50]

[46] Cf. the draft, in her own hand, of a letter to Prince de Ligne, dated 2 December 1788: 'J'été élevée dans l'amour et le respect pour les républiques, mais l'expérience m'a coinvaincu que plus il y a de monde de rassemblé pour raisonner et plus on entend déraisonner'. (*Sb. R.I.O.*, XXVII, p. 535).

[47] *Gramota na prava i vygody gorodam Rossiyskoy Imperii* (The Charter of Rights and Privileges to the Towns of the Russian Empire), *P.S.Z.*, XXII, No. 16,188, 21 April 1785. The Town Councils were abolished in the reign of Paul I, in 1798.

[48] Cf. Semennikov, 'Literaturno-obshchestvennyy Krug Radishcheva', Literaturnyy Arkhiv, *A. N. Radishchev-Materialy i issledovaniya* (Radishchev's Literary and Social Circle', Literary Archives, A. N. R. – Materials and Investigations), M.-L., 1936, p. 282f.

[49] *P.S.Z.*, XXI, No. 15,379.

[50] I. A. Chistovich, *Istoricheskaya zapiska o Sovete v tsarstvovaniye Imp. Yekateriny II*

An interesting comment on Catherine's attitude in an incident involving a "*podmyotnoye pis'mo*"[51] at the time of the Pugachov uprising is found in the despatches of the then British envoy at St. Petersburg, Sir Robert Gunning. These mention an anonymous letter, found in the empress's apartments, which

"... contained very heavy accusations not only against the Procurator General, but against many other People in Power; shewing their abuse of it, and the great Corruption that prevails in each of the Departments, and hinting that Prince Orlov, Patriotick as he affected to be, connived at it. Though the Author of this has not appeared to make good his charge, he has said no more than what is in the Mouth of every one unemployed here; Indeed the Liberty of Speech can no where be carried farther, but the Empress as much through Policy as Moderation has hitherto passed it by unnoticed. Her Maxim is that whilst ill Humours are allowed to have this Vent, their Effects are not to be apprehended."

The author of the letter "not appearing to make good the Charges it contained, as he has promised to do, it was by the Empresses's Order burnt by the common Hangman."[52]

It is, of course, an undisputed fact that, especially where freedom of speech was concerned, Catherine applied different standards in dealing with the lower – or, more correctly, uneducated – as opposed to the upper, or educated, strata of society. This differentiation is evident in her theoretical views. As rightly pointed out by Nezelyonov, in Catherine's *Notes Concerning Russian History* and in her historical plays "simple people" appear as generally disorderly, stupid, and naive, in contrast to their enlightened and sophisticated rulers.[53] In practice Catherine did not hesitate to apply drastic measures to curb undesirable rumours and "loose talk" amongst the uneducated, especially in emergencies such as the Moscow riots of 1771 or the Pugachov revolt.

Thus after the riots of September 1771 Catherine, writing to the newly appointed Governor of Moscow, Prince M. N. Volkonsky, instructed him to investigate the sources of wild rumours circulating in city, and, at his

(Historical Note on the Council during the Reign of the Empress Catherine II), St. P., 1870, p. 8.

[51] Cf. p. 2 above.

[52] Public Record Office, London, S.P. 91/95. (Despatches by Sir Robert Gunning to the Earl of Suffolk dated at St. Petersburg, January 14/25, 1774, and January 17/28, 1774).

[53] Nezelyonov, 'Literaturnyye napravleniya v yekatorininskuyu epokhu' (Literary Trends in the Age of Catherine), *Istorichesky Vestnik* (Historical Messenger) XVI, (1884), pp. 16-17.

discretion, to subject the rumour-mongers to public corporal punishment by the Police.[54]

In her note to Potyomkin dating from 1774, on the subject of a self-appointed successor to Pugachov, one Metel'ka, she approved of the action taken by Pyotr Panin who "considering such rumours inimical to public peace forbade any such felonious talk, including the very utterance of the name "Metel'ka"."[55] Some of her earlier measures such as the "Manifesto on Silence" of 1763, quoted earlier, or the Senate edict of 22 August 1767 forbidding the peasants to present her with complaints against the landlords fall into the same category.[56]

Unless we apply twentieth-century "Western" standards to the Russian eighteenth-century conditions, we must agree that the difference in treatment of the uneducated, as opposed to the educated parts of society was to a large extent justified.[57] Catherine's views on this score were in keeping with the then accepted ideas and were, if anything, more enlightened and humane than those of some of her subjects now considered "progressive" by some writers. To quote one example: Dmitri Anichkov (1733-1788), since 1772 Professor of Logic, Metaphysics and Pure Mathematics at Moscow University, held in high esteem by the Soviet scholars because of his non-noble origin and allegedly materialistic views (mainly due to his dissertation "On the Origins of Natural Religion" – of which more below), wrote in his *Speech on Various Reasons Impeding the Extension of Human Knowledge... Delivered on 30 June 1774:* "Everyone knows with how many diverse prejudices the simple people are contaminated. Everywhere and among every kind of simple people it is possible to observe innumerable errors, arising for the most part from their lack of understanding and undue credulity. This is because simple people, having coarsely constructed

[54] Such totally fantastic and unsubstantiated rumours were earlier the direct cause of the riots and of the murder of the then Archbishop of Moscow, Ambrosius. (Bartenev, *Os'madtsatyi Vek* (The Eighteenth Century), Book I, pp. 63f.

[55] *Sb. R.I.O.*, XXVII, p. 17. At the same time Catherine did not forget her humane principles: writing to Prince A. A. Vyazemsky in (probably) the autumn of 1775, she positively forbade the use of severe punitive measures which he had advocated against the suspected participants in the rebellion. In another undated note she demanded definite proofs of criminal intent in cases of peasants accused of sedition and a precise formulation of charges against them 'especially since this concerns matters involving thoughts and not actions'. (Bartenev, *op. cit.*, Book 3, pp. 390 and 391 respectively).

[56] *P.S.Z.*, XVIII, No. 12,966. This, in effect, only reminds those concerned of the existing laws (notably of the *Ulozheniye* of 1649) and calls for their strict observance.

[57] Dashkova expressed the same idea in different terms when she told Diderot in Paris: '... it is knowledge which produces liberty and not liberty knowledge, the former unaccompanied by the latter, never yet failed to produce anarchy and confusion'. (*Memoirs of the Princess Dashkaw...*, ed. by W. Bradford, London, 1840, p. 165).

brains and overabundance of blood, will believe anything without any further reflection..."[58]

The next medium of expression to be considered is the theatre. Here, Catherine's attitude was analogous to that in the field of literature and periodical press. The theatre was a tool she herself used very extensively, and it is therefore resonable to assume that she appreciated its value in influencing public opinion. Consequently, as in the literary sphere, she could be expected to foster its development by granting it a relatively high degree of freedom, provided she could supervise its use. In cases where such supervision was difficult, she would tend to be less generous. Thus, for example, in 1769 when granting a five-year charter to the Italians Belmonti and Cinti to operate a theatre in Moscow, she took care to ensure "que la plus exacte bienséance y soit gardée et que les pièces nouvelles soient représentées après que le maréchal comte Soltikof les aura fait passer par la censure."[59]

On the other hand, in the case of Fonvizin's famous comedies *Brigadier* and *The Minor* – especially the latter – Catherine proved to be more liberal than some of her subjects. As pointed out by Semyontkovsky, it was only thanks to her that these plays could be performed at all.[60] *The Minor* was staged for the first time in St. Petersburg, in September 1782,[61] with resounding success, but encountered difficulties in Moscow. There its planned performance at Maddox's theatre[62] was held up by Professor Chebotaryov[63] who appears to have taken exception to some lines by the principal character Starodum. Fonvizin's letter to Maddox written at

[58] *Izbrannyye proizvedeniya russkikh mysliteley vtoroy poloviny XVIII veka* (Selected Works of Russian Thinkers of the Second Half of the Eighteenth Century), ed. by I. Ya. Shchipanov, M., 1952, p. 160 f.

[59] Catherine's note in her own hand to the Military Governor of Moscow, P. Saltykov, dated 18 June 1769. (*Sb. R.I.O.*, XIII, p. 16).

[60] R. I. Semyontkovsky, 'Nash pervyi skeptik (o Fonvizine) (Our First Sceptic (About Fonvizin), *Istorichesky Vestnik* (Historical Messenger), LXI, p. 127.

[61] D. D. Yazykov, ' "Nedorosl' na stsene i v literature' ('The Minor' on Stage and in Literature) *Ist. Vestnik* (Historical Messenger), X, p. 141. The text of the play was published in the following year, also in St. P., at Schnorr's private press. Makogonenko, asserts on the basis of a comparison between this printed version and a MS copy of *Friend of Honest People*..., recently discovered in the archives of Prince P. A. Vyazemsky, that certain strong satirical sallies against Catherine's courtiers have been left out of the former. (*Denis Fonvizin-tvorcheskiy put'* (Denis Fonvizin - His Creative Progress), M.-L., 1961, pp. 262ff.).

[62] Michael Maddox (Mikhail Yegorovich Medoks, 1747-1822), an Englishman and originally an itinerant showman, arrived in Russia in 1776 and, by 1780 built his own theatre in Moscow (it was destroyed by fire in 1806). See O. Chayanova, *Teatr Maddoksa v Moskve 1776-1805 gg.* (Maddox's Theatre in Moscow 1776-1805), M., 1927; also 'Michael Maddox, Impresario,' *The Times*, 9 February 1956.

the time, implies that the censor suspected him of having added these lines to the original text used for the performances at St. Petersburg.

Another instance of the high degree of freedom accorded playwrights working "in the shadow of the throne" is the incident involving the play *Sorena i Zamir* written by a protegé of Dashkova N. P. Nikolev and performed with great success in Moscow in February 1785. The Military Governor Bruce objected to some lines in it, critical of absolute monarchy, stopped the performances, and sent the manuscript of the play to Catherine with a letter requesting her to ban it. The empress refused to do this and reproached Bruce for his action,[64] whereupon the performances were resumed. In the following year the text of the play was published in *Rossiysky Teatr*[65] (Russian Theatre).

The Police Statute of 1782, as already noted, permitted popular theatricals "provided the Police do not find anything there that contravenes the law or is harmful to individuals." Another relevant legislative act is Catherine's personal edict on the establishment of a special committee for directing the activities of state-controlled theatrical and musical companies, issued in 1783.[66] While it is primarily concerned with administration, it also states plainly that the government does not hold a monopoly in this field; on the contrary, anyone was permitted "to organize suitable public entertainments, under the sole condition that they abide by the Government legislation and by the regulations laid down in the Police Statute." It is possible to see in this a manifestation of the same spirit, favourable

[63] Khariton Andreyevich Chebotaryov (1746-1815), Professor of Russian Literature, Librarian, and theatrical censor at Moscow University (since 1778). Member of the Moscow masonic circle.

[64] 'I am surprised Count Yakov Alexandrovich, that you stopped performances of a tragedy which obviously had been well received by the public. The meaning of lines such as those noticed by you has no relation to your Sovereign. The author attacks the despotic rule of tyrants, whereas you refer to Catherine as "mother" '.

[65] For the details of this incident and the correspondence between Catherine and Bruce see Longinov, 'Materialy dlya istorii russkogo prosveshcheniya i literatury v kontse XVIII v.' (Source Materials for the History of Education and Literature in Russia at the end of the 18th Century), *Russkiy Vestnik* (The Russian Messenger), XXV, 1860, pp. 639 f. Cf. also Skabichevsky, *op. cit.*, p. 39 f.

[66] *P.S.Z.*, XXI, No. 15,783 of 12 July 1783. There were seven such companies at the time, namely: (1) The Italian Opera; (2) The Russian Theatre; (3) The Italian Opera Comique; (4) The French Theatre; 5) The German Theatre; (6) The Ballet Companies; and (7) The Orchestra. Before the establishment of this Committee there existed the post of a Chief Director of Spectacles *(Glavnyy Direktor Spektakley)* held from 1766 to 1779 by I. P. Yelagin (1725-1794), and, from 1779 to 1782 by V. I. Bibikov (1740-1787). The latter (brother of Alexander, Marshal of the 'Great Commission') was instrumental in establishing a school of dramatic art in St. Petersburg in 1779. Both occasionally acted in the capacity of theotrical censors. (*Russkiy Biografichesky Slovar'* (Russian Biographical Dictionary), St. P., 1908.)

to private enterprise, as in the edict on free printing presses issued some six months earlier.

On the side of society, apart from the already quoted examples of the use of this medium by authors such as Fonvizin and Nikolev, we must note the significant general increase in the number of theatres and performances during this period. While it is impossible to attempt an accurate estimate of this increase, there is abundant contemporary evidence of theatrical companies being maintained by nobles on their estates, at educational institutions of all levels, military units, factories, etc. [67] What is indeed remarkable is that with all this, there is no record, before the 1790s, of any repressive or restraining action on the part of the government. This surely must be taken as an indication that its practice in this sphere was quite liberal at the time.

In turning to the educational field the first point to be noted is that there is no appreciable change in the number or character of institutions of higher learning, in relation to the earlier period. [68] Both the Academy of Sciences and Moscow University are left, relatively speaking, to fend for themselves and, in the absence of any specific encouragement from the government side, society shows little interest in higher education. [69] The administrators in charge of the institutions concerned continue, at least in the earlier part of this period, to maintain a fairly strict degree of control over public utterances of the academic staff. Thus, in the 1770s at the University of Moscow, all speeches to be delivered by the professors had to undergo the scrutiny of the Academic Conference. "The Curator [Adadurov] several times reminded the Director [Kheraskov] that the censorship of speeches must be vigilant, and that the professors who deliver them must not be permitted to make any audacious pronouncements." [70] The professors themselves did not lack vigilance. At the Conference of 24 August 1769 six of them lodged a solemn protest against the publication of a dissertation by the already mentioned Anichkov "On the Origin of Natural Religion" after it had already been passed by the faculty. The outcome was that Anichkov was made to remove two footnotes and the

[67] According to Haumant there were no less than fifteen established theatres in Moscow alone in 1787. (*La Culture Française en Russie (1700-1900)*, Paris, 1910, p. 82.)

[68] Unless we count the Mining Academy opened in 1774 which although, strictly speaking, an institution of higher education, had little or no significance in the context of freedom of expression.

[69] Thus in 1782 and 1783 there were only two students at the University attached to the Academy of Sciences. In 1787, 82 students attended Moscow University as compared with about 100 in 1758. (A. S. Arkhangel'sky, *Imperatritsa Yekaterina II v istorii russkoy literatury i obrazovaniya* (The Empress Catherine II in the History of Russian Literature an Education), Kazan', 1897, pp. 13 f.).

dissertation was reprinted in this revised form.[71] It seems highly likely, however, that such manifestations of a cautious attitude were engendered mainly by fear of attracting adverse publicity or unwelcome government attention to the University. Anyhow, the situation seems to have improved gradually and took a pronounced turn for the better with the appointment of Catherine Dashkova to the Directorship of the Academy of Sciences and of the newly established Russian Academy in 1783. Dashkova's role in reviving the former and developing the latter, and in her enlightened attitude to free exchange of opinion, must be considered as definitely positive.

In the field of primary education the Statute on Primary Schools of 1786,[72] displayed the traditional principle of tight administrative control. The duties of teachers were laid down in great detail, and the same applied to the curricula, textbooks, etc.[73] On the other hand, a certain measure of de-centralisation was introduced by delegating the supervisory functions to Inspectors elected by citizens of the towns concerned.

On the side of society again the same tendency towards independence which we have noted in other fields, can be seen in the educational activities of the free-masons, both in Moscow and in St. Petersburg. In the former capital the "Association of University Alumni" established in 1781, incorporated both current and former students of the University, as well as some professors (e.g. Schwartz). This circle actively participated in the publication of two periodicals, *Twilight Glow* and the already mentioned *Industrious Man At Rest*. It was connected with the "Learned Society of Friends" which was, by itself, involved in the educational field, through grants of scholarships, despatch of promising students to foreign universities, establishment of a teachers' college, etc. In St. Petersburg one of its members, M. I. Antonovsky, founded the "Society of Friends of Literature", in about 1784, which counted Radishchev amongst its

[70] S. Shevyryov, *Istoriya Imp. Moskovskogo Universiteta 1755-1855,* (History of the Imp. University of Moscow), M., 1855, p. 151.

[71] The professors concerned were Dilthey, Kerstens, Rost, Barsov, Reichel, and Schaden. For the text of Anichkov's dissertation see A. P. Gagarin, 'Pervaya filosofskaya dissertatsiya zachchishchavshayasya v Moskovskom Universitete' (The First Philosophical Dissertation Defended at Moscow University), *Vestnik Moskovskogo Universiteta* (Messenger of Moscow University), 1952, No. 7, pp. 151-173. For the extent of the changes in the dissertation see E. A. Bobrov, 'Autodafe nad filosofskoy knigoy' (The burning of a Philosophical Book), *Istoricheski Vestnik* (Historical Messenger), 96 (1904), pp. 606-7.

[72] *P.S.Z.*, XXII, No. 16,421.

[73] Thus Section 33 of the Statute decreed that 'All Teachers shall, in all respects, follow the prescribed method of teaching and shall not use books other than those listed in this Statute'.

members.[74] The activities of all these groups were, as we have noted earlier, adversely affected by Catherine's anti-masonic moves of 1785-86 and afterwards became less significant.

An interesting example of ideas concerning academic freedom is provided by the project of new universities drawn up by a committee headed by O. P. Kozodavlev (identical with one of the editors of *Sobesednik* mentioned earlier).[75] This advocates almost unlimited freedom for University teachers, as for example: "Teachers shall be free from compulsion as regards both the mode of teaching and textbooks. Freedom of thought is beneficial to learning in general...". And, with reference to the proposed faculties of law: "Teachers of jurisprudence must have absolute freedom of opinion..." The supervisory functions of the administrative head are to be limited to ensuring that the teachers see the instructions issued for them and that they perform their respective duties. The project also favours opening the universities to all social groups, including peasants in bondage, since "learning is called free because everybody is free to acquire it, and not because it is the exclusive privilege of free people." Although the project did not materialise, it is certainly noteworthy on account of the liberal spirit in which it was written, and of the fact that it was prepared by an officially appointed governmental committee, for consideration on the highest level.

We have seen that the most outstanding general feature of the whole period is the spectacular growth of means of expression (with the exception of the sphere of higher education). In this chapter, in addition to describing various practical manifestations of attitudes towards freedom of expression in relation to this process, I have tried to present a balanced view of the principal causes of this growth. It seems that these are to be found in government policies as well as in the practical work done by members of society. Without the opportunities created by the government legislation the achievements of Novikov and associates would have been unthinkable, yet the overwhelming majority of writers on this subject only stress the latter while ignoring the former. With special reference to the publishing field, credit must be given to Catherine for progressive liberalisation

[74] Cf. Semennikov, 'Literaturno-obshchestvennyy krug...' (...Literary and Social Circle...), pp. 215 f.

[75] In the latter 1780-s the government was considering opening three new universities (at Pskov, Chernigov, and Penza) and appointed a committee to draw up a Project of the Charter of Russian Universities *(Proyekt Ustava Russkikh Universitetov)*. This was prepared between February 1786 and February 1787, Kozodavlev being its principal autor. (Sukhomlinov, *Istoria Ross. Akademii* (History of the Russian Academy), VI, St. P., 1882, p. 54 and *passim*).

leading to the edict of 1783, and for the fact that it was not, up to the time of French revolution, adversely affected by her anti-masonic campaign. Novikov and associates, whose activities represent the practical application of the most important tendency towards autonomy, stressed in the previous chapter, deserve highest commendation for making most of the opportunity and for their pioneering work in the field of private initiative. The masonic aspect of their activities played a certain positive part in their quest for independence; but, on the other hand, it evoked suspicion from above and in the end proved their undoing.

CHAPTER VI

THE "REACTION" OF THE "NINETIES"

The present chapter will outline the history of free expression in the last period of Catherine's life and reign under the following headings: government theory, government practice, and the evolution of the idea within society.

The first of these points concerns predominantly the change in Catherine's views, its character, extent, and discernible causes. There is a general agreement among historians concerning the fact that Catherine's views had become more "conservative" or "reactionary" towards the end of her life and this I propose to accept as a broad assumption. The controversies revolve around the character, extent, and reasons for this change and this is where it becomes necessary to state the case rather more explicitly.

In dealing with the character of the change in Catherine's attitude we might ask this preliminary question; did it occur suddenly, e.g. as a direct result of the French revolution, or was it a lengthy process originating somewhere at the time of the Pugachov uprising, or even earlier, but merely accelerated by the events in France?

A type of answer to this question which is fairly frequently encountered is the statement of the French historian Ch. de Larivière, who wrote: "Ce changement ne s'accomplit pas à la façon d'un coup de foudre, et il serait difficile d'en préciser la date fixe. Deux crises capitales, cependant semblent avoir décidé de cette évolution: la révolte de Pougatchev et la Révolution française."[1]

With certain qualifications, concerning the actual significance of the

[1] *Catherine Le Grand d'après sa correspondance - Catherine II et la Révolution Française*, Paris, 1895, p. 1. For a critical review of Larivière's book and discussion of some of its more controversial aspects cf. A. Brikner, 'Yekaterina II i frantsuzskaya revolyutsiya' (Catherine II and the French Revolution), *Istoricheski Vestnik* (Historical Messenger) LXI, 1895), esp. pp. 413-415.

Pugachov uprising, this thesis has been accepted by the great majority of non-marxist historians and its validity, in the most general context, cannot be denied. The situation is somewhat different within the more limited terms of reference of our subject: there is no evidence of any gradual evolution of Catherine's views on this score before 1789 as, it is to be hoped, will be clear from what has already been said here. In effect, it can be suggested – always strictly within the limits of our subject – that the change in Catherine's views did not represent a long-term gradual process; that indeed, it occurred, if not as a *coup de foudre,* nevertheless quite rapidly, as a result of an entirely new situation.

The extent of this change, in the purely theoretical sense, is difficult to assess. Much of the evidence here is indirect or overlapping with practical moves or actions; nonetheless the assertion can be made that it was, in fact, quite small. First of all, Catherine's hostility towards the French revolution does not make her anti-liberal: it has been shown, with justice, more than once that in revolutionary extremism she recognised a force inimical to liberalism.[2] This is clearly reflected in her correspondence with Grimm: she wrote, for example, in May 1791:

> "...puisque ces messieurs [members of the National Assembly] sont des républicains déterminés, ils doivent aimer, respecter et encourager la vérité, et s'ils ne le feront pas, je dirai qu'ils ne sont rien du tout... ils sont bien propres à discréditer pour longtemps la liberté et à la rendre odieuse à tous les peuples..."[3]

and again, in 1794:

> "...le monde ne manquera jamais de maître, et encore vaut-il mieux le déraisonnement momentané d'un que le déraisonnement de beaucoup, qui met une vingtaine de millions d'hommes en fureur pour le mot de liberté dont ils n'ont pas même l'ombre, et après lequel ces insensés courent sans jamais l'acquérir."[4]

Thus Catherine's negative attitude towards the French revolution was not due to a change in her outlook from "liberal" to "reactionary", but rather to the not entirely unjustified belief that the revolution led not towards liberty, but towards anarchy eventually to be replaced by a despotic form of government. Needless to say, this belief was shared by a great many liberally-minded men and women of her age. Considering further that she looked at these events from the point of view of her

[2] This point has been stressed by V. Leontowitsch in his *Geschichte des Liberalismus in Russland,* Frankfurt, 1957, pp. 31ff. Cf. also Brikner, *op. cit.,* pp. 414 f.

[3] Letter No. 204, 12 May 1791, *Sb. R.I.O.,* XXIII, p. 488.

[4] Letter No. 222, 11 February 1794, *Ibid.,* p. 593.

professed political creed, i.e. "enlightened absolutism", and that she did not have the benefit of retrospect or knowledge of 19th century social and political theories, her attitude towards the revolution *per se* cannot be cited as an evidence of her departure from her earlier "liberal" principles.

Some manifestations of a conservative outlook, rare in her earlier writings, but increasingly prominent in her correspondence of this last period, can certainly be interpreted as indicative of a change of views. A good example are some of her remarks to Radishchev's *Journey from Petersburg to Moscow,* e.g.: "... all that had been constructed and established in the world so far, had been done on the basis of past needs and experiences and not just because someone had wanted it to be so; if things were to be made different they could only become worse, for the "better" is an enemy of the existing "good". It is preferable to hold on to what we know than to try and open the door to the unknown." [5]

I shall return to the question of the extent of the change in Catherine's theoretical views during the discussion of the practical aspect. For the time being I propose to look at the reasons for this change.

The first of these is undoubtedly the age factor. Catherine had reached her sixtieth birthday a few months before the events which – as it must have been evident even then – were to prove of epochal significance. The purely physiological aspect of aging would clearly tend to make her attitudes progressively more conservative: a good illustration of this process is provided by the tenor of her letters to Grimm. This in the seventeen-nineties is appreciably different to that of the 'seventies and early' 'eighties: she often reminisces, philosophises, at times sounds irritable, but the old light and frequently jocular tone of earlier days is absent.

The second principal cause of the change in Catherine's attitude was the influence of her entourage, first and foremost that of her last favourite, Platon Zubov. The full significance of this factor has not always been appreciated in spite of the rather abundant contemporary evidence. [6] Zubov relieved his predecessor Dmitriev-Mamonov in June 1789. His influence on Catherine had been considerable from the beginning, but increased greatly after Potyomkin's death in 1791. Zubov was an eager partisan of autocracy and decidedly conservative in his views.

[5] *Vorontsov Archives,* V, p. 411.

[6] For example, Pyotr Vasil'yevich Zavadovsky (1738-1813, close to Catherine from approximately 1774 until her death, one time favourite, displaced by Potyomkin, later chairman of the Commission on Popular Education) wrote to Semyon Vorontsov in January 1792: '.... Zubov has been in control of all internal and external affairs without exception ... Not one of the earlier favourites, not even the omnipotent Prince Potyomkin himself had ever controlled such a wide field ...' (*Vorontsov Archives, XII, p. 75).*

In addition to this, some key positions in internal administration came to be occupied by people like Bruce and Prozorovsky[7] of a strictly conservative and anti-liberal outlook.

Finally, one very important factor contributing to the change in government attitude towards freedom of expression in this last period was Catherine's preoccupation with external affairs to the exclusion of internal ones. This can be dated at least to 1787, the year of great diplomatic activity followed by the outbreak of the second Turkish war. From mid-1789 until the end of her life, the events in France and their interaction with other international problems obviously intensified this preoccupation.[8] In other words, during the period with which we are now concerned, internal matters had, firstly, to be subordinated to the exigencies of foreign policies, and secondly, little time was left for them. In consequence Catherine had gradually lost touch with affairs at home, leaving this field mainly to Zubov, and, in emergencies, would tend to follow his advice or that of her senior administrators. Therefore the definition of the term "government" used so far has to be altered somewhat with reference to this last period: while it is still "Catherine with her circle of immediate

In a subsequent letter to the same addressee, Zavadovsky had this to say: 'It used to be throught earlier that no one would be able to concentrate in his hands as much power as did Potyomkin, but the present favourite is incomparably more powerful. The late Potyomkin controlled only the military departments whereas this one has concentrated in his hands all matters without exception.' (*Ibid.*, p. 104). The Chancellor Bezborodko confirms this in June 1795: '... the control of all affairs, most of all the internal ones, has been usurped by this new and omnipotent gentleman.' (*Vorontsov Archives*, XIII, p. 243). A prominent military figure of the late 18th and early 19th centuries, S. A. Tuchkov, wrote in his memoirs: 'Catherine II... had full confidence in her favourite Prince Zubov and desired to have all the most important matters of state referred to him'. (*Zapiski Sergeya Alekseyevicha Tuchkova 1766-1808* (Memoirs of S. A. Tuchkov 1766-1808), ed. by K. A. Voyensky, St. P., 1908, p. 114).

7 Prince A. A. Prozorovsky (1732-1809) was Military Governor of Moscow from 19 December 1790 until 21 March 1795. Potyomkin. upon learning of his appointment, wrote to Catherine: 'Your Majesty has taken out the oldest cannon from your armoury, it is certain to fire at the targets you choose, as it has none of its own. Only take care that it does not stain your name with blood in the eyes of posterity'. One of the measures initiated by Prozorovsky during his tour of duty in Moscow was the surreptitious opening and reading of private mail. (*Russkaya Starina* (The Russian Past). IX, pp. 263 f, editor's footnote, presumably by V. Semevsky). Bruce, already referred to earlier, was Military Governor of St. Petersburg in the early 1790-s.

8 It is evident from her correspondence that she had feared the spread of French revolution to other European countries, from which only the Turks would gain. She appears to have been genuinely convinced that they would invade Europe were it to fall victim to 'the French anarchy'. (Cf. *Sb. R.I.O.*, XLII, pp. 94ff). Zavadovsky, writing to S. Vorontsov in early 1792 informed him that the events in France are absorbing all Catherine's attention and advised him, whenever an opportunity presents itself, to make remarks hostile to the revolution, 'which, in itself, will make your despatches agreeable [to her]'. (*Vorontsov Archives*, XII, pp. 76 f).

advisors", the stress moves to "the advisors" and away from "Catherine".

Of the three factors believed to have caused the change in Catherine's theoretical views on civil liberties only the first, i.e. age, represents a gradual process of longer standing, the other two coming into play only from 1789 towards. This would support my assumption that the change itself was rapid rather than gradual.

I shall next recount the most important practical measures undertaken by the government in relation to freedom of expression during the period in question. In cases such as those involving Radishchev and Novikov, about which a great deal had been written I shall limit myself to the most salient points without repeating what is generally known.

Chronologically, Radishchev's case is the first to have occurred.[9] Catherine's recorded utterances and the final sentence passed make it clear that his offence was considered to have been purely political and was evaluated in relation to the international situation obtaining at the time. After reading the first thirty pages of *Journey* Catherine is reported to have exclaimed: "...this is sowing the seeds of the French malady, disregard for authority; the author [must be] a Martinist."[10] And a few days later she told Khrapovitsky that Radishchev "praises Franklin as a leader and represents himself as possessing the same qualities."[11] Catherine's edict containing the ultimate sentence speaks of Radishchev's crime as a "violation of his oath of loyalty" (i.e. high treason) in that he had published a book "filled with most damaging theories [aimed at] disturbing the public peace, diminishing the respect for authority, creating a popular dissatisfaction, and with improper utterances against the status and power of the sovereign."[12] All this was technically consistent with the accepted standards and the "three-fold limiting clause" which did not permit any open criticism of the established system of government.

No steps seem to have been taken to trace copies of Radishchev's book which had in the meantime found their way into private hands. References to it made openly in contemporary private letters make it clear that a

[9] Radishchev's book *Journey from Petersburg to Moscow* was printed in his private press and passed by the St. Petersburg Chief of Police N. Ryleyev in July 1789. It appeared on sale in May-June 1790. The author was arrested on 30 June. Catherine's edict sentencing him to 10 years' exile in Siberia is dated 4 September 1790. For a recent account in English of the events surrounding Radishchev's arrest and exile see A. McConnell, *A Russian Philosophe - Alexander Radishchev*, The Hague, 1964. This work also contains a useful bibliography.

[10] *Dnevnik A. V. Khrapovitskogo 1782-1793* (A. V. Khrapovitsky's Diary, 1782-1793), St. P., 1874, p. 338. (Entry for 26 June 1790).

[11] *Ibid.*, p. 340. (7 July 1790)

[12] Personal edict of 4 September 1790, *P.S.Z.*, XXIII, No. 16,901.

number of such copies were in circulation throughout the seventeen-nineties.[13]

One interesting point is that Radishchev in his written "confession" adressed to Catherine from prison whilst awaiting the final verdict, defends his plans to liberate peasants by attributing similar ideas to herself. If these "have not yet been fulfilled it can be only that some important considerations are preventing their being put into effect." The same applies to his views on censorship: „If I wrote against censorship it is because I thought I was doing the right thing; I believed it to be unnecessary: if it did not exist then everyone would be answerable in person, without having to rely on censors."[14]

It seems fair to assume that in a document of this kind Radishchev would obviously avoid saying anything that might aggravate the empress even further. He is, in fact, apologetic on other counts, trying to play down their significance. His firm stand on the subjects of serfdom and censorship must be interpreted as indicating that he considered his ideas acceptable to Catherine. If they were not, then he either suffered from a gross misapprehension – which is not likely – or she must have changed her views quite recently.

In 1791 occurred what was probably the first instance in Catherine's reign of administrative interference with the publication of foreign news by a newspaper. This happened when the compilation of news items for *St. Petersburg News* was entrusted to the Translators' Department, newly established at the Academy of Sciences.[15] The directives issued at the time banned from publication all items, whether original or translated, appertaining to: (1) the Court and Russian Empire in general; (2) Russia's

[13] Cf. for example 'Russkiye vol'nodumtsy v tsarstvovaniye Yekateriny II' (The Russian Freethinkers in the Reign of Catherine II), *Russkaya Starina* (The Russian Past), IX, (1874), p. 70. S. Glinka recounts in his memoirs how, upon his graduation from the Cadet Corps in 1794, all his 'treasures' he was taking home consisted of 'Knyazhnin's [play] *Vadim*, *Journey from Petersburg to Moscow* which was then creating much commotion..., and Sterne's *Sentimental Journey*'. (*Zapiski S. N. Glinki* (Memoirs of S. N. Glinka), St. P., 1895, p. 132).

[14] *Vorontsov Archives*, V, pp. 426-8.

[15] The *Perevodcheskiy* Department was organised in 1790 by Dashkova, with the Academician Protasov at its head. It replaced the former *Perevodcheskaya Ekspeditsiya*. (Semennikov, *Sobraniye starayushcheyesya o pervode inostrannykh knig uchrezhdyonnoye Yekaterinoy II, 1768-1783 gg.* (Society for Translation of Foreign Books Established by Catherine II), St. P., 1903, p. 25).

[16] *Zhurnal kantselyaryi Imp. Akademii Nauk* (Journal of the *Kantselariya* of the Imperial Academy of Sciences), 1791, No. 602, quoted by Semennikov in 'K istorii tsenzury v yekaterininskuyu epokhu' (A Contribution to the History of Censorship in the Age of Catherine), *Russkiy Bibliofil* (Russian Bibliophile), 1913, No. 1, p. 52.

allies; (3) anything potentially offensive to European courts, monarchs, or their families. At the same time the editors were instructed to "abbreviate translations of news items about the disorders now prevailing in France and to use every opportunity to insert a report or a comment which would show how harmful this insanity is to [the French] themselves.[16]

Novikov's lease of the Moscow University Press expired, as will be remembered, in May 1789. Catherine's decision not to renew it is recorded by Khrapovitsky already in October 1788.[17] The Printing Company was disbanded, by common consent of the shareholders, in November 1791. Novikov then went to live on his estate near Moscow where he was arrested, apparently on Prozorovsky's own initiative, at the end of April 1792. The search at his home revealed a number of books printed at the masonic "secret" press, including those condemned earlier. Prozorovsky's report on the arrest and the initial interrogation of Novikov was, according to Khrapovitsky, shown by Catherine to Zubov practically as soon as it was received, on 2 May 1792.[18] Catherine then instructed Prozorovsky to hand over the case to the appropriate judicial authority, whose verdict "shall be submitted to you for review after which you will forward it to the Senate for decision."[19] To this Prozorovsky replied arguing that the case was too "complicated" to be handed over to the courts and recommended that it be handled by a "special committee composed of trustworthy people." Catherine agreed and ordered Novikov to be moved to the fortress of St. Peter and Paul on 18 May 1792. It may therefore be said that Prozorovsky's argument prevailed here over Catherine's professed principles of legality – something that would have been unlikely to happen a few years earlier.

Shortly afterwards, on 20 May 1792, Prozorovsky wrote again to Catherine urging her to "limit the activities of purveyors of foreign books and to abolish the [existing] facilities at ports of entry for importation of books, especially those originating from France." "Although," the letter went on, "I have employed all available means, it is impossible to stop this traffic completely, mainly because such books are being sold secretly..., and it would be safe to say that any and all books now appearing in France can be purchased here in this way."[20]

[17] 'Novikov not to have the University press. C'est un fanatique'. (Khrapovitsky, p. 173).

[18] *Ibid.*, p. 400.

[19] Longinov, *Novikov*, p. 071.

[20] V. V. Sipovsky, 'Iz proshlogo russkoy tsenzury' (From the Past of Russian Censorship), *Russkaya Starina*, (The Russian Past), XCVIII, (1899), p. 164. The author considers this letter to be the starting point of the history of organised censorship in Russia.

No immediate action followed these recommendations, but they were embodied in the edict establishing censors' offices in 1796.

The questionnaires prepared by Catherine for Novikov's interrogation show clearly that she was concerned primarily, if not exclusively, with the political aspects of his case. These can be reduced to two main points: (1) what were the political objectives of Moscow Rosicrucians, did they owe allegiance to a foreign power or participate in an international plot? and (2) their connections with the Crown Prince Paul and his "party".[21] The action against Novikov must thus be viewed within the context of international relations and the political situation at home and abroad. Of the six points listing Novikov's crimes in Catherine's edict committing him to prison, only one is concerned with his publishing activities. ("That they had published forbidden, immoral, and anti-Orthodox books, and after having been explicitly forbidden on two occasions to do so, continued to sell them, for which purpose they had established a secret printing press").

An aftermath of Novikov's case of a more direct interest was the investigation by Prozorovsky, and the subsequent trial, in 1792, of Moscow booksellers involved in this case. It was, in fact, the first trial in Russian history involving offences against publishing laws (in this case the edict of 27 July 1787, which forbade lay publishers and booksellers to deal in literature pertaining to Orthodox faith). Heavy sentences imposed on the accused by lower courts were subsequently "humanised" at higher levels so that final sentences were relatively mild. The books seized were examined by both Church and lay censors and the greater part of them destroyed by burning in the following year.[22]

By 1792 we already have an instance of a repressive governmental action involving the works of Catherine's old friend and mentor Voltaire. As a result of a complaint by a local administrator, (the Governor of Tambov, V. S. Zveryov), Catherine ordered confiscation of a complete edition of Voltaire's works published by Rakhmaninov at his private press, on the grounds that they were "harmful and filled with demoralisation". The press itself was closed as a result.[23]

In 1793 occurred the often-quoted incident involving Knyazhnin's tragedy *Vadim Novgorodsky*. In June of that year Dashkova, according to

[21] *Sb. R.I.O.*, XLII, pp. 224ff. Cf. also Longinov, pp. 327ff.

[22] The list of these books was published in *Chteniya v Imp. Ob. Ist. i Dr. Ross.* (Lectures at the Imperial Society of Russian History...), No. 3 for 1871. In November 1793, 18,656 volumes were burnt, 1,964 handed over to Zaikonospasskaya Religious Academy, and 5,194 to Moscow University.

[23] Semennikov, 'Dopolnitel'nyye materialy...' (Supplementary Source Materials...), p. 80. Cf. also above **p. 95.**

her own story, gave her permission to the bookseller Glazunov to have the text of the play printed at the Academy press. (Glazunov had purchased the manuscript from Knyazhnin's successors, the poet himself having died in 1791). Some months later, in November, she received a note from Catherine to the effect that a play which "on dit très mordante contre l'autorité souveraine" had been published at the Academy and was now on sale. At their subsequent meeting Catherine appeared quite incensed and accused Dashkova of having published "des injures et atrocités contre moi." The detailed account of the affair is given by Dashkova in a letter to her brother A. R. Vorontsov.[24] Even allowing for a certain amount of distortion in her own favour, it is clear from Dashkova's story that Catherine had become emotional out of all proportion to the significance of the play – something that would have been most unlikely a few years earlier – and that her thinking was strongly influenced by the events in France. In the same letter there is a confirmation of the influence then exerted upon Catherine by her close associates: "des gens sans mérite, sans capacité, ne pouvant se rendre nécessaires, viennent l'inquiéter par des terreurs officieuses et qu'elle était fort inquiétée."[25] In her memoirs, Dashkova, relating the same events, says that "...Marshal Count Ivan Soltikoff whom no one could accuse of ever having read a book in his life" had told [Platon] Zubov that Knyazhnin's play had "a dangerous tendency in the present times."[26] In essence, the objection to Knyazhnin's play was political: it was supposed to be inimical to the existing form of government. The Senate edict committing it to be destroyed by burning refers to it as "a book filled with insolent and damaging utterances against the lawful autocratic power." It may be interesting to note that, in spite of all this, the text of the play was never officially banned.[27] The withdrawal of copies that had already found their way to booksellers was being done discreetly: the Procurator-General Samoylov, writing to Prozorovsky in Moscow, instructed him to impound the 400 copies known to have

[24] *Vorontsov Archives*, V, pp. 216ff.

[25] *Ibid.*, p. 224. Catherine possibly had some reasons to be nervous. It may be recalled that Gustav III of Sweden was assassinated in March 1792. In April of that year, Catherine in a letter to Grimm, spoke of a 'Jacobin Plot' to kill her whereby 'three or four people' had been despatched to St. Petersburg for that purpose. (*Sb. R.I.O.*, XXIII, p. 565).

[26] *Memoirs of the Princess Dashkaw ...*, Ed. by Mrs. W. Bradford, London, 1840, Vol. I, p. 362.

[27] It was published in 1793 both in a book form (73pp.) and in *Rossiyski Featr* (Russian Theatre), Part 39, pp. 123-195. (Longinov, 'Materialy dlya istorii russkogo prosveshcheniya i literatury v kontse XVIII v.' (Source Materials for the History of Education and Literature in Russia at the End of the 18th Century), *Russkiy Vestnik* (The Russian Messenger), XXV, (1860) p. 643).

been taken there by Glazunov, but urged him to act "with circumspection and without any publicity, in accordance with the authority granted to you, [but] without bringing the Imperial order into it." In effect, out of the 400 copies taken to Moscow, only 160 were confiscated at various bookshops. No attempt was made to trace the copies already sold.[28] Perhaps this reflects a certain amount of concern with the public opinion, a phenomenon extremely rare in Russia in the earlier days.

One direct consequence of the affair of *Vadim Novgorodsky* was increased caution and vigilance within the Academy of Sciences. Thus the publishing of the fifth edition of Novikov's *Painter* already authorised in August 1793 was held up until November of that year. It was then referred to Academician Kotel'nikov for examination and eventually published with some ommissions in the text which can presumably be attributed to censorship. Also, from approximately the same time, the Academy which had so far been acting independently of police censorship prescribed by the edict of 1783, began to demand a police clearance from persons wishing to use its printing facilities.

The translation of Milton's *Paradise Lost* already published earlier (in 1780) by Novikov was submitted for printing at the Academy in 1795. It was censored by the Acedemician Inokhodtsev who refused to pass it on both religious and literary grounds.[29]

Another illustration of Catherine's sensitivity to anything suggesting accord with French revolutionary ideas is the incident involving Derzhavin's paraphrase of Psalm 81 which he gave to Catherine, together with some other poetry in manuscript form in 1795.[30] Unbeknown to Derzhavin, this same psalm had been also paraphrased in Paris some years earlier where it was circulated by the Jacobins. Catherine took a strong exception to this poem but was eventually pacified by an explanatory letter from the poet.

In 1796 we have an instance of a direct censorial interference by

[28] E. Yefremov in *Russkaya Starina* (The Russian Past), III (1871), p. 725ff. In the meantime a review of the play, albeit unfavourable, appeared in *St. Petersburgskiy Merkuriy* (St. Petersburg Mercury. Part III, 1793, pp. 124-144). This review, written by Klushin, met with no interference on the part of the authorities.

[29] Semennikov, 'K istorii tsenzury . . .' (A Contribution to the History of Censorship . . .), p. 52ff.

[30] In fact it had already been published earlier, in 1780, in *St. Petersburg Messenger (Vestnik)* edited by G. Brayko and in the periodical *Zerkalo Sveta* (The Mirror of Light, 1787, part IV, p. 1. (Cf. G. R. Derzhavin, *Stikhotvoreniya* (Poems), M., 1958, pp. 41 and 476 f. and Berkov, 'Zhurnalistika 1770-kh-1790-kh gg. (The Periodical Press of the Years 1770-1790), in *Ocherki po istorii russkoy zhurnalistiki i kritiki* (Studies in History of Russian Periodical Press and Criticism) L., 1950).

Catherine, in a spirit directly contrary to her earlier pronouncements. A book, *The Newest Narrative Geography,* published early that year by an anonymous group of "learned Russians", was withdrawn from sale, on Catherine's orders, in April of that year. The Academy was then given the task of revising the book, with the instructions to "wholly delete the article about France... and not to leave anything that is directed against autocracy or public morals before printing it again and releasing it for public sale." This revision took so long that it was finally abandoned in the reign of Paul, in 1799, and the book was never published again.[31]

The most important legislative act of this period and, at the same time, the most retrogressive practical measure concerning freedom of expression for the whole of Catherine's reign, was undoubtedly her edict of 16 September 1796.[32] It affected both the freedom to publish and the freedom to read and its opening words: "In order to put an end to various inconveniences resulting from the free and unrestricted publication of books..." signified a conscious reversal of earlier policies in this field. The edict consists of eight sections, as follows:

(1) Censors' offices to be established at St. Petersburg, Moscow, Riga, Odessa, and Radzivillov Customs Office; each to consist of three censors: one appointed by the Church and two laymen.
(2) All private printing presses to be closed, since and "adequate number" of printing presses exists at various educational institutions for the printing of "useful and necessary" books.
(3) No book written or translated within the Empire to be published without prior examination and approval by one of the Censors' offices, with the "threefold limiting clause" to apply.
(4) The same principle to apply to imported books.
(5) The establishment of new printing presses is permitted, under the auspices of Governor's offices in *Gubernia* capitals only, and for the purpose of expediting official correspondence, subject to the rules of Section (3) above.
(6) Synodal printing presses and those at religious schools to be left under the supervision of ecclesiastical authorities.

[31] Semennikov believes the 'learned Russians' to have been members of the *Obshchestvo druzey slovesnykh nauk* (Society of Friends of Literature) with which Radishchev was connected in the 1780s. Semennikov, 'K istorii tsenzury...' (A Contribution to the History of Censorship), p. 66, cf. also his *Radishchev-ocherki i issledovaniya* (Radishchev - Studies and Investigations), M.-Pbg., 1923, p. 9; and N. G. Vysotsky, 'Zapreshchonnyye pri Yekaterine Velikoy knigi' (Books Banned in the Reign of Catherine the Great) *Russkiy Arkhiv* (Russian Archive), Book 3, M., 1912, pp. 252-255.

[32] *P.S.Z.*, XXIII, No. 17,508.

(7) The Chief Postmaster to be instructed to apply analogous measures to periodicals carried through official mails.
(8) The whole to be strictly enforced by the governors and other officials concerned, with judicial sanctions against the offenders.

This decree thus establishes an official system of governmental censorship of printed matter, for the first time in Russian history. It was followed by a Senate edict which directed the Censors to be appointed in each case, respectively by the Synod, the Senate, and the institutions of higher learning.[33] They were thus to be persons of a relatively high standing and education.

As we shall see in the next chapter, the actual establishment of censors' offices encountered numerous difficulties and the edict of 16 September 1796 did not become fully effective for quite a long time. It was repealed by Alexander I after it had been in force for a little over five years.[34]

Even if this Act represents a measure dictated largely by current political considerations, its spirit is quite contrary to the principles professed by Catherine in the earlier years of her reign. Therefore, at least by implication, the extent of change in her "theoretical" outlook to which I had referred earlier must have been by that time very considerable indeed.

In spite of such adverse measures the actual degree of freedom available in this last period of Catherine's reign was still relatively high. For example, Kapnist's *Ode on Slavery* which was received favourably by Catherine in mid-1780s, could still be published in 1796, whereas half a century later, in 1849, it was prohibited by censors. Sergei Glinka (1776-1847) recounts in his memoirs how, at the time of the French revolution, the Officer Commanding the 1st Cadet Corps, Count v. Anhalt (a relative of Catherine's), "...in order to acquaint us with the current situation had set up in our common room a special table with all foreign periodicals. It was then, whilst at the Corps, and not later that I had learned about personalities active on the general European scene at the time. On the same table were to be found the Russian monthlies: Krylov's *Spectator,* Klushin's *Mercury, Academic News,* and Karamzin's *Moscow Journal.*"[35] The titles of books kept by young Glinka at the Cadet Corps and later taken home have already been mentioned. Clearly, at the height

[33] October 22, 1796, *P.S.Z.*, XXIII, No. 17,523. Three censors were to be appointed by the Academy of Sciences to serve at St. Petersburg, Riga, and Odessa, and two by the University for Moscow and Radzivillov (a small town in Volhynia).

[34] Personal edict of 9 February 1802, *P.S.Z.*, XXVII, No. 20,139. It is interesting that it refers to an 'external political situation' which had evoked the edict of 1796, but had since ceased to exist.

[35] *Zapiski Sergeya Nikolayevicha Glinki* (Memoirs of S. N. Glinka), St. P., 1895, p. 76 f.

of Catherine's "reaction", it was still quite a natural thing for a graduate of an elite military school to own and carry officially proscribed literature.

Even at the end of her reign Catherine was not insensitive to abuses of civil liberties. For example we have a note, in her own hand, dated 23 August 1795, objecting strongly to unauthorised house searches by St. Petersburg police and ordering their immediate cessation.[36]

A Scotsman, Dr. Matthew Guthrie who was the chief physician to the First (Army) Cadet Corps for over a quarter of a century (from 1778 until about 1806) tells in one of his unpublished works, written in the early eighteen-hundreds, of Catherine's treatment of revolutionary agitators in the seventeen-nineties:

> "... indeed the propagand [sic] made us but short visits, as they did not like Catherine's jokes, who used to send the Physician of the mad house to feel the pulse of all those who were found preaching *holy insurrection the most sacred of Duties of her Subjects* ... The Doctor was commonly accompany'd with a couple of stout keepers from Bedlam who immediately carryd the Patient there, and a blister on the head with a few purges and watergrouse soon brought him to his right senses, and made him as harmless as a child. For he was so laughed at by his Disciples on reappearing in public that he quickly took the road to Prussia there to write secret memoirs of the Court of Russia, and abuse the whole Empire by every possible falsehood that rage could invent ..."[37]

And when some citizens of the Capital began sporting "jacobin cloaks", "that sagacious Princess got rid of [them] by only ordering the City watchmen with their long beards to put on the same kind of wrapper and strut alongside of the fantastic young men who were so attired in the Imperial Gardens and Public Walks, always open to the public. They took the hint and we saw no more jacobin cloaks during her Reign."

We shall now turn to the examination of relevant ideas within society. Here the most prominent spokesman of the "independent" trend, already noted in the earlier period, is undoubtedly Radishchev who devoted a whole chapter (*Torzhok*) of his *Journey* to censorship and related problems.[38]

Referring to the current situation in Russia, Radishchev notes that while everyone is now free to own the means of printing, their output is still subject to supervision. This ought to be abolished entirely. Quoting

[36] *Vorontsov Archives*, XII, p. 386.

[37] *BM Add. Mss.* 14,389, Fol. 109.

[38] Quotations used here are from A. N. Radishchev, *Puteshestviye iz Peterburga v Moskvu* (Journey from Petersburg to Moscow), in *Russkaya Proza XVIII veka* (Russian Prose of the 18th Century), M.-L., 1950.

from Herder, he says: "In the realm of truth and spirit no earthly power is capable of giving decisions and it should not attempt to do so... Improvement can be achieved only through education... the sounder the government, the more favourable it will prove towards freedom of thought and writing..."

Radishchev considers police organs unsuited for the performance of censorship duties: a poorly educated police official can cause an immense amount of harm by arbitrarily banning some work of great value.[39]

He represents Catherine's "Great Instruction" as being in full accord with his own views: "Let them print anything that enters their heads... words do not always become deeds and thoughts are not criminal." Persecution of written word only creates martyrs whereas errors and falsehoods, if permitted to be uttered without hindrance, will the sooner be recognised for what they are and their true nature will be exposed. In case of libellous writings, the offended party has recourse to the court of law.

"In limiting freedom of publishing timorous governments fear not the blasphemy, but the criticism of their own actions." A good and sound government does not fear criticism; consequently the degree of the government's sensibility to this criticism can be taken as a measure of its soundness.

On the subject of satire aimed at specific persons Radishchev feels that it can be of two kinds: just or slanderous. Both ought to be permitted: in case of the latter the offended party has recourse to legal proceedings. An unjustified verbal attack on a person, delivered in a highly abusive language, "such as is commonly used in the market-places", is not a matter for the public prosecutor, but for a civil action; moreover it must be remembered that it is not the judge who appears as a plaintiff, but the allegedly offended party. In a footnote Radishchev quotes an incident involving John Dickinson[40] who had defended his actions in an open verbal contest with the authors of pamphlets attacking him, and proved their accusations to be groundless. Generally, American influences on Radishchev's views in this and allied fields are quite prominent.

At times Radishchev's argument in favour of absolute freedom of the press becomes a trifle specious, as for example when he treats of writings involving what Catherine's edicts called "Good Manners" (public decency).

[39] This passage was not included in the original edition submitted to the police (cf. Semennikov, *Radishchev...*, p. 32).

[40] John Dickinson (1732-1808) a prominent Philadelphia lawyer, governor of Pennsylvania 1782-1785, author of numerous papers and pamphlets on constitutional law.

He admits that pornography is harmful to young people, but argues that the real evil here lies in the facility with which they are able to satisfy their aroused desires through intercourse with prostitutes – in whom both Russian capitals abound. Since, as pointed out by Catherine in her "Instruction", what really counts is deeds and not words, the proper remedy would be to abolish prostitution and to leave books alone: no one has yet contracted a venereal disease from a book.

With this unlimited freedom of thought and expression the final judgement between good and evil, truth and falsehood is to rest with society at large. "If everyone is allowed to think and express his thoughts publicly without hindrance, it naturally follows that everything that is thought of or invented will be generally known; what is great will remain great, the truth will not be obscured. Rulers of nations will not dare to deviate from the path of righteousness and will stand in awe; for their evil ways and deceit will be exposed."

Radishchev follows these reflections with a survey of the history of censorship in the civilised world. Here considerable attention is devoted to the young American republic, but Russia is left out of the account.[41] There is, however, one interesting remark showing a good appreciation of Catherine's role in the Russian context. Addressing contemporary "enlightened monarchs" Radishchev exclaims: "What does it profit you to struggle against yourselves and to destroy with your left hand what your right hand had implanted?"

The chapter ends on a note indicating the author's belief in the incompatibility of freedom of expression with absolute monarchy: "In whose head can there be more incongruities than in that of a tsar?"

The admittedly Western-European origins of Radishchev's ideas are a separate problem which is beyond the scope of the present work. Of greater relevance is the fact that, since his book became known to many educated Russians at the time, these ideas received a fairly wide circulation even if their effect was dampened by the restrictive policies of the government. In advocating unlimited freedom of expression (he sounds almost like John Stuart Mill) Radishchev went further than the most liberal constitutional acts of his period.[42]

[41] For Radishchev's sources on the history of censorship cf. A. N. Radishchev, *Puteshestviye . . .*, Vol. II, Materialy k izucheniyu Puteshestviya (Commentary by Ya. Barskov) (Source materials for the Study of *Journey . . .*), M.-L. 1935, p. 445. As shown by P. E. Shchegolev in his article 'Rukopis' *Puteshestviya . . .* (The Manuscript of *Journey)*, attached to its 1905 edition, (p. LXXXI) this part of the chapter *Torzhok* was added by Radishchev *after* the book had been passed by the police 'censor'.

[42] The French Declaration of Human Rights while proclaiming complete freedom of

A very significant point in his thinking is the clear realisation of the conflict between society's desire for freedom and the state power. His views can therefore be seen as a logical development of the trend seeking independence from the sponsorship of that power noted earlier, for example, in Novikov. The importance of Radishchev's ideas in the context of our subject lies not so much in their extreme character as in the demonstration of the principle that an extension of civil liberties can only be achieved in opposition to the claims of the state and not as a result of voluntary – and therefore only temporary – concessions on its part.[43]

No satisfactory answer can be provided to the rather fascinating question of the extent to which Radishchev's views were in accord with those of contemporary Russian society. Indirectly, it is interesting to note some reactions to his arrest and exile and to compare them with comments of the representatives of later generations. The contemporary view seems to have been that Radishchev's "crime" was insignificant and the punishment severe out of all proportion. Thus Semyon Vorontsov wrote to his brother Alexander, from England, on 1/12 October 1790: "La condemnation du pauvre Raditchef me fait une peine extrême. Quelle sentence et quel adoucissement pour une étourderie! Que fera-t-on pour un crime et pour une révolte en forme?"[44]

Glinka in his memoirs, from which I have quoted earlier, takes a similar view and expresses the opinion that Catherine would have been more lenient with Radishchev had it not been for the insistence of some unnamed "persons" close to Catherine, other than Potyomkin.[45]

Radishchev himself did not of course see anything extraordinarily audacious in the act of the publication of his book. Yet, as pointed out by Semennikov, subsequent generations of Russians, from Pushkin to Lunacharsky, could not comprehend his daring.[46] Radishchev's contemporaries,

conscience, speech, and writing implied a limitation in the definition of freedom which it conceived as 'the right to do everything that does not harm others'. (Art. IV). Expression of opinions must be free provided it 'does not disturb the public order established by law'. (Art. X). Freedom of expression granted in the U. S. Bill of Rights is limited by the co-existing rights of others, the demands of national security, and public decency. (Cf. Robert E. Cushman, *Civil Liberties in the United States*, Cornell U. P., 1956, p. 2).

[43] For another recent discussion in English of Radishchev's views on these and other matters see Jesse V. Clardy, *The Philosophical Ideas of Alexander Radishchev*, N. Y., 1964.

[44] *Vorontsov Archives*, IX, p. 181.

[45] i.e. obviously Platon Zubov. Glinka, incidentally, was on friendly terms with Radishchev's son Paul.

[46] Pushkin in his article 'Alexander Radishchev' wonders if Radishchev's action of publishing the book was not one of 'a madman' and suggests that perhaps Radishchev himself did not grasp the gravity of his offence: 'how else can we explain his unconcern and the extraordinary idea of sending the book to all his friends'. (A. S. Pushkin,

some of them, like his friend Alexander Vorontsov, occupying high administrative positions, sympathised with many of his ideas, but one generation later, Pushkin – who is not normally regarded as a reactionary – made these comments after reading Radishchev's chapter *Torzhok:* "This is concerned with freedom of publishing. It is curious to read ideas on this subject of a man who granted such freedom to himself by printing in his own press a book in which the audacity of thought and expression exceeds all limits."[47]

Of numerous other instances illustrating changed attitudes within society it may perhaps be worthwhile to quote two, involving persons whose social origin and education – the latter especially in the sense of exposure to Western-European ideas – were considerably more modest than those of Radishchev's. One, Fyodor Krechetov, about whose life little is known, wrote a letter, in 1789, to the Secretary of St. Petersburg nobility asking him to sponsor a petition to the empress which was enclosed. This, among other things, suggested that censorship of all books be carried out by a free popular assembly composed of persons of "all ranks, calling, and [degrees of] learning."[48] Krechetov wrote this whilst under investigation on criminal charges proferred by the Church authorities (for having included sacred words used in Orthodox liturgy in the title of one of his publications). Some answers given by him to his interrogators show an attitude which would be unthinkable in Russia one generation earlier. For example, to the question: "To what end did you make notes

Sochineniya (Works), ed. by V. Vengerov, Vol. V, pp. 338 f). Lunacharsky could not understand the mildness of the punishment: '... rather must one wonder that he was pardoned after all and the death penalty commuted to 10 years' *katorga* [sic] at Ilimsk'. (*Aleksandr N. Radishchev, pervyi prorok i muchennik revolutsiyi,* Rech' proiznessyonnaya na otkrytii pamyatnika v Petrograde 22 sentyabrya Narodnym Kommissarom A. Lunacharskim (A. N. Radishchev, the First Prophet and Martyr of Revolution. A Speech made at the Unveiling of the Monument in Petrograd on the 22 of September, by the People's Commissar A. Lunacharsky), Petrograd, 1919, p. VI). Such utterances represent valuable, if unconscious, tributes to the liberal climate of Catherine's regime.

47 *Mysli na doroge* (Throughts While Travelling), quoted in *Puteshestviye ...*, (Journey) II, – Materyaly k izucheniyu *Puteshestviya* (Source Materials to the Study of *Journey*), M.-L., 1935, p. 466. It has recently been argued that Pushkin tried to camouflage his real (sympathetic) view of Radishchev by such apparent criticisms in order to outwit the censor (McConnell, *op. cit.*, pp. 194-196, and, by the same author, 'Pushkin's Literary Gamble', *American Slavic & East European Review,* XIX, (1960). Whether or not one accepts this argument, the fact remains that Radishchev's action would appear incomparably more audacious under the conditions prevailing in Russia in 1836 than under those of 1790.

48 N. Chulkov, 'F. V. Krechetov-zabytyy radikal'nyy publitsist XVIII veka' (F. V. Krechetov the Forgotten Radical Writer of the 18th Century), *Literaturnoye Nasledstvo,* (Literary Heritage) 9-10, 1933, p. 459.

from the book *On the Government and on Various Kinds Thereof*[49] tending more towards harm than good?" Krechetov replied: "I have been making extracts not only from this, but from all kinds of books and materials, good and bad, not for the purpose of causing harm, but for the benefit of mankind."[50]

Pyotr Andreyevich Slovtsov, born in 1767, son of a priest, educated at Tobol'sk and St. Petersburg religious seminaries, occupied in the early 1890s the position of a teacher of philosophy at the seminary of Tobol'sk. While there, in 1793, he preached a sermon, remarkable for its frankness, which led to his denunciation by the Governor of Tobol'sk and subsequent investigation. This, among other things, is what Slovtsov said:

> "Peace among the people may represent only a forced silence which lasts only as long as it is not ruptured by dissatisfaction gradually eroding society's patience. When not all citizens live under the same laws, when distinctions, advantages, and pleasures are reserved for one group, whilst to the others are left labour, the full severity of law, and unhappiness . . . To sound the trumpets of victory in foreign countries . . . and to spread one's own glory beyond the boundaries of one's power is usually considered to add to nation's happiness. But this avails nothing . . . The might of the monarchy is an instrument of evil, leading to internal decay . . . what appears to be its most glorious age, usually becomes the hour of its doom . . ."[51]

Already in one of his earlier sermons Slovtsov openly condemned the autocracy, demanded concessions for the peasants, strict observance of existing laws, the removal of court favourites, etc. Addressing Catherine he declared that unless she steps down from her throne "to wipe the tears of the humblest of your subjects, if your education will only lead to augment your lust for power and you will use it . . . to destroy completely the idea of freedom . . . then, with all your faculties, you will only be a lucky villain."[52]

[49] Adapted from the French *Encyclopaedia* by Ivan Tumansky, translator attached to the Senate, and published in 1770, It contained translations of articles on Democracy, Despotic Rule, Monarchy, Oligarchy, Autocracy, Tyranny, etc.

[50] L. Svetlov, 'A. N. Radishchev i politicheskiye protsessy XVIII veka' (A. N. Radishchev and the Political Trials in the 18th Century), *Iz istorii russkoy filosofii XVII-XIX vekov* (From the History of Russian Philosophy of the 18th-19th Century), ed. by I. Ya. Shchipanov, M., 1952, p. 60. From the records of Krechetov's interrogation we also learn that he did not think that Radishchev had done anything wrong by adding several pages to his book *after* it had been passed by the censor, and believed that his (Radishchev's) sentence was too harsh. (*Ibid*, p. 57 - original source: *Ts. G.A.D.A.*, G.A., part VII, case 2813, fols 189-190.)

[51] *Chteniya v Imp. Obshchestve Istorii, etc.*, (Lectures at the Imperial Society of History . . .), 1873, Book 3, pp. 150-153.

[52] *Russkaya Starina* (The Russian Past), Feb. 1902, p. 287. Also Svetlov, p. 48.

Slovtsov was summoned to St. Petersburg where he was interrogated, in 1794, and although confined for a time to a monastery, was eventually promoted to the post of a lecturer in rhetorics at the Senior (Aleksandrovskaya) Seminary at St. Petersburg. Later he became a friend of the statesman Speransky.

In the field of instruments of expression there is very little change up to the time of the edict of 1796. Apart from the few private printing presses in the provinces already mentioned in the last chapter, only one was opened in St. Petersburg, by Krylov and associates for the publication of *Spectator*, in 1792.[53]

The output of printed books fell slightly in the 'nineties in comparison to the record-setting late 'eighties, but was still higher than before 1785.[54] But 1793 was the record year for the number of novels published. Almost the same level was maintained throughout 1794 and 1795, but it dropped significantly in 1796.[55]

The number of periodicals published fell after Novikov's disappearance from the scene. About five new ones appeared during the period in question, but none of these lasted beyond 1795.

In closing this account of the last years of the reign of Catherine II we may recall that Russia was not the only country in which measures restricting free expression were introduced as a result of the events in France. In England the Traitorous Correspondence Bill was put in effect in 1793, after the outbreak of the war with France, and the Habeas Corpus Act was suspended in the following year. In the United States the notorious Alien and Sedition Acts were passed a few years later, in 1798.

Perhaps the most important feature of this last period is the fact that the development of the idea within society (more exactly its educated and articulate component) became both more rapid and more far-reaching than was compatible with the existing political system. The level this development achieved was, on the whole, equal with that of the ideas then current

[53] Its output was quite negligible: about 10 titles, all insignificant editions, in the approximately four years of its existence. (Cf. G. Kenevich, 'Materialy dlya biografii Krylova (Materials for Krylov's Biography), *Sbornik statey chitannykh v otdelenii russkogo yazyka i slovesnosti Imp. Akademii Nauk* (Collection of Papers Presented in the Department of Russian Language and Literature at the Imperial Academy of Sciences), St. P., 1869, p. 298).

[54] On the average 299 books per year were published in 1791-1795, as compared to 366 in the period 1786-1790, and 197 in 1781-1785. (*Russkaya kniga* . . ., (Russian Books), M., 1924, table on p. 346.)

[55] Cf. V. Sipovsky, *Iz istorii russkogo romana i povesti* (From the History of the Russian Novel and Tale), Part I, St. P., 1903, pp. 26ff.

in Western Europe and North America. The sharpness of the resulting conflict was accentuated by external political circumstances (both in the sense of causing a change in government attitude and arousing the more extreme tendencies within society) but there can be no doubt that is was bound to have occurred in any case.

CHAPTER VII

THE BALANCE SHEET OF CATHERINE'S REIGN FREEDOM OF EXPRESSION UNDER PAUL I

Catherine II occupied the Russian throne for over one-third of the eighteenth century; practically all significant developments relevant to freedom of expression occur within that period. In trying to sum up its effects we may start from the self-evident assumption that in an absolute monarchy much more depends on the personality of the ruler than elsewhere; consequently it is the ruler who must take the greatest share of praise or blame for any achievements or lack thereof in any given field. To put this a little differently, the part played by the government in the developments with which we are here concerned is the most significant of all the factors involved; since the terms "Catherine" and "government" are, for the present purpose of a general summing-up, practically synonymous, her attitudes and actions are obviously crucial to the whole problem.

As has been suggested, for all practical intents and purposes, the idea of freedom of expression did not exist in Russia by 1762, at least not in an articulate form. Before Catherine there was neither a tangible demand for it on the part of society nor any significant tendency on the government side to relax its restrictive policies. In the "Great Instruction" Catherine made a statement of theoretical principles which was liberal by the standards of contemporary European courts and quite revolutionary in relation to the Russian scene.

This awakened the undoubtedly existing but dormant desire for free expression within society: aided by the fact that, at least approximately until the late 1780s, the government did practice what it preached, by the concurrent rise in education, and increased cultural intercourse with the rest of Europe, its appetites developed rapidly. Twenty years after the "Great Instruction" the ideas and demands voiced within society were running well ahead of anything the government might be prepared to grant within the existing political system. Were we to assume that Catherine's theoretical views did not change at all in the whole course of her reign, she would still, *in relation to society,* appear "progressive" at the beginning and "reactionary" at the end. In fact, as we know, both her views and her practical policies underwent a change in the last years which only served further to emphasize the inevitable conflict.

In the realm of practical policies Catherine's legislative measures were consistent with her theory, as professed in the "Great Instruction", for approximately the first twenty-five years of her reign. In the last decade a strong restraining trend sets in, culminating in the edict of 16 September 1796 which – in relation to 1783 – amounts to a reversal of the earlier policies. But, in the final account, the degree of freedom of expression existing in November 1796 (at the time of Catherine's death) still compares favourably with the 1750s in Russia and, most certainly, with contemporary France where, by 1793, nothing was left of the liberties proclaimed four years earlier.

In any case, the incidence of restrictive legislation cannot, by itself, serve as an indicator of freedom of expression actually available. If we compare the situation existing in Russia in the first half of the century – when no such legislation pertaining to publishing was in force – with that in 1796, we must come to the conclusion that, in spite of Catherine's "reaction", the degree of freedom was incomparably higher at that latter time. Other examples, from various historical periods including the present one, could be quoted to illustrate this point, as anyone reading this will realise upon a moment's reflection. More helpful in attempting to assess the extent of freedom of written word is the simple truth that, when the government's policies are truly repressive, there will be few, if any, spectacular cases involving suppression of "undesirable" literature, since the overwhelming majority of writers will not consciously court trouble and will either avoid potentially dangerous subjects, or simply remain silent. (In the history of Russian letters the two outstanding – if not exactly comparable – examples of such a situation are the periods 1848-1855, and 1946-1953). There is little evidence of this kind of "self-imposed censorship" during Catherine's reign, at least until about 1792.

References have been made earlier to the complexities inherent in Catherine's dual role, as a ruler and as a writer. Her direct participation in literary activities must be regarded, on balance, as a positive factor. She both encouraged others by her example and helped to arouse interest in publications for which she was known to be writing.[1] On the other hand,

[1] For example, when Dashkova begged Catherine not to stop contributing to the *Sobesednik* (Letter dated 29 September 1783 quoted by Pekarsky in *Materialy dlya istorii zhurnal'noy...*, (Source Materials For the History of Catherine II's Journalistic...

it is a fact that an absolute monarch does not divest himself of his or her status by temporarily joining the ranks of the country's *literati*. While Catherine did not avoid argument with other writers, any such argument or polemic in which she was involved would naturally assume a very special character. It could not, for example, be allowed to become too exacerbated or personal, nor could she permit herself to become involved in quarrels between others. This became clear in relation to the satirical journals of 1769-1774. In the case of *Sobesednik* such a situation was largely to blame for that journal's demise: a quarrel between L. A. Naryshkin and Dashkova in which Catherine took the side of the former. To this we must add the incident with Fonvizin's questions which clearly had introduced a political angle. Although they were, in fact, answered, the continuation of the exercise was obviously incompatible with Catherine's position as an absolute monarch. It was putting her on the defensive and forcing her to produce excuses and explanations for her policies, quite an impossible situation.

Catherine's literary efforts may, at least up to a point, be regarded as an integral part of her attempts to direct the practical use of the freedom she had granted into the desired channels. While she, no doubt, thought herself justified in this, feeling that without her there would not have been any freedom at all, they amounted, in effect, to interference by governing authority and thus represented a certain limiting factor.

No autocratic ruler, however liberal he may be in theory, can accept in practice the concept of freedom – of any kind – as a natural right of his subjects; he must essentially regard it as a concession, as a delegation of a part of his own powers. The recipients can retain it only as long as they do not appear to abuse it. It is, of course, beyond dispute that, in the final account, the fate of civil liberties in any country depends on the political system.

In relation to the media of expression Catherine's reign is marked by a most spectacular growth. Schloezer, writing some time after her death, refers to the "new world" that had come into being after Catherine's accession, with the result that "in the next twenty-five years Russian

Activities), p. 19), saying that, without her, the journal will have to close, her remarks cannot be regarded as pure flattery. Both the volume of Catherine's contributions and their 'reader appeal', quite apart from their intrinsic value, were very significant indeed.

[2] *A. L. Schloezer's oeffentliches und privat-Leben...*, Erstes Fragment, Goettingen, 1802, p. 301. In actual fact, the number of books (volumes, not titles) published between 1762 and 1800 exceeded the whole output, from the introduction of printing into Russia until 1761, about three and a half times. (Cf. *Knizhnaya torgovlya* (The Book Trade), ed. by Muratova and Nakoryakova, M.-L., 1925, p. 92).

printing presses published more works of all kinds than under all the earlier governments since the introduction of printing into Russia."[2]

In relation to the period immediately preceding, the annual output of books increased more than tenfold,[3] the number of printing presses about five times. Although no reliable figures exist concerning the increase in the number of theatres, this was also very spectacular. In addition there appeared elected bodies of citizens at various levels, some of them relatively short-lived as the Great Commission, others more durable as the town councils created in 1785, a very important factor in the development of freedom of speech. Only in the field of higher education there is, remarkably enough, no appreciable progress, in the sense of an increase in the number of establishments or the growth of the existing ones. (Although, as we have seen, three new universities had been planned in the late 1780s).

Catherine cannot, of course, take the sole credit for these achievements – especially in the publishing field where private initiative played a large part – but the fact that her role was most important cannot seriously be denied.

In spite of the retreat from the earlier liberal practices in the last period of the reign and of other negative factors, Catherine's overall contribution to the development of both the theory and practice of free expression in Russia must be regarded as the outstanding positive factor. Its most valuable long-term effect was, as already pointed out, the effect it had on society. In this sphere Catherine's policies pursued up to about 1790, contributed most prominently to bringing the idea to the level where it could not be seriously damaged by a decade or so of repression. Her part in bringing this about has been played down by most historians; yet it is impossible to escape the conclusion that without her things would have been very different indeed. Wtihout being unduly speculative or fanciful we could visualise three other regimes that might have existed in Russia in the second half of the century: the continued reign of Peter III, that of his son from about mid-'seventies on, or some modified system with increased participation of the aristocracy and a corresponding limitation of the monarch's powers, such as almost did come into being at the time of the accession of Anna Ioannovna, and as longingly portrayed in Shcherbatov's utopia *Journey to the Land of Ophiria*. Could we reasonably expect the conditions for the development of freedom of expression in either of these cases to be as favourable as they were under Catherine? Without taking any credit away from people like Novikov, it was Catherine who was responsible for creating conditions in which they and the trends they represented could prosper and develop – at least up to a point. This point is obviously the conflict between the society's desire for freedom and the claims of an authoritarian state; in the specific context of freedom of expression, it is reached when that freedom threatens to be used for the propagation of ideas advocating a change in the political system. It is a point beyond which civil liberties cannot progress in such a state without a change in the system of government.

To conclude this evaluation, it may be worthwhile to quote a contemporary assessment of Catherine's reign, made by none other than Radishchev, in a note written in 1801 or 1802: ". . . it will be to her great credit before distant posterity that in her *Instruction* she had stressed the basic principles on which societies are founded, and their purpose. Her wish was to reign over a contented people or, to use a better expression, to let them govern themselves, leaving to herself only the task of supervising everything." Radishchev is even prepared to find justification for the fact that, in the course of her long reign, ". . . and especially at its end [Catherine] . .. departed from many of her principles," in pointing out that she must then have been upset by "external and internal disorders" and, apart from everything else, was paying her debt to nature. And "who among the mortals"– he asks – "has ever succeeded in remaining unchanged throughout his whole life?" [4]

II

The theoretical aspect of government attitude towards free expression in the reign of Paul I is something which defies any attempt at a reasonably accurate analysis. The meaning of the term "government" may, for our purpose, be identified with the person of the tsar. [5] Insofar as it is possible to discern any general trends in the spectacularly inconsistent policies of

[3] 366 titles per year in 1790, as compared with 30 in 1760. (*Russkaya kniga* (Books in Russia), p. 346.

[4] Semennikov, *Radishchev . . .*, pp. 122-3.

[5] Under Paul the Senate lost a great deal of its executive significance, although it still acted much as before on matters which did not attract his immediate attention. The Council of State and within it the Procurator-General, can be said to have participated to some extent in the process of government, at least in the earlier part of the reign. But, all in all, the situation was much as succintly put by a contemporary foreign visitor: 'Russia has no definite political system. All her policies consist of the Emperor's whims'. (E. Shumigorsky, 'Zapiska bavartsa o Rossii vremyon Imp. Pavla' (translated from French) (A Bavarian's Memoir on Russia at the Time of Emperor Paul), *Russkaya Starina* (The *Russian Past)*, XCIX, 1899, p. 359).

the new ruler, the most obvious one was to try and undo what his mother had done. Another – strictly speaking a derivative of the first – was the tendency to favour the lower classes at the expense of nobility. In the field relevant to our subject it is possible to point to two instances illustrating this second trend.

Shortly after his accession, Paul appears to have conceived the idea that, in order to learn of the true state of affairs within his realm, the sovereign must try to eestablish a direct contact with his subjects, bypassing the court and administrative organs which could not be trusted. To this end he had a box installed in one of the windows of the Winter Palace where any passer-by could deposit written complaints, requests, etc. Paul himself kept the key to this "letter box" and made a point of going over its daily intake every evening between 6 and 7 p.m. Some of his resulting decisions were then published in *St. Petersburg News*. This primitive – if not entirely valueless – method of communication with the more humble of his subjects came to an end when various rude or abusive notes began to find their way into the box – possibly, as suggested by one historian, not without the assistance of those who were likely to suffer through its continued existence. [6]

On the other hand, in May 1797, on his return journey to St. Petersburg from Moscow, Paul decreed to the Procurator-General "not to accept from anyone anywhere any petitions signed by several names." [7] The effect of this was to abolish the right hitherto enjoyed by the nobility to adress collective petitions directly to the tsar.

With his outlook fundamentally an antithesis of everything liberal, Paul could not have been expected to pursue any but restrictive policies in relation to freedom of expression. Already at the time of his coronation in 1797, he announced to his former teacher, the Metropolitan Platon, that he had "made it his guiding principle not to increase the existing number of printing presses." [8] With the exception of some instances where he

[6] Cf. Shumigorsky, *Imperator Pavel I* (The Emperor Paul I), St. P., 1907, pp. 100f. It is possible that the prominent English merchant W. Eton, who had spent many years in Russia and lived there during the reign of Paul, had this contraption in mind when ho noted that 'every person in the Empire may now write to their Sovereign, and if they receive no answer, may address themselves personally to him'. (W. Eton, *A Survey of the Turkish Empire*..., London, 1799, p. 465).

[7] Shil'der, *Imperator Pavel Pervyi (Emperor Paul the First)*, St. P., 1901, p. 351.

[8] Snegiryov, *Zhizn' moskovskogo mitropolita*..., (Life of the Metropolitan [Platon] of Moscow), Part I, p. 95. But on the same occasion, he permitted the teaching of French at the seminary attached to the monastery of the Holy Trinity and St. Sergius, forbidden by Catherine a few years earlier.

was countermanding his mother's decisions (as in the amnesty for Novikov and Radishchev), or acting on the spur of the moment (as in the incident involving the play *Chicane* by Kapnist),[9] his practical measures had an overwhelmingly restrictive character.

One of such measures was the decree issued in the first year of his reign forbidding the use, in writing, of certain words and expressions. Among them were the words "society" (*obshchestvo*) for which no substitute was provided, and "citizens" (*grazhdane*) to be replaced by "inhabitants" (*zhiteli* or *obyvateli*).[10]

Early in 1797 Paul reaffirmed the edict of 16 September 1796, stressing the point that no other than officially sponsored printing presses were to be permitted, and granting jurisdiction over matters pertaining to censorship to Dept. III of the Senate.[11] The relevant act also lists the censors – with the exception of the ecclesiastical ones who had not yet, by that time, been appointed.[12] Here we come across some already familiar names of people with previous experience in such matters, such as the Academicians S. Kotel'nikov and P. Inokhodtsev. The censors' qualifications were high, and in this respect the new laws could be regarded as superior to the earlier legislation whereby similar duties were delegated to police officials, on the whole completely unsuited for this task. The more important practical difference, however, was that the old laws were applied very loosely, whereas now the government had every intention to have the new ones enforced to the letter. But even so, it took six months from the time the new law was promulgated merely to have the censors appointed, and considerably longer, as we shall see, to get the whole machinery working.

In the meantime, Paul issued a personal edict directing that all books recommended for prohibition by the censors, or considered "doubtful", be referred for the final decision to the Council of State.[13] Within that body a special committee was formed for dealing with censors' reports, under the chairmanship of the Procurator-General. Its minutes were regularly perused by Paul himself. In a way this shows the high degree of importance attached to these matters and can be taken as indicating the concern that

[9] It was staged in 1798, but forbidden after a few performances, and its author banished to Siberia. As a result of Paul's being persuaded to see the play for himself, the sentence on Kapnist was rescinded and he himself promoted to the post of the Director of Imperial Theatres at St. Petersburg. The ban on the play was also lifted.

[10] Cf *Russkaya Starina*, (The Russian Past), III, (1871), pp. 720f; Skabichevsky, p. 84.

[11] *P.S.Z.*, XXIV, No. 17,811 of 16 February 1797.

[12] This was done shortly afterwards, by the edict of 29 March 1797 (*P.S.Z.*, XXIV, No. 17,895).

[13] 3 July 1787, *P.S.Z.*, XXIV, No. 18,032.

no publication be condemned without reference to the highest level. On the other hand, it may be regarded as a manifestation of Paul's tendency to supervise personally all branches of administration or, conversely, his reluctance to delegate responsibility.[14]

In essence, the principal object of government legislation beginning with Catherine's edict of 16 September 1796, was the protection of society from subversive ideologies infiltrating from abroad. This was to be achieved mainly by denying entry into the country to undesirable literature. Strictly speaking therefore, all these measures affected the freedom *to read* imported publications more than that to utter or *express* ideas within the country. This concern to protect society from insidious foreign, i.e. French, influences showed itself in the practical aspect of the new restrictive measures.

First of all, and not at all surprisingly, if we bear in mind the usual gap between the promulgation of the law and its implementation and enforcement, the whole new system of censorship did not become fully operative for quite a considerable time. A number of supplementary acts was required to appoint the censors, fix their salary scales, secure appropriate accommodation, etc.[15] The censors themselves, especially the "learned" ones (i.e. the members of the Academy or of Moscow University) showed, on the whole, remarkably little enthusiasm for their task. For example, the Academician Ya. D. Zakharov appointed censor for the Radzivillov office in 1797, sent a letter of protest directly to the tsar. In it he pleaded lack of qualifications for the appointment which, in his view, required ". . . a sound and thorough knowledge not of just three, but of several languages, and knowledge of all literature, as well as mythology, poetry, and other branches of learning."[16]

His case was referred to the Academy Conference which not only found him unsuitable, but recommended that all members of the Academy should be exempt from censorship duties:

[14] The same tendency is evident in Paul's policies towards the Academy of Sciences. Here the post of Director (held by P. P. Bakunin) was abolished, and the aged President, K. G. Razumovsky, replaced by G. L. Nicolai. Paul usurped some of their functions, such as the confirmation of newly elected members.

[15] Such, in addition to those already mentioned, were the edicts of 5 October 1797 (*P.S.Z.*, XXIV, No. 18,186); 11 December 1797 (*Ibid.*, No. 18,265); 11 February 1798 (*P.S.Z.*, XXV, No. 18,367).

[16] V. V. Sipovsky, 'Iz proshlogo russkoy tsenzury' (From the Past of Russian Censorship), *Russkaya Starina* (The Russian Past), XCVIII, (1899), p. 169.

"La conférence serait aussi obligée de dire la même chose de tous les autres académiciens, dont chacun s'est dévoué a une science particulière, dont l'avancement d'après le rêglement est le but essentiel de l'Académie des Sciences et qui n'a point de rapports aux objets de la censure."

The St. Petersburg office could not become operational for a considerable time since one of the censors, M. Tumansky[17] began his new career by departing on a prolonged holiday. The Moscow office, in the person of Professor Prokopovich-Antonsky, was reprimanded shortly after it had begun to function for the extreme brevity and vagueness of their reports. At Radzivillov the censors apparently preferred to seek advancement by other means than sheer application to their work, and consequently produced very few reports.[18]

Only the Riga office showed extraordinary zeal.[19] For this reason its transactions achieved the greatest notoriety. This zeal was due almost entirely to the personality of the "civilian" censor Fyodor Tumansky, called by one historian, "the monster in the history of Russian censorship". But even there the proceedings were held up by the delay in the appointment of the ecclesiastical censor and by the fact that no provisions had been made for accommodation, heating, etc.

The general scheme of censorship in the reign of Paul was thus as follows: the censors' offices forwarded reports on books and publications recommended for banning or considered "doubtful" to the Censorship Committee of the Council of State (*Tsenzurnyi Komitet pri Sovete Ye. V.*). This Committee presided over by Kurakin, and later by Lopukhin, was empowered to approve or reject the censors' recommendations.[20] The final decision, however, rested with the emperor himself to whom all minutes of the Committee's proceedings were referred to as a rule.

During the period 25 June 1797 to 14 November 1799 the number of titles of books on which reports were received totalled 639. Of these 552 originated from the Riga office, leaving only 87 to the remaining four put together.[21] The total number of books and publications reecived at Riga

[17] Former Deputy-Governor of St. Petersburg, not to be confused with Fyodor Tumansky mentioned below.

[18] Sipovsky, pp. 170f.

[19] The Riga office queried about 13% of the books received in 1797-98 and 23% in the following year. The corresponding figures for St. Petersburg are 2% and 1% while the activities of the remaining offices were even less significant. As far as works published within the Empire were concerned, the figures available for St. Petersburg for 1798 show that of 218 titles only 7, i.e. just over 3% were questioned by the censors. (*Ibid.*, p. 446).

[20] They were upheld in the majority of cases.

[21] According to the data from 'Sbornik predstavleniy tsenzorov' (Collection of Censors'

in 1798-99 exceeded the corresponding figure for St. Petersburg by about one-third.[22]

The following are some examples of censors' reports:

(1) "*Journal for Factories, Manufactures, Fashion, and Trade:* On the first line of page 306 [the author] cunningly criticises a sacred text by the insertion of a question mark." – The Committee passed this item.

(2) "*The Case of Frederick II Saved from Death During the Seven Years' War:* ... on p. ... [the author] detracts from the glory of the victorious Russian army, ... on p. ... he reaffirms the superiority of Prussian Forces over the consistently victorious Russian ones ..."

According to the minutes this book was passed "on orders from His Majesty", no doubt a reflection of Paul's admiring attitude towards the late Frederick II and his army.

(3) "*Du contrat social ou principes du droit politique* par J.J.Rousseau." The censors' recommendation that it be prohibited was rejected by the Committee on the grounds that Rousseau's works had been circulating freely within Russia "and are already available in many libraries."[23]

(4) Four books against which the Riga censors produced rather vague accusations (e.g. "crafty philosophising", [exposing serious matters to] ridicule", etc.), but which appear to have been generally sympathetic to French revolutionary ideas were banned by the Censorship Committee. Twenty-one other books against which no objections had been raised, but which happened to belong to the same shipment, were also summarily condemned. A marginal note by Paul directs the books to be burned and their owners, when traced, to be prosecuted for having ordered them.

(5) "*Selected Literary Works by English Writers:* [evidently in German]: This book contains, among others, a separate novel "Voyage to Lilliput" in which [the author] strives to ridicule various courtly institutions, as for example, on page ... [where he states] in an insulting manner, that jumping on strings is an exercise performed only by great men."

(6) "*National Gallery,* Stuttgart, 1794". This book, objected to by the censors because it described Russia as a despotic country, in the same

Submissions), published by G. K. Repinsky in 'Tsenzura v Rossii pri Imperatore Pavle 1797-1799' (Censorship in Russia in the Reign of Emperor Paul), *Russkaya Starina* (The Russian Past), XIV, (1875), pp. 454ff, from which the examples that follow have been taken.

22 The respective figures are 30,219 and 18,985 (Sipovsky, p. 446).

23 A contemporary poet, V. V. Popugayev, welcomed this decision with the *Ode on the Occasion of the Council's Decision to Allow 'Contrat Social'* where he struck an optimistic note that appears hardly justified under the circumstances: 'O Russians, you are not forbidden to read the works of great men of genius, you are free to follow boldly in their footsteps ...'

category as Turkey, "where the nobles are cruel and the peasants unhappy", was the only one, out of a shipment of twenty-five, which was passed by the Council. However, Paul, upon perusing the minutes, noted that it should also be prohibited, and directed that "from now on all books where the year of publication is marked as one of the years of the French republic shall be banned,"

(7) on the other hand, the ban on the book by Arndt *On the True Christianity* imposed still in the reign of Elizabeth[24] was now lifted by Paul, most probably because it had been upheld by his mother in 1784.

(8) When the St. Petersburg censors wrote to the Council of State asking for a ruling on Voltaire's writings, it was decided that, since many copies of his books had been on the market in Russia already for a long time, it would be pointless to ban them now; but Paul, again no doubt in the spirit of "anti-Catherinism", forbade their further imports, adding that they ought to be treated as prohibited books.

(9) The Moscow censors received a manuscript of a novel, in French by a "Miss (*Devitsa*) Demidova of Kaluga." This was sent to the Committee as a "doubtful" case. The latter, in prohibiting the book's publication, noted that "if it was in fact written by a *devitsa* then she was occupying herself with matters which are none of her concern."

In general, it can be said that the publications queried by censors were those which contained – or were suspected to contain – (a) French revolutionary propaganda, (b) anything offensive to the national pride, (c) criticism, direct or implied, of the Russian political and social system, (d) religious free-thinking, (e) anything concerning the Russian or any other European reigning family, and, last but not least, (f) criticism of Russia's allies (most notably England).

The principles on which this system of censorship was based must be classified as fair and reasonable, especially if we remember that it had been originally conceived – at least ostensibly – as an emergency measure evoked by a specific international political situation. Neither an imported nor a domestic book or publication could be condemned out of hand in the first instance, but any recommendation for prohibition had, in effect, to be referred to the highest authority in the land. The censors themselves were appointed from among persons of high educational qualifications and social standing. With one conspicuous exception of Fyodor Tumansky in Riga, they were inclined to be reasonable, as witness the small proportion of publications questioned by them. (It must also be remembered that

[24] Cf. p. 10 above.

unless this happened at the censor's office level, a book would, in all probability, escape prohibition). The fact that the final decisions, while unpredictable and often haphazard, tended to be restrictive, is attributable, of course, to Paul's personal characteristics.

So far we have been dealing with legislation deriving from Catherine's edict of 1796. It was not long, however, before the new government began to introduce its own measures which gradually altered the situation in the direction of increasing the severity of the existing laws. Its main aim was the same: the prevention of the influx of French revolutionary ideas.

Thus Paul's personal edict of 17 May 1798[25] ordered the establishment of censors' offices in every port, for the examination of imported books, newspapers, and periodicals. It provided penalties for recipients of such material failing to submit it for examination, and also "for admission of harmful books", thus making the censors responsible for their mistakes. It is quite clear from the text of the edict that it was directed primarily, if not exclusively, at French literature considered subversive. (The notion of what was "subversive" was, as we have seen, extremely broad and ill-defined: by that time it applied to practically anything published in France during the last decade, and to much else besides). It did not, obviously, become operative at once: it was not until almost a whole year later, in April 1799, that there appeared a Senate edict[26] establishing censors' offices at Kronstadt, Revel, Viborg, Frederickshamn, and Archangel, with the stipulation that no printed matter must be imported via ports which had no censorship facilities. This last act is remarkable also for its departure from the earlier principle concerning the appointment of censors: it left this to the local governors who were considered best qualified "to find suitable candidates possessing the knowledge of foreign languages." As it often happens, the satisfaction of increased demand could only be achieved at the expense of quality.[27]

Finally, the edict of 18 April 1800[28] cut the Gordian knot by simply forbidding imports from abroad of "all kinds of books and [sheet] music, until further notice."

[25] *P.S.Z.*, XXV, No. 18,524.

[26] *Ibid.*, No. 18,939.

[27] Notwithstanding this the tendency to appoint persons of relatively high official status and qualifications appears to have persisted. The censors appointed shortly afterwards at Vilno (for the examination of books imported via Polangen) consisted of two Poles, one of them ex-*Podczaszy* of Kovno, and the other a priest with the degree of a Doctor of Theology, one retired colonel with a German-sounding name, and one Jewish censor originally from Leipzig. (*P.S.Z.*, XXV, No. 19,010).

[28] *P.S.Z.*, XXVI, No. 19,387.

One other general point that can be made about censorship in the reign of Paul is that it was preventive rather than corrective, in the sense that its principal aim was to stop the influx of undesirable ideologies from abroad, while little or no effort was made to control the internal circulation or to expurgate publications available within the country. The old confusion between the function of the censor and those of a literary critic, or the idea that one of the former's tasks is to watch over the literary standards, nevertheless appeared to persist. It showed itself in some of the censors' actions (as in the case involving Karamzin quoted below) and also in at least one official act: Paul's edict to the Synod of 14 March 1799.[29] This established the office of an ecclesiastical censor in Moscow "... for the examination, consideration, and correction" of translations from foreign languages concerning the Church and its teachings as well as of anything written by members of the clergy or originating from Church-controlled institutions. The censors were to ensure that such writings did not contain anything contrary to religion, laws of the realm, common decency, "and to literature itself."

On the side of society there is, understandably, little in the way of recorded utterances to show its reaction. The period of four years was, of course, too short to produce any significantly new attitudes. There is no doubt about the resentment felt by men of letters at the oppressive character of the regime. For example, Karamzin, in his letters to Dmitriev, refers to his encounters with censorship complaining bitterly about their interference: "if the censors will continue deleting and correcting [the new edition of *Letters of Russian Traveller*] I would much rather abandon the whole thing than agree to such a sordid operation ..."[30] Thus freedom undreamt of some fifty years earlier was, by the end of the century, regarded as a natural right and any limitation of it strongly resented.

The demand within society for unrestricted access to written matter was by now too strong to be eradicated by repressive policies and was simply driven underground. Hence the appearance of a number of secret circles devoted to various currently illegal pursuits, among them the reading of forbidden books. One such example is the group uncovered in late 1798, composed of Army officers headed by a Colonel A. M. Kakhovsky, who used to gather to read banned Russian and foreign books, notably works

[29] *P.S.Z.*, XXV, No. 18,888.

[30] *Pis'ma N. M. Karamzina k. I. I. Dmitrievu,* (N. M. Karanzin's Letters to I. I. Dmitriev), ed. by Ya. Grot and P. Pekarsky, St. P., 1866, Letter No. 89, p. 104. Cf. also letters Nos. 77 (p. 84) and 86 (p. 97).

by Montesquieu, Helvétius, Holbach, and Radishchev's *Journey from Petersburg to Moscow.*[31]

One Russian periodical of special interest in this period is *St. Petersburg Journal* edited in 1798 by I. P. Pnin and A. F. Bestuzhev. It displayed a considerable concern with the problem of freedom and especially with its following three aspects: freedom of thought and expression, freedom of education, and free participation of society in the process of government.[32] A sample passage referring to freedom of speech reads: "Wise men... ought to be at liberty to say what they think. When they are not able to speak freely their teachings cannot be perfect." Especially interesting is a series of contributions which appears under the collective title "Letters from Torzhok"[33] an obvious reference to the chapter "Torzhok" in Radishchev's *Journey*. Here the main idea is that the limits of the freedom to write ought to be "self-imposed" by authors as a matter of conscience and good taste, rather than be defined by the state. This, of course, shows a close affinity with the views expressed earlier by Radishchev. It is another example of the level reached by liberal ideas among the educated part of Russian society by the end of the century. Another point that might be considered remarkable is that ideas of this kind could still be freely expressed in print in the year 1798.

Another noteworthy phenomenon is the sympathetic attitude of the people towards violations of Paul's censorship laws (no doubt, at least partly, due to the highly unpopular character of the regime). This is how Heinrich Storch, a German resident of St. Petersburg at the turn of the century, described the effects of the total ban on importation of printed matter proclaimed in 1800:

> "Since it paid to run the risks involved in importation of books, only for the sake of the most piquant items, the very strictness of the law resulted in a situation where, of all literary works, only those against which the prohibition had been made in the first place, would enter the Empire. Some booksellers, amongst whom there were also [French] immigrants, engaged in this dangerous but profitable trade with unheard of boldness. Their shops were known practically to everyone, yet no one could be found to denounce them."[34]

[31] L. Svetlov, 'Radishchev i politicheskiye protsessy...' (Radishchev and the Political Trials...), p. 68.

[32] Cf. Kizevetter, 'Iz istorii russkogo liberalizma-Ivan Petrovich Pnin (1773-1805 gg.)' (From the History of Russian Liberalism - I. P. Pnin), *Istoricheskiye ocherki* (Historical Studies), M., 1912, p. 77. Also Berkov, *Istoriya russkoy zhurnalistiki* (History of Russian Periodical Press), p. 285 f.

[33] In Parts III and IV of *the Journal* (1798).

[34] Quoted by I. Ayzenshtok in 'Frantsuzskiye pisateli v otsenkakh tsarskoy tsenzury

Finally, a brief look at publishing statistics. In the period 1796-1800, 1166 titles had been published, an average of 233 titles per year, as compared with 1494 or 299 per year in 1791-1795, a decrease of some 20 percent. Considering the fact that private printing presses were closed at the end of 1796, this is not a very significant decrease. The average figure of 233 titles published per year in the last years of the century still compares favourably with that of 105 titles per year some three decades earlier.[35]

In closing this account we might ask the question: to what extent did Paul's regime vary from that of Catherine as far as freedom of expression was concerned? The fact that it was more openly despotic and, at the same time, basically opposed to Catherine's policies accounted for its radically different general climate. The restrictive policies of the last few years were not sufficient to deny the previous regime its generally liberal character in the eyes of contemporaries. To the educated strata of Russian society, directly affected by all other unpleasant aspects of the new reign, the difference must have seemed very considerable indeed. If, in fact, the policies of Paul's government did not vary much from those of Catherine's in 1796, they nevertheless represented a complete reversal in relation to the period before 1790. In the narrower field of freedom to read and to publish, the all-important factor was the introduction of organised censorship which although decreed in the previous reign only became operative in the present.

A contemporary British witness, the Rev. L. K. Pitt, then chaplain to the "British Factory" in St. Petersburg, in his unpublished account of the "Commencement of the Reign of Emperor Paul",[36] written presumably in late 1800, speaks of the "inconsistency, the violence and the ungovernable precipitation" as marking "the rash imbecility of the Supreme Power." Referring to the abuses of civil liberties by Paul, and in particular to the Edict of 18 April 1800 prohibiting "every source of information to be derived from foreign publications," Pitt, somewhat extravagantly, compares the internal situation in Russia to that in France under Robespierre. Although Pitt's views were at that time undoubtedly affected by Paul's recent reversal of his policies towards England, he could not have been far from the truth in his conclusion:

"...that it has pleased the Almighty to confer the Sceptre of power on one incapable of the lowest office in which the exertion of sound reason is required. The

(French Writers As Seen by the Tsarist Censorship), *Lit. Nasledstvo* (Lit. Heritage), 33-34, M. 1939, p. 775.

[35] *Russkaya kniga*, (Books in Russia), table on p. 346.

[36] B. M., *Add. Mss. 9255*, Fols. 174-183.

public voice confirms this necessary conclusion, and those who approach nearest to the sources of information feel most sensibly the painful conviction."

As already pointed out, the reign of Paul I was too short to have any perceptibly adverse effect on the concept of freedom of expression already well developed and appreciated by society. Consequently, when the regime ended abruptly in early 1801, it did not take people long to revert to their former ways. The reaction in Moscow to the news of Paul's death, recorded by a contemporary observer, may serve to illustrate this point:

"On Thursday 14 March, after dinner, came the first news of the death of Emperor Paul I. The whole city became a scene of unusual activity. At first [the people] only whispered and were afraid to talk openly, ... [but by the next day, March 15th] Moscow resembled a republic in its behaviour, opinions [voiced], and its freedom... Many young people appeared already in round hats about which they would not even dare think earlier. The police looked upon this forbidden attire with equanimity..." [37]

[37] M. F. de Pule, 'Otets i syn' [Memoirs of Ivan Alekseyevich Vtorov] (Father and Son), *Russkiy Vestnik* (The Russian Messenger), CXVII, M., 1875, pp. 123-4.

CONCLUSION

In relation to the history of freedom of expression in Russia, the eighteenth century falls into two distinct epochs, with the late 1760s as the dividing line between them. The first is the transitional period where new trends, set in motion by a drastic alteration of the existing system of values, are at work without, as yet, producing any appreciable changes; the second is one where the results of this process assume a definite shape. A similar chronological division applies, of course, to other sectors of Russian cultural life affected by "secularisation". It can be seen as simply the time-lag between the major political and social upheaval and its consequences in the cultural field.

Conceived as one of the civil liberties, freedom of expression is clearly a secular concept; as such it was incompatible with the medieval system of values or, perhaps more correctly, irrelevant to it. (This is my justification for having left something like 98 % of the population of eighteenth-century Russia outside the scope of this work). With reference to the three simplified situations, ranging from complete "unfreedom" to the maximum possible freedom, about which I spoke in the Introduction, the first part of the century represents a transition from (1) to (2): the time when the old ideological unity was breaking up and the one, universally accepted, set of values no longer existed. Consequently, dissent and its corollary – repression became especially prominent.

In the middle and early second half of the century the new concepts and ideas inherent in the modernised culture of the "upper classes" become clearly discernible and begin to appear in an articulate form. Thus, Catherine II, in enunciating the concept of freedom of expression in her *Instruction,* performed essentially a function analogous to that performed, for example, by Lomonosov and Sumarokov in the field of language and literature. The *Instruction,* however, because of the position occupied by its author, amounted to much more than just a definition of a theoretical principle, or a set of principles: it also represented a grant, or at least an offer, of a relatively very considerable extension of freedom in the realm of thought, speech, and the press. At the same time, by reaffirming the inviolability of the existing political system, Catherine drew a clear dividing line between the civil and the political liberty and thus set a defnite limit beyond which the newly-granted freedom could not progress. In comparison to the history of civil liberties in most European countries (of which, if we are to believe the first article of the *Nakaz*, Russia was now one), the situation where a declaration of civil rights and liberties emanates voluntarily from the State, represented by the absolute monarch, is nothing short of paradoxical. It does not have its roots in the demand for more freedom by society (or even its small privileged segment) against the claims of the state and, for this reason, it is not accompanied by a liberalisation of the political system; it simply represents a voluntary concession on the part of the "autocratic" ruler. However, once this concession had been made in the civil field, it could only be a matter of time before voices would be heard asking for liberalisation in the political one. When this happened, the state bent on the preservation of its authoritarian character, had no choice but to resort to restrictive measures.

It was indeed fortunate that this did not occur for some twenty years, during which time the idea had made a most remarkable progress. We must remember that this was also the peak-period of Western-European influences on Russian intellectual life. These influences were manifold in character: in Western Europe and notably in France ideas were then very much in a state of flux, even though the general trend was easily discernible. This was towards further secularisation of thought as a result of the development and consolidation of the anthropocentric *Weltanschauung*, away from the heritage of the Middle Ages. Upon being imported into Russia, these ideas acted as an accelerator on a parallel process already very much in evidence. It is therefore not surprising that in 1789, in Russia, we have Radishchev who, in his demand for freedom of expression, goes further than the French Declaration of Human Rights; yet, barely a generation earlier, at the time of the "Great Commission", no one except Catherine seemed to be concerned with such problems. By the beginning of the last decade of the century a situation was reached where the continuation of the government's liberal policies in this sphere might present a positive threat to its survival.

The inevitable crisis was precipitated and aggravated by the external political events, the most important of these being obviously the French revolution and the consequent spreading of radical political ideas from

France. The self-preservation of the regime in Russia demanded drastic measures to protect its subjects from this "contamination". This and a number of subsidiary factors, such as the increased influence on policy-making exerted by conservative elements, steeped in traditional attitudes, brought about a radical change in policies amounting, in many respects, to a reversal of those pursued earlier. The resulting restraints on free expression at home, with concurrent attempts to prevent the flow of undesirable ideas from abroad, were applied for approximately the last decade of the century. In its last few years they were emphasised by the irresponsible despotism of Paul I. The important thing, however, was that, by that time, the concept of freedom of expression and the appetite for it were sufficiently well developed among the educated not to be vitiated by this turn of events. In fact, from that time onwards, the intellectually advanced elements in Russian society were to remain conscious of the value of and the consequent need for free expression and its subsequent history was to be one of an almost continuous – and, on the whole singularly unrewarding – struggle between the resulting aspirations and the claims of the authoritarian state.

The printed word was the most important medium of expression in the second half of the century and, consequently, a great deal of attention had to be devoted to censorship in its various forms. Censorship, as I have pointed out earlier, affects both the freedom to read and the freedom to write. The latter is more strictly relevant in the context of "expression", but both had to be considered because of ther close connection with each other. Pre-publication censorship affects the freedom to write, post-publication that to read. Assuming that the prime purpose of censorship is to protect the reading public from undesirable or harmful influences, this can be achieved by either banning the offending material altogether, or by re-editing it. Then, there is this very important question: at what administrative level are to be found those who are qualified to classify written matter as harmful or otherwise? In a highly centralised state the natural tendency would be towards the highest level and this – with the notable, if unsuccessful, attempt at "decentralisation" made by Catherine in delegating the supervision over the output of printing presses to the local police organs – is what happened in Russia. Other specific features of Russian eighteenth-century censorship were: it tended to be pre-publication, at least up to the time of the French revolution; it also tended to amend rather than to suppress. In the last decade of the century the emphasis moved to post-publication censorship affecting the freedom to read (since it was mostly foreign material that was involved), but the tendency to "correct" manuscripts, both from the ideological and the purely literary point of view, proved persistent. Organised censorship in Russia, in the strict sense, begins of course only with the edict of 16 September 1796. Implicit in it was the "Platonic" principle that it is the state and not the author who is ultimately responsible for what is being published. The opposite view is represented by Radishchev (and a few years later, in the nineteenth century, by P. I. Pnin) who, as we have seen, placed the responsibility squarely on the author.

A major point made in this study is that Catherine's policies towards freedom of expression were more liberal, and her contribution to its growth was more positive and significant than it is generally believed. This should not be surprising if we accept the fact that Catherine was a spiritual child of the Enlightenment (the principal ideological source of liberalism); the real question is whether or not she practiced what she preached. Much of the evidence brought forward on the preceding pages has led me to believe that her actions in this particular respect were generally consistent with the theory she professed, through the greater part of her reign. Such a conclusion challenges much that has often been taken for granted. If it is to be refuted, I trust it will be on the basis of firm historical evidence and not that of preconceived ideas or ideological considerations.

The post-eighteenth century history of freedom of expression in Russia is, as is well known, far from propitious. After the initial effort of Alexander I to live up to his promise that "everything will now be as it was in Grandmother's time," by re-instating the law of 1783 concerning printing and publishing, the restraints began to be reimposed as early as 1804, becoming quite oppressive in the latter part of his reign. With a few relatively brief periods of respite (such as the early years of the reign of Alexander II and the period 1905-1922) this situation has basically prevailed to this day, albeit with a widely varying degree of repression. The question must thus be asked: is there some special factor in Russian life, or a trait in the national character, which has been consistently inhibiting this particular freedom?

The close organic connection between the civil and political liberty referred to earlier, in other words, the essential incompatibility between a highly authoritarian political system and the freedom of those living within it, is undoubtedly a part, perhaps the major part, of the answer. Another part, it might be suggested, is to be sought in a less easily definable but no less evident factor, namely in the extraordinary (if perhaps not surprising) tenacity of the old "medieval" culture. Its underlying patriarchal principle seems to be continuously reasserting itself in Russian life, in ways that are sometimes positive, but, perhaps more frequently, decidedly negative. Prominent among the latter is the trait that Dobrolyubov called *samodurstvo* – a practically untranslatable term denoting an arbitrary, overbearing, and bullying attitude often found in those in authority at all levels, beginning with the family and ending at the top of the governmental structure. The paternalistic, conservative outlook normally associated with pre-Petrine society seems to have survived the onslaught of European ideas and, if anything, is now stronger than ever. It is this continued spiritual survival of old Muscovy, in its least attractive aspects, that bears a great deal of responsibility for the vicissitudes of freedom of expression in Russia in the eighteenth century and ever since.

SELECTED BIBLIOGRAPHY

1. Bibliographies

Bibliothèque Impériale Publique de St. Petersbourg, *Catalogue de la Section de Russica ou écrits sur la Russie en langues étrangères,* 2 vols., St. Petersburg, 1873.

Horecky, P. L., *Basic Russian Publications,* Chicago U. P., 1962.

Ikonnikov, V. S., *Opyt russkoy istoriografii* (A Tentative Russian Historiography), 2 vols., Kiev, 1891-1908.

Maichel, K. (J. S. G. Simmons ed.), *Guide to Russian Reference books,* Stanford, Vols. I (1962) and II (1964).

Mintslov, S. P., *Obzor zapisok, dnevnikov, vospominaniy, pisem i puteshestviy otnosyashchikhsya k istorii Rossii i napechatanykh na russkom yazyke* (Survey of Notes, Diaries, Memoirs, Correspondence and Travelogues Concerning the History of Russia and published in Russian), Novgorod, 1911.

Neustroyev, A. N., *Istoricheskoye razyskaniye o russkikh povremennykh izdaniyakh i sbornikakh za 1703-1802 gg.* (Historical Investigation of Russian Periodical Publications and Collections of Articles for the Period 1703-1802), St. P., 1874.

–, *Ukazatel' k russkim povremennym izdaniyam i sbornikam*... (Index of Russian Periodical Publications...), St. P., 1898.

Sopikov, V. S., *Opyt rossiyskoy bibliografii (1813)* (Tentative Russian Bibliography), ed. by P. Rogozhin, St. P., 1904.

Svodnyi katalog russkoy knigi grazhdanskoy pechati XVIII veka, 1725-1800 (Union Catalogue of Russian 18th Century Books in Secular Type, 1725-1800), 5 vols., M., 1963-67.

Vengerov, S. A., *Russkiye knigi... (1703-1893)* (Russian Books...), 3 vols., St. P., 1887-1892.

2. Primary Sources

(a) unpublished:

Bentham Papers: British Museum, *Additional Manuscripts,* 33,529; 33,540; 33,541; 33,552; 33,554; 33,557; 33,558.

Coxe Papers: B.M., *Add. MSS.*, 9078; 9079; 9254; 9255; 9256; 9557.

Gunning Papers: B.M., *Egerton MSS.*, 2703; 2705; 2706.

Guthrie Papers: B.M., *Add. MSS.*, 14,390.

Public Record Office Manuscripts: S.P. 91/95.

(b) published:

Bartenev, P., see: *Os'mnadtsatyi vek.*

Bibikov, A. A., *Zapiski o zhizni i sluzhbe Aleksandra Il'icha Bibikova* (Memoirs on the Private- and Service-Life of A. I. Bibikov), St. P., 1817.
Bolotov, A. T., *Zhizn' i priklyucheniya...* (The Life and Adventures...), *Russkaya starina* (The Russian Past), I-VII, St. P., 1870-1874.
–, *Ibid.*, 'Academia', Moscow-Leningrad, 1931.
Carr, John, *A Northern Summer or Travels Round the Baltic...*, London, 1805.
Catherine II of Russia, [Miscellaneous notes], *Russkaya starina* (The Russian Past), XIII, St. P., 1875.
–, *Sochineniya Imperatritsy Yekateriny II* (Works of Empress Catherine II), ed. by A. N. Pypin, 12 vols., St. P., 1901-1907.
–, *Sochineniya Imperatritsy Yekateriny II - proizvedeniya literaturnyye* (Literary Works), ed. by A. I. Vvedensky, St. P., 1893.
–, *Documents of Catherine the Great,* ed. by W. F. Reddaway, Cambridge, 1931.
Chteniya v Imperatorskom Obshchestve Istorii i Drevnostey Rossiyskikh pri Moskovskom Universitete (Lectures at the Imperial Society of Russian History and Antiquities at the University of Moscow), M., 1861, 1862, 1870, and 1873.
Coxe, W., *Account of the Russian Discoveries between Asia and America,* London, 1780.
–, *Travels in Poland, Russia, Sweden, and Denmark,* 5 vols., London, 1802.
Dashkova Ye. R. (Catherine), *Memoirs of the Princess Dashkaw...*, ed. by W. Bradford, 2 vols., London, 1840.
De Ligne, Prince, *His Memoirs, Letters, and Miscellaneous Papers,* selected and translated by Katharine Prescott Wormeley, 2 vols., London, 1899.
Derzhavin, G. R., *Zapiski Gavriila Romanovicha Derzhavina 1743-1812* (Memoirs of G. R. D.), Moscow, 1860.
Dobrynin, G., 'Istinnoye povestovaniye ili zhizn' Gavriila Dobrynina im samim napisana, 1752-1827', (A True Narrative or the Life of G. D. Written by Himself), *Russkaya starina,* III, 1871.
Eton, W., *A Survey of the Turkish Empire...*, London, 1799.
Fonvizin, D. I., *Sochineniya, pis'ma i izbrannyye perevody Denisa Ivanovicha Fonvizina* (Works, Letters, and Selected Translations by D. I. F.), ed. by P. A. Yefremov, St. P., 1866.
Glinka, S. N., *Zapiski Sergeya Nikolayevicha Glinki* (Memoirs of S.N.G.), St. P., 1895.
Gribovsky, A. M., *Vospominaniya i dnevniki Adriana Moiseyevicha Gribovskogo* (Recollections and Diaries of A. M. G.), M., 1899.
Grot, Ya. K., *Pis'ma Lomonsova i Sumarokova k I. I. Shuvalovu* (Letters by Lomonosov and Sumarokov to I. I. Shuvalov), St. P., 1862.
Harris, James, *Diaries and Correspondence...*, 4 vols., Lond., 1844.
Illustrations of the Literary History of the Eighteenth Century, 8 vols., London, 1828.
Karamzin, N. M., *Pis'ma N. M. Karamzina k I. I. Dmitrievu* (Karamzin's Letters to I. Dmitriev), ed. by Ya. Grot and P. Pekarsky, St. P., 1866.
Khodnev, A. I., *Istoriya Imperatorskogo Vol'nogo Ekonomicheskogo Obshchestva s 1765 do 1865 goda* (History of the Imp. Free Economic Society 1765-1865), St. P., 1865.
Khrapovitsky, A. V., *Dnevnik A. V. Khrapovitskogo 1782-1793* (Diary of A. V. Kh.), St. P., 1874.
Krestinin, V., *Kratkaya Istoriya o Gorode Arkhangel'skom* (A Brief History of the City of Archangel), St. P., 1792.
Kunik, A., *Sbornik materialov dlya istorii Imperatorskoy Akademii Nauk v XVIII veke* (Collected Source Materials for the History of the Imp. Academy of Sciences in the 18th Century), St. P., 1865.
Lomonosov, M. V., *Polnoye sobraniye sochineniy* (Complete Collected Works), 10 vols, M.-L., 1951-1957.
Lopukhin, I. V., *Zapiski...* (Memoirs...), London, 1860.
Macartney, G., *An Account of Russia 1767,* Lond., 1768.

Materialy po istorii SSSR (Source Materials for the History of the USSR), V, Dokumenty po istorii XVIII v. (Documents on 18th cent. History), M., 1957.
Nichols, J., *Literary Anecdotes of the Eighteenth Century, 9 vols.*, Lond. 1812-1815.
Os'mnadtsatyi vek (The Eighteenth Century), ed. by P. Bartenev, 2 vols., M., 1868-1869.
Penchko, N. A. ed., *Dokumenty i materialy po istorii Moskovskogo Universiteta vtoroy poloviny XVIII veka* (Dokuments and Source Materials Concerning the History of the University of Moscow in the Second Half of the 18th Century), 2 vols., M., 1960-1962.
Polnoye sobraniye zakonov Rossiyskoy Imperii (Complete Collection of Laws of the Russian Empire), 45 vols., St. P., 1830.
Poroshin, S., *Semyona Poroshina zapiski...* (Memoirs of S.P.), St. P., 1844.
Privilegiya i ustav Imperatorskoy Akademii tryokh znatneyskikh khudozhestv... (The Charter and Statute of the Imperial Academy of the Three Most Prominent Arts...), St. P., 1765.
Protokoly Zasedaniy Akademii Nauk s 1725-1803 g. (Minutes of the Meetings of the Academy of Sciences), 4 vols., St. P., 1897-1900).
Pule, de, 'Otets i syn (otryvki iz zapisok I. A. Vtorova)' (Father and Son – Extracts from I. A. Vtorov's Memoirs), *Russkiy Vestnik* (The Russian Messenger), CXVII, 1875.
Radishchev, A. N., *Radishchev-materialy i issledovaniya* (R.-Materials and Investigations), M.-L., 1936.
–, *Puteshestviye iz Peterburga v Moskvu* (Journey from Petersburg to Moscow), 2 vols., ed. by Ya. L. Barskov, M.-L., 1935.
Repinsky, G. K., 'Tsenzura v Rosii pri Imperatore Pavle' (Censorship in Russia in the Reign of Emperor Paul), *Russkaya starina*, XIV, 1875.
Richardson, W., *Anecdotes of the Russian Empire*, London, 1874.
Rovinsky, D. A., *Russkiye narodnyye kartinki* (Russian Popular Illustrations), 5 vols., St. P., 1881-1893..
Sbornik Imperatorskogo Russkogo Istoricheskogo Obshchestva (The Collection of the Imperial Russian Historical Society), 148 vols., St. P., 1867-1916.
Schloezer, A. L., *August Ludwig Schloezer's oeffentliches und Privat-Leben...*, Goettingen, 1802.
Segur, de, L.-P., *Memoirs and Recollections*, 3 vols., Lond., 1825.
Shcherbatov, M. M., *Neizdannyye sochineniya* (Unpublished Works), M., 1935.
Shcherbatov, M. M., 'O povrezhdenyi nravov v Rossii' (On the Corruption of Morals in Russia), *Russkaya starina*, I, 1870.
–, 'Pis'mo k vel'mozham pravitelyam gosudarstva' (A Letter to the Mighty Rulers of State), *R. starina*, V, 1872.
–, *Raznyye sochineniya* (Miscellaneous Works), M. 1860.
Shumigorsky, E. S., 'Zapiska bavartsa o Rossii vremyon Imperatora Pavla' (Memoir on Russia at the Time of Emp. Paul, by a Bavarian). *R. starina*, XCIX, 1899.
Skalon, S. V. 'Vospominaniya S. V. Skalon (urozhdyonnoy Kapnist)' (Recollections of S. V. Skalon, born Kapnist), *Istoricheskiy vestnik* (The Historical Messenger), XLIV, 1891.
Smolyaninov, V. I. ed., *Vosemnadtsatyi vek (Arkhiv kn. Kurakinykh)* The Eighteenth Century (Kurakin Archives), 2 vols., St. P. 1904-1905.
Snegiryov, I. M., *Zhizn' moskovskogo Mitropolita Platona* (Life of Metropolitan Platon of Moscow), M. 1856.
Sukhomlinov, M. I., *Istoriya Rossiyskoy Akademii*, (History of the Russian Academy), 8 vols., St. P., 1874-1887.
–, *Materialy dlya istorii Imp. Akademii Nauk* (Source Materials for the History of the Imp. Academy of Sciences), 10 vols., St. P., 1885-1897.
The Spectator, Volume the First, London, 1744.
Thesby de Belcour, F. A., *Tagebuch eines franzoesischen Offizieres...*, Amsterdam, 1776.

Tooke, W., *Russia: or a Compleat Historical Account of All the Nations which Compose that Empire,* 2 vols., London, 1780.

–, *View of the Russian Empire,* 3 vols., London, 1799.

Tuchkov, S. A., *Zapiski Sergeya Alexeyevicha Tuchkova 1766-1808* (Memoirs of S. A. Tuchkov 1766-1808), ed., by K. A. Voyensky, St. P., 1908.

Vorontsov (family), *Arkhiv knyazya Vorontsova* (Archives of Prince Vorontsov, i.e. Vorontsov Archives), ed. by P. Bartenev, 40 vols., M., 1870-1895.

Vsyakaya vsyachina 1769 g. (All Sorts of Things, 1769), M., 1893.

Yazykov, D. D., '"Nedorosl" na stsene i v literature' (*The Minor* on Stage and in Literature), *Istor. Vestnik,* X., 1882.

3. Secondary Sources

Akademiya Nauk SSSR (USSR Academy of Sciences), *Istoriya Akademii Nauk SSSR* History of the USSR Ac. of Sc., (1724-1803), M.-L., 1958.

–, *Istoriya russkoy literatury* (History of Russian Literature), III & IV, M.-L., 1941-1947.

–, *XVIII vek, sbornik,* 1-5, (The 18th Century - A Collection), M.-L., 1935-1962.

Amburger, E., *Geschichte der Behoerdeorganisation Russlands von Peter dem Grossen bis 1917,* Leiden, 1966.

Anderson, M. S., *Britain's Discovery of Russia 1533-1815,* Lond., 1958.

–, 'Some British Influences on Russian Intellectual Life and Society in the 18th Century', *The Slavonic & East European Review,* XXXIX, Lond., 1960.

Arkhangel'sky, A. S., *Imperatritsa Yekaterina II v istorii russkoy literatury i obrazovaniya* (The Empress Catherine II in the History of Russian Literature and Education), Kazan', 1897.

Arsen'yev, A. V., 'Starinnyye dela ob oskorblenii Velichestva (1701-1797 g.)' (Old Cases of Lèse-Majesté), *Ist. vestnik,* IV, St. P., 1881.

Bentham, M. S., *The Life of Brig.-Gen. Sir Samuel Bentham, K.S.G.,* London, 1862.

Berkov, P. N., *Istoriya russkoy zhurnalistiki XVIII v.* (The History of the Russian Periodical Press of the 18th Cent.), M., 1952.

–, *Vvedeniye v izucheniye istorii russkoy literatury XVIII veka* (An Introduction to the Study of History of Russian 18th Century Literature), Chast' (Part) I, L., 1964.

–, See also: Novikov, N. I.

Bil'basov, V. A., *Istoriya Yekateriny Vtoroy* (History of Catherine the Second), I-II, Berlin, 1900.

–, *Ditto,* XII, Berlin, n.d.

–, 'Pervyye politicheskiye pis'ma Yekateriny II' (The First Political Letters of Catherine II), *Zhurnal Ministerstva Narodnogo Prosveshcheniya* (Journal of the Ministry of Public Education), CCLII, St. P., 1887.

–, 'Rossiya i Angliya v XVIII veke' (Russia and England in the 18th Cent.), *R. starina,* LXXX, 1893.

Billington, J. H., *The Icon & The Axe,* N. Y. & Toronto, 1966.

Blank, P. E. 'Yekaterininskaya Kommissiya 1767-1769' (Catherine's Commission of 1767-1769), *Russkiy vestnik* (The Russian Messenger), CXXI, St. P., 1876.

Blum, K. L., *Ein Russischer Staatsmann,* 4 vols., Leipzig & Heidelberg, 1857-1858.

Bobrov, E. A., 'Autodafe nad filosofskoy knigoy' (The Burning of a Philosophical Book), *Ist. vestnik,* XCVI, 1904.

Bochkaryov, V. N., 'Russkoye obshchesvo yekaterininskoy epokhi i frantsuzskaya revolutsiya' (Russian Society of the Period of Catherine and the French Revolution), *Otechestvennaya voyna i russkoye obshchestvo 1812-1912* (The Patrotic War and Russian Society, 1812-1912), M., 1911.

Brueckner (Brikner), A., *Die Europaeisierung Russlands,* Gotha, 1888.

–, 'Yekaterina II i frantsuzskaya revolutsiya' (Catherine II and the French Revolution), *Ist. vestnik*, LXI, 1895.

–, *Istoriya Yekateriny II* (History of Catherine II), St. P., 1885.

–, 'Vskrytiye chuzhikh pisem i depesh pri Yekaterine II', (The Perusal of Foreign Letters and Despatches in the Reign of Catherine II), *R. starina*, VII, 1873.

Chechulin, N. D., *Nakaz Imperatritsy Yekateriny II dannyi Komissii o sochinenii proyekta novogo Ulozheniya* (Instruction by the Empress Catherine II Given to the Commission for the Compilation of the New Code of Laws), St. P., 1907.

Chechulin, N. D., *Russkiy sotsiyal'nyi roman XVIII veka* (The Russian Social Novel of the 18th Century), St. P., 1900.

Cherniavsky, M., *Tsar & People: Studies in Russian Myths*, N. Y., 1969.

'Chetyryokhsotletiye tsenzury' (The Four-Hudredth Anniversary of Censorship), *Ist. vestnik*, XXIII, 1886.

Chistovich, I. A., *Istoriya Sanktpeterburgskoy Dukhovnoy Akademii* (History of the St. Petersburg Seminary), St. P., 1857.

–, *Istoricheskaya zapiska o Sovete v tsarstvovaniye Imperatritsy Yekateriny II-y* (Historical Note on the Council [of State] in the Reign of the Empress Catherine II), St. P., 1870.

Coxe, W., 'Zapiski Uilliyama Koksa (Coxe)' (Memoirs of William Coxe), *R. starina*, XVIII, 1877.

–, see also: Viktorov, V.

Cushing, G. F., 'Books and Readers in 18th Century Hungary', *The Slavonic & E. E. Review*, XLVII, 1969.

Cushman, R. E., *Civil Liberties in the United States*, Cornell, 1956.

De Larivière, Ch., *Catherine Le Grand d'après sa correspondance - Catherine II et la Révolution Française*, Paris, 1895.

Demkov, M.I., *Istoriya russkov pedagogii*, Chast' II - novaya russkaya pedagogiya (XVIII v.) - (History of Russian Pedagogy - Part II - The Modern Russian Pedagogy), M., 1910.

Derzhavin, G. R., *Stikhotvoreniya* (Poems), M., 1958.

Dobrolyubov, N. A., *Sobraniye sochineniy* (Collected Works), I, M.-L., 1961.

Drizen, N. V., 'Ivan Perfil'yevich Yelagin (1725-1794', *R. starina*, LXXX, 1893.

Dukes, P., *Catherine the Great and the Russian Nobility*, Cambridge, 1967.

Engel'gardt, N., *Ocherk istorii russkoy tsenzury v svyazi s razvitiyem pechati (1703-1903)* - (An Outline of the History of Russian Censorship in Relation to the Development of Printing), St. P., 1904.

Epokha prosveshcheniya, see: Levin, Yu. D.

Florovsky, A. V., *Sostav Zakonodatel'noy Kommissii 1767-1774 gg.* (Composition of the Legislative Commission for the years 1769-1774), Odessa, 1915.

Fonvizin, D. I., *Sobraniye sochineniy* (Collected Works), ed. by G. P. Makogonenko, 2 vols., M.-L., 1959.

–, See also: Makogonenko, G. P.

Gagarin, A. P., 'Pervaya filosofskaya dissertatsiya zashchishchavshayasya v Moskovskom Universitete' (The First Philosophical Dissertation Defended at Moscow University), *Vestnik Moskovskogo Universiteta* (Moscow University Messenger), No. 7, 1952.

Gellhorn, W., *Individual Freedom and Governmental Restraints*, Baton Rouge, 1956.

–, *The States and Subversion*, Cornell, 1952.

Gennadi, G., *Spravochnyi slovar' o russkikh pisatelyakh i uchonykh* (Reference Dictionary of Russian Writers and Scholars), 2 vols., Berlin, 1870-1876.

Gol'tsev, V. A., *Zakonodatel'stvo i nravy v Rossii XVIII veka* (Legislation and Customs in 18th Century Russia), St. P., 1896.

Grot, Ya. K., *Literaturnaya zhizn' Krylova* (Krylov's Literary Life), St. P., 1868.

–, 'Satira Krylova i yego "Pochta Dukhov", *Sbornik statey chitannykh v otdelenii russkogo yazyka i slovesnosti Imp. Akademii Nauk* (Krylov's Satire and his *Mail of*

Ghosts, Collection of Papers Read at the Department of Russian Language and Literature of the Imp. Academy of Sciences), VI, St. P., 1869.
–, 'Zhurnal'nyye trudy Krylova', (Krylov's Works in the Periodical Press), *Ditto.*
Haumant, E., *La Culture Française en Russie (1700-1900),* Paris, 1910.
Hazard, P., *European Thought in the Eighteenth Century from Montesquieu to Lessing,* Cleveland & N. Y., 1963.
Istoriya Pravitel'stvuyushchego Senata za dvesti let: 1711-1911 (History of the Governing Senate for the Two Hundred Years: 1711-1911), 2 vols., St. P., 1911.
'Istoricheskiy ocherk russkogo zakonodatel'stva o pechati' (A Historical Study of Russian Legislation Pertaining to the Press), *Ist. vestnik,* IV, 1881.
Istoriografiya istorii SSSR (Historiography of the History of the USSR), ed. by V. I. Illeritsky and I. A. Kudryavtsev, M., 1961.
Ivanov-Razumnik, R. V., *Istoriya russkoy obshchestvennoy mysli* (History of Russian Social Thought), 2 vols., St. P., 1908.
Kafengauz, B. B., *I. T. Pososhkov - zhizn' i deyatel'nost'* (The Life and Activities of I. T. P.), M.-L., 1950.
Karatygin, P. P., 'Tsenzura vremyon Imperatora Pavla' (Censorship at the time of Emperor Paul), *Ist. vestnik,* XXII, 1885.
Kizevetter, A. A., *Istoricheskiye ocherki* (Historical Studies), M., 1912.
–, 'Pervoye pyatiletiye pravleniya Yekateriny II, (The First Five Years of the Government of Catherine II), *Sbornik statey posvyashchonnykh Pavlu Nikolayevichu Milyukovu 1859-1929* (Collection of Papers in Honour of P. N. Milyukov), Prague, 1929.
Klyuchevsky, V. O., *Sochineniya* (Works), 8 vols., M., 1959.
Knorring, N. I., 'Yekaterininskaya zakonodatel'naya Kommissiya 1767 goda v osveshchenii inostrannykh rezidentov pri russkom dvore' (Catherine's Legislative Commission of 1767 Through the Eyes of Foreign Envoys to the Court of Russia), *Sb. statey . . . Milyukovu* (Collection of Papers . . . Milyukov), Prague, 1929.
Knizhnaya torgovlya (The Book Trade), ed. by V. M. Muratova and N. N. Nakoryakova, M.-L., 1925.
Koyalovich, M. O., *Istoriya russkogo samosoznaniya po istoricheskim pamyatnikam i nauchnym sochineniyam* (History of Russian National Consciousness on the Basis of Historical Records and Works of Scholarship), St. P., 1901.
Lappo-Danilevsky, A. S., *Ocherk vnutrennoy politiki Imperatritsy Yekateriny II* (An Outline of the Internal Policies of Empress Catherine II), St. P., 1898.
Larivière, De, see: De Larivière.
Lekhtblau, L. V., *Russkiye satiricheskiye zhurnaly XVIII veka* (Russian Satirical Journals of the 18th Century), M., 1940.
Leontovitsch, V., *Geschichte des Liberalismus in Russland,* Frankfurt, 1957.
Levin, Yu. D., 'Angliyskaya prosvetitel'skaya zhurnalistika v russkoy literature XVIII veka' (The English Periodical Press of the Enlightenment [as reflected] in Russian 18th Century Literature), USSR Academy of Sciences, *Epokha prosveshcheniya* (The Age of Enlightenment), L., 1967.
Likhachova, Ye., *Materialy dlya istorii zhenskogo obrazovaniya v Rossii (1086-1856)* Source Materials for the History of Women's Education in Russia), 3 vols., St. P., 1890.
Lipinsky, M. A., *'Novyye dannyye po istorii Yekaterininskoy Kommissii o sochinenii proyekta novogo ulozheniya'* (New Data on the History of Catherine's Commission for the Compilation of New Code of Laws), *Zhurnal Ministerstva Narodnogo Prosveshcheniya* (Journal of the Ministry of Public Education), CCLII, St. P., 1887.
Literaturnoys Nasledstvo, Sbornik, (Literary Heritage - A Collection), 9-10, M., 1933; 29-30, M., 1937; 33-34, M., 1939.
Lively, J., *The Enlightenment,* N. Y., 1966.
Longinov, M. N., 'Materialy dlya istorii russkogo prosveshcheniya i literatury v kontse XVIII v.' (Source Materials for the History of Russian Enlightenment and Literature

at the End of the 18th Century), *R. vestnik*, XXII, 1859 and XXV, 1860.
–, *Novikov i moskovskiye martinisty* (Novikov and the Moscow Martinists), M., 1867.
–, *Russkiy teatr v Peterburge i Moskve (1749-1774)*, The Russian Theatre in St. Petersburg & Moscow), St. P., 1873.
Lough, J., *An Introduction to Eighteenth Century France*, Lond., 1960.
Luzny, R., *Rosyjskie czasopismiennictwo satyryczne XVIII w.* (Russian Satirical Periodicals of the 18th Century), Wroclaw-Kraków, 1960.
Makogonenko, G. P., *Denis Fonvizin-tvorcheskiy put'* (Denis Fonvizin - His Creative Progress), M.-L., 1961.
–, *Nikolay Novikov i russkoye prosveshcheniye XVIII veka* (N. N. and the Russian Enlightenment of the 18th Century), M.-L., 1951.
–, See also: Novikov, Fonvizin.
Martem'yanov, T. A., 'Iz istorii tsenzury russkoy narodnoy pesni' (From the History of the Censorship of Russian Folk Song), *Ist. vestnik*, XCVIII, 1904.
Masaryk, T. G., *The Spirit of Russia*, 3 vols., Lond., 1955-67.
Maykov, L. N., *Ocherki iz istorii russkoy literatury XVII i XVIII stoletiy* (Studies in the History of Russian Literature of the 17th and 18th Centuries), St. P., 1889.
Mazour, A. G., *Modern Russian Historiography*, N. Y., 1958.
McConnell, A., *A. Russian Philosophe - Alexander Radishchev*, The Hague, 1964.
Mel'gunov, S. P., *Religiozno-obshchestvennyye dvizheniya XVII-XVIII vv. v Rossii* (Religious and Social Movements in Russia in the 17th and 18th cents.,), M., 1922.
Mel'gunova, P. E., et al., *Russkiy byt po vospominaniyam sovremennikov, XVIII vek* Russian Life in the Recollections of Contemporaries, 18th Century), 2 vols., M., 1914.
Mel'nikova, N. I., *Izdaniya Moskovskoga Universiteta 1756-1779* (Moscow University Publications), M., 1955.
Milyukov, P. N., *Glavnyye techeniya russkoy istoricheskoy mysli* (The Main Trends of Russian Historical Thought), St. P., 1913.
–, *Ocherki po istorii russkoy kul'tury* (Studies in the History of Russian Culture), 3 vols., Paris, 1930-37.
–, 'The Influence of English Political Thought in Russia', *The Slavonic Review*, V., Lond., 1926.
Moskovskiy Universitet 1755-1930, Yubileynyi sbornik (Moscow University 1755-1930 - Jubilee Collection), Paris, 1930.
Nezelyonov, A. I., 'Literaturnyye napravleniya v Yekaterininskuyu epokhu' (Literary Trends in the Age of Catherine), *Ist. vestnik*, XVI, 1884.
–, *Nikolay Ivanovich Novikov - izdatel' zhurnalov 1769-1785 g.*, (N. I. Novikov - The Publisher of Journals), St. P., 1875.
Nezelyonov, A. I., 'Novikov v Petropavlovskoy kreposti' (N. in the Fortress of St. Peter and Paul), *Ist. vestnik*, X, 1882.
Novikov, N. I., *Izbrannyye pedagogicheskiye sochineniya* (Selected Pedagogical Works), compiled by N. A. Trushin and edited by F. Shabayeva, M., 1959.
–, *Izbrannyye sochineniya* (Selected Works), ed. by G. P. Makogonenko, M.-L., 1951.
–, *Novikov i ego sovremenniki* (N. and His Contemporaries), M., 1961.
–, *Satiricheskiye zhurnaly N. I. Novikova* (N. I. Novikov's Satirical Journals), ed. by P. N. Berkov, M.-L., 1951.
–, see also: Longinov, Makogonenko, Nezelyonov.
'Ocherki starinnogo byta - kaznyonnaya tetradka' (Sketches of the Old Way of Life - A Copybook Condemned), *Ist. vestnik, XXXIII, 1886.*
Orlov, V., ed., *Poety-Radishchevtsy* (Poets of the Radishchev School), L., 1961.
Papmehl, K. A., 'The Problem of Civil Liberties in the Records of the "Great Commission"', *The Slavonic & E. E. Review*, XLII, Lond., 1964.
–, Samuel Bentham and the *Sobesednik* (1783)', *Ibid.*, XLVI, Lond., 1968.
Pekarsky, P. P., *Dopolneniya k istorii masonstva v Rossii XVIII stoletiya* (Supplementary

Notes to the History of Freemasonry in 18th Century Russia), St. P. 1869.
–, *Istoriya Imperatorskoy Akademii Nauk v Peterburge* (Mistory of the Imp. Academy of Sciences in Petersburg), 2 vols., St. P., 1873.
–, *Materialy dlya istorii zhurnal'noy i literaturnoy deyatel'nosti Yekateriny II* (Source Materials for the History of Catherine II's Journalistic and Literary Activities), St. P., 1863.
–, *Nauka i Literatura v Rossii pri Petre Velikom* (Learning and Literature in Russia at the Time of Peter the Great), 2 vols., St. P., 1862.
–, *Redaktor, sotrudniki i tsenzura v russkom zhurnale 1755-1764 gg.* (The Editor of, the Contributors to, and the Censors of a Russian Journal of the years 1755-1764), St. P., 1867.
Peshtich, S. L., *Russkaya istorigrafiya XVIII veka* (Russian Historiography of the 18th Century), 2 vols., L., 1961 & 1965.
Pozdeyeva, I. V., 'Izucheniye drevney istorii i drevnikh yazykov v Moskovskom Universitete v 50-ye - 70ye. gg. XVIII v.' (The Study of Ancient History and Languages at Moscow University in the 50-s through 70-s of the 18th Century), *Vestnik drevney istorii Akademii Nauk SSSR* (USSR Academy of Sciences, The messenger of Ancient History), No. 3., N., 1962.
Pypin, A. N. *Istoriya russkoy literatury* (History of Russian Literature), 4 vols., St. P., 1907.
–, *Russkoye masonstvo* (Russian Freemasonry), Petrograd, 1916.
Radishchev, A. N., *Izbrannyye sochineniya* (Selected Works), M.-L., 1949.
Raeff, M., 'Les Slaves, les Allemands et les "Lumieres" ', *Canadian Slavic Studies, I*, 1967.
–, 'State and Nobility in the Ideology of M. M. Shcherbatov', *American Slavic & East European Review*, XIX, 1960.
Rogger, H., *National Consciousness in Eighteenth Century Russia*, Harvard, 1960.
Ruggiero, de, G., *The History of European Liberalism*, Boston, 1966.
Russkaya kniga ot nachala pis'mennosti do 1800 goda (Books in Russia from the Earliest Writings to 1800), ed. by V. Ya. Adaryukov and A. A. Sidorov, M., 1924.
Russkaya Proza XVIII veka, (Russian Prose of the 18th Century), 2 vols., M., 1950.
'Russkiye vol'nodumtsy v tsarstvovaniye Yekateriny II' (The Russian Freethinkers in the Reign of Catherine II), *R. starina*, IX, 1874.
Russkoye narodnoye poeticheskoye tvorchestvo (Russian Folk Poetry), ed. by P. G. Bogatyryov, M., 1954.
Sacke, G., 'Zur Charakteristik der gesetzgebenden Kommission Katharina's II von Russland' *Archiv fuer Kulturgeschichte*, XXI, Leipzig & Berlin, 1931.
Semennikov, V. P., 'Dopolnitel'nyye materialy dlya istorii provintsiyal'nykh tipografiy XVIII i nachala XIX veka' (Supplementary Source Materials to the History of Provincial Printing Presses of the 18th and Early 19th Centuries), *Russkiy Bibliofil* (Russian Bibliophile) No. 7., St. P., 1913.
–, 'K istorii tsenzury v Yekaterininskuyu epokhu' (A Contribution to the History of Censorship at the Time of Catherine), *Ibid.*, No. 1, 1913.
–, *Knigoizdatel'skaya deyatel'nost' N. I. Novikova i tipograficheskoy kompanii*, (The Publishing Activities of N. Novikov and of the Printing Company), Petersburg, 1921.
–, 'Literaturnaya i knigopechatnaya deyatel'nost' v provintsii v kontse XVIII i nachale XIX vekov' (Literary and Publishing Activities in the Provinces in the Late 18th and Early 19th Cent.), *R. Bibliofil*, 1911, No. 6.
–, *Materialy dlya istorii russkoy literatury i dlya slovarya pisateley epokhi Yekateriny II* (Source Materials for the History of Russian Literature and for the Dictionary of Writers of the Period of Catherine II), St. P., 1914.
–, Radishchev - *ocherki i issledovaniya* (Radishchev - Studies and Investigations), M.-Pbg., 1923.

–, *Russkiye satiricheskiye zhurnaly 1769-1774 gg.* (Russian Satirical Journals of the Years 1769-1774), St. P., 1914. (Appendix to *R. Bibliofil*, No. 1-4).
–, *Sobraniye starayushcheyesya o perevode inostrannykh knig uchrezhdyonnoye Yekaterinoy II, 1768-1783 gg.* (Society for Translation of Foreign Books Established by Catherine II), St. P., 1913. (Appendix to *R. Bibliofil*, Nos. 5-8).
Semyontkovsky, R., 'K istorii liberalizma' (A Contribution to the History of Liberalism), *Ist. vestnik*, LI, 1893.
–, 'Nash pervyi skeptik' (Our First Sceptic), *Ist. vestnik*, LXI, 1895.
Shchipanov, I. Ya., ed., *Izbrannyye proizvedemya russkikh mysliteley vtoroy poloviny XVIII veka*, (Selected Works of Russian Thinkers of the Second Half of the 18th Century, M., 1952.
–, ed., *Iz istorii russkov filosofii XVII-XIX vekov* (From the History of Russian Philosophy of the 17th-19th Centuries), M., 1952.
Shevyryov, S., *Biograficheskiy slovar' professorov i prepodavateley Imp. Moskovskogo Universiteta 1755-1855* (A Biographical Dictionary of the Professors and Teachers at the Imp. University of Moscow), M., 1855.
–, *Istoriya Imp. Moskovskogo Universiteta 1755-1855* (History of the Imperial University of Moscow), M., 1855.
Shil'der, N. K., *Imperator Pavel Pervyi* (Emperor Paul the First), St. P., 1901.
Shumigorsky, E. S., *Imperator Pavel I* (Emperor Paul I), St. P., 1907.
Simmons, E. J., *English Literature and Culture in Russia (1553-1840)*, Harvard, 1935.
Sipovsky, V. V., *Iz istorii russkogo romana i povesti* (From the History of the Russian Novel and Tale), Chast' I-XVIII vek (Part I - 18th Cent.), St. P., 1903.
–, 'Iz proshlogo russkoy tsenzury' (From the Past of Russian Censorship), *R. starina*, XCVIII, St. P., 1899.
Skabichevsky, A. M., *Ocherki istorii russkoy tsenzury (1700-1863 gg.)* (An Outline of the History of Russian Censorship), St. P., 1892.
Solntsev, V., ' "Vsyakaya vsyachina" i 'Spektator" ', *(All Sorts of Things* and *The Spectator), Zhurnal Ministerstva Narodnogo Prosveshcheniya* (Journal of the Ministry of Public Education), Part 279, St. P., 1892.
Soloviev, A. V., *Holy Russia - The History of a Religious-Social Idea*, The Hague, 1959.
Solov'yov, S. M., *Istoriya Rossii s drevneyshikh vremyon* (History of Russia from the Earliest Times), 29 vols. in 15 books, M., 1960-1966.
Strange M., *La Révolution Française et la societé russe*, M., 1960.
Sumarokov, A. P., see: Grot, Ya. K.
Svatikov, S. G., *Obshchestvennoye dvizheniye v Rossii (1700-1895)* - (The Social Movement in Russia), Rostov n/D., 1905.
Svetlov, L., 'A. N. Radishchev i politicheskiye protsessy XVIII veka' (A. N. R. and the Political Trials of the 18th Century), *Iz istorii russkoy filosofii XVII-XIX vekov* (From the History of Russian Philosophy in the 17th-19th Centuries), ed. by I. Ya. Shchipanov, M., 1952.
Tikhomirov, M. N., *Istochnikovedeniye istorii SSSR s drevneyshikh vremyon do kontsa XVIII v.* (The Study of Sources for the History of the USSR From the Earliest Times to the End of the 18th Cent.), M., 1940.
–, *Istoriya Moskovskogo Universiteta* (History of the University of Moscow), I., M., 1955.
Tikhonravov, N. S., *Sochineniya* (Works), II & III, M., 1898.
Timir'yazev, V. A., 'Didro i Yekaterina II' (Diderot and Catherine II), *Ist. vestnik*, LXXVII, 1899.
Timofeyev, S. P., 'Posledniy predstavitel' russkoy satiry proshlogo veka' (The Last Representative of Russian Satire of the Past Century), *Ist. vestnik*, XXXIII, 1886.
Vasilenko, N., 'Rost frantsuzskogo vliyaniya v Rossii do frantsuzskoy revolutsii' (The Growth of the French Influence in Russia Before the French Revolution), *Otechestven-*

naya voyna i russkoye obshchestvo 1812-1912 (The Patriotic War and Russian Society), M., 1911.

Veselovsky, A., *Zapadnoye vliyaniye v novoy ruskoy literature* (Western Influence in Modern Russian Literature), M., 1896.

Viktorov, V., 'Sochineniya Villiyama Koksa o Rossii' (The Works on Russia by William Coxe), *Ist. vestnik,* LXXIV, 1898.

Vysotsky, N. G., 'Zapreshchonnyye pri Yekaterine Velikoy knigi' (Books Banned in the Reign of Catherine the Great), *Russkiy arkhiv* (Russian Archives), Book 3, M., 1912.

Yefremov, P. A., *Materialy dlya istorii russkoy literatury* (Source Materials for the History of Russian Literature), St. P., 1867.

Yeleonsky, S. F., 'Iz istorii massovoy literatury XVIII veka. Lubochnyye listy' (From the History of Mass-Literature of the 18th Century. The Woodcuts), *Izvestiya Akademii Nauk SSSR, otd. Literatury i yazyka* (Bulletin of the Academy of Sciences, Dept. of Literature and Language), XIV, Vyp. 5, M., 1955.

Zenkovsky, V. V., *Istoriya russkoy filosofii* (History of Russian Philosophy), 2 vols., Paris, 1948.

INDEX

GPSR Compliance

The European Union's (EU) General Product Safety Regulation (GPSR) is a set of rules that requires consumer products to be safe and our obligations to ensure this.

If you have any concerns about our products, you can contact us on ProductSafety@springernature.com

In case Publisher is established outside the EU, the EU authorized representative is:

Springer Nature Customer Service Center GmbH
Europaplatz 3
69115 Heidelberg, Germany

Batch number: 10830943

Printed by Printforce, the Netherlands